Antillus Stone

Jake Stone

Book 1

Viam Invenire, Vim Vivere

Life's Journey, Forged with Courage
Discover Your Way. Unleash Your Potential

Eric Jones

Dedication

Life can be rewarding, and sometimes it can be complex. I would like to dedicate this book to all the strong individuals who had a hand in shaping my life.

I had a very humble upbringing, and my grandmother was always someone who was diligently in my corner. Her strength, wisdom, and dedication to our family were unparalleled. I try to follow the example of my grandparents because I stand on the shoulders of giants, and I keep going each day, knowing that they are with me. In writing this book, I wanted to explore the nature of right and wrong and what it means to be family so that the reader could potentially find a piece of themselves within the context of exploring the souls of these characters. In my old age, I can genuinely say that art does indeed imitate life; in this way, I invite the reader to look for their own reflection in this work.

Every day brings new challenges, but it also brings possibilities. I would also like to dedicate this book to every person who wakes up in the morning and puts on their shoes to go to work. This could mean going to an actual job or having to toil and labor for their own benefit or that of someone else. My grandparents taught me the value of hard work. This life's journey is not easy; it requires work and effort, and sometimes it requires character. I want to provide a setting for the world to relax. When you finish your day and take those shoes off, breathe and come with me to explore your imagination.

I have been blessed with a good family, the world's best grandparents, and daughters who are forever my advocates. I hope that something contained within these pages will make a difference in the readers' lives so they can find a way to relax and gain the satisfaction and fulfillment it took me to learn much later in life. I appreciate your time and efforts in embarking on this journey, and I hope your time is well spent.

Cast of Characters

Jake Stone	Main Character
Isabella Franco	Jake's Girlfriend
Mary Clayton	Jake's Rich Aunt
Titiano Clayton	Jake's Cousin - Friend
Rodney Hatcher	Aunt Mary's Butler
Paul Stone	Jake's Dad
Pam Stone	Jake's Mom
Randy Barnes	Jake's Sensei Uechi-Ryu

FBI

Agent Jackson	Main FBI Agent
Patrick Flanagan	Agent Jackson's Partner
Agent Collins	FBI Task Force Lead
Shawn Brady	FBI Bureau Chief
Wendy	Station Clerk

Capoli Family

Vincent Capoli	Powerful Mafia Don
Martin Capoli	Vincent Capoli's Son
Francesca Capoli	Vincent Capoli's Daughter
Knuckles McGee	Capoli Family Enforcer
Johnny Viola	Operations Lead

About the Book

Antillus Stone is a gritty crime thriller born from my fascination with classic mob stories and their exploration of moral complexity. As an author, I wanted to delve into the blurred lines between heroism and villainy, examining how ordinary people can be drawn into extraordinary circumstances.

The story follows Jake Stone, a recent finance graduate whose life takes an unexpected turn in the bustling streets of New York City. A chance encounter thrusts Jake into the orbit of the powerful Capoli crime family, setting off a chain of events that will test his principles, loyalties, and the lengths he'll go for love.

Antillus Stone is more than just a crime saga. It is a deep dive into the human psyche, exploring how our choices shape us and the fine line between justice and vengeance. Through Jake's journey, readers will grapple with questions of morality in a world where right and wrong are rarely black and white. My motivation for writing this book was deeply personal. It's an introspective exploration of factors in my life that I felt compelled to express through fiction. I've always been drawn to stories that challenge our perceptions of circumstances, and I wanted to create a narrative that would resonate with readers on multiple levels.

In crafting Jake's character, I sought to create a relatable protagonist—someone with dreams and ambitions suddenly thrust into a world he never expected to inhabit. His struggle to navigate the criminal underworld while maintaining his moral compass reflects our internal battles when confronted with difficult choices. The novel also explores themes of loyalty, family, and the power of love in the face of adversity. Through Jake's relationships with the Capoli family and his partner Isabella, we see the complexities of human connections and the sacrifices we're willing to make for those we care about.

Antillus Stone is my tribute to the classic mob genre, reimagined for a modern audience. It's a story of love, loyalty, and the price of power in a world where shadows shift, and alliances are never certain. Prepare for a thrilling journey that I hope you will enjoy until the last page and perhaps leave you with a unique perspective to draw your moral boundaries.

Contents

Chapter 1: City Lights and College Dreams

As he stood there, gazing up at the towering skyscrapers that lined the streets of New York City, his mind wandered into the deep abyss of uncertainty. Jake Stone had just wrapped up an intense five years at the University of Redlands in California, diving deep into the world of finance and coming out with an MBA to show for it. But his next steps weren't exactly laid out in black and white after graduation. So, he decided to take a pretty big leap and moved to New York City.

He was going to live with his aunt in a city that's as intimidating as it is exciting. New York was a whole new ball game for Jake, a place buzzing with opportunities he had only dreamt of while hitting the books back in California. For him, it felt like stepping into a world where all his hard-earned finance knowledge could really come into play.

As Jake Stone stepped off the train at the subway station, lugging his suitcases behind him, he was immediately struck by the relentless pace with which people moved here. The subway station was a hive of activity; people rushed past without a second glance, too absorbed in their own worlds to notice someone struggling with baggage. Jake couldn't help but feel a bit lost in the flow, dodging commuters who seemed to have no time to spare for a second look, let alone for someone who might have accidentally bumped into them.

Out from the subway station onto the bustling sidewalks of New York, his eyes darted from the kaleidoscope of signs to the sea of diverse faces, each carrying their own unique story. The city's unrelenting pulse seemed to echo in his chest, a mix of raw excitement and butterflies. "Man, this place is both terrifying and thrilling," he thought, feeling the weight and wonder of the city.

As Jake Stone stood in the middle of the thronging crowd, he experienced a surge of wonder that moved through him. At that time, he was overcome by the persistent energy of the city's population as well as the buildings that towered above him, reaching for the clouds. It was a striking contrast to the peaceful and open fields of upstate New York, where he had spent his childhood. Before he moved to California to attend college, Jake's life had been centered around the rhythms of a farm, which was a world apart from the hectic pace of New York City.

Grabbing his luggage while absorbing the scene, he realized just how different this part of New York was from the one he knew. The people here seemed to be from a different breed altogether: focused, fast-moving, and seemingly oblivious to anything that didn't directly concern their immediate goals.

Despite the initial shock of the city's indifference to small courtesies, especially evident in this rush hour madness, Jake couldn't help but feel a spark of ambition ignite within him. The towering buildings around him were more than just architectural marvels; they represented the city's immense potential and opportunities.

To many, his decision to chase his dreams in New York City was borderline crazy. But Jake couldn't shake off the belief that sometimes the open sea is the safest harbor in life. "You've got to make things happen, Jake. No one's going to hand it to you on a silver platter," he reminded himself, feeling a spark of determination. He was here to put his hard-earned finance degree to good use, and he had every intention of exploiting every opportunity that came his way.

He looked around, sensing that New York's countless avenues were like hidden doors waiting to be opened. "All it takes is a bit of courage, a bit of luck," he mused, feeling a sense of adventure like misplaced butterflies. It was now time to put in the work. And seize any opportunity that came his way. "Life is all about taking chances. After all, fortune favors the brave," he thought, a smile tugging at his lips.

Jake had spent his entire childhood surrounded by the oak trees and undulating hills of his parents' farm. He had spent his boyhood and early adulthood secluded in a rural area, doing little more than observing the endless changing of the seasons. While he enjoyed the close-knit community and assisting with tasks, he had always believed that a more meaningful existence awaited him beyond the boundaries of his home.

New York was unlike anything he could have dreamed of in his young, naïve mind back on the farm. He was aware that it would be difficult to relocate to such an intimidating municipality without family funds or connections. However, Jake had developed a strong work ethic and resiliency through his early involvement in farming. Although certain individuals believed he was insane for sacrificing expansive fields for congested sidewalks, he maintained that the perseverance and tenacity that had propelled him through countless lengthy days of manual labor would now push him forward.

In the country, Jake had always been defined by his family and their multigenerational tie to the land. There, he had an identity to live by, but for the first time in New York, neither his name nor his history were recognized. Unpredictably forging his own path was simultaneously intimidating and emancipating. He was ready to prove that a small-town boy from humble roots could make waves in the big city if given half a chance.

Growing up on the farm had given Jake an uncontrollable strength of character. Regardless of the weather, arduous days spent administering to the fields or repairing machinery had fortified his physical and mental health. He had lost count of the storms he had endured, ranging from debilitating summer downpours to blizzards in the winter that confined most of us to our homes. However, labor never ceased on the farm, irrespective of the weather conditions.

Experiences on the farm instilled in Jake the assurance that he could endure any adversity that the city presented. Although some individuals might be intimidated by the rain and snowfall in New York, he had learned from past encounters that weather is a lot like life; sometimes you endure everything bad, but you also enjoy the good times when they come. Since he could recall, he had been forced to endure harsh conditions, strengthening his resilience beyond what could be achieved in a classroom or textbook.

He had also experienced restless nights spent feverishly repairing equipment or completing assignments prior to a rapidly approaching deadline. The arduous, long hours of physical and mental labor had strengthened his resolve. His steely disposition would prove opportune as he maneuvered through the fierce competition and fast-paced atmosphere of his novel urban setting.

Emerging from the subway station into the heart of the city, Jake Stone felt an invigorating sense of challenge. The towering skyscrapers, those behemoths of concrete and glass, didn't intimidate him as one might expect, given his rustic background. Instead, he faced the cutthroat competition and the diverse throngs of city life with a readiness born of his country upbringing. His modest origins, far from being a drawback, fueled his determination to succeed. This metropolis, with all its intensity and bustle, was simply another landscape to conquer, no match for his tenacity and resolve.

Jake wasn't just another face in the crowd. His dreams were as big as the city's towering skyscrapers. He was here to make something of himself, to prove that a farmer's son could make it big in the big city. His rural upbringing wasn't a setback; it was his secret weapon. It had taught him about hard work and about sticking to it even when things get tough. He was ready to take on this concrete jungle, to build a life that was all his own, powered by the grit and determination he brought from the fields to the city streets.

Making his way to the new residence, Jake Stone, an ambitious farm boy from rural upstate Ithica, New York, was prepared to embark on his odyssey. This young man had an unending love for finance that stemmed from an innate curiosity for the complex interplay between numbers and markets rather than merely being a career decision. He found a certain beauty in the measured risk and reward of investing and a certain rhythm in the fluctuating equities.

Just yesterday, he was sitting under the soft light of his desk lamp with his textbooks spread out. Throughout the course of his MBA, he would spend his university nights immersed in the theories of financial gurus, trying to find ways to put complicated ideas into practice through his simulations and projects.

"Jake, I need your opinion on this financial matter," his roommate had made a comment.

"It's a tough world out there," as they were both up late making notes.

With his fixed gaze fixed on the charts and graphs, Jake had merely grinned. "It's like the farm," he said. "To grow anything from mere seeds, you must first sow it, then water it, and tend to it consistently. Knowing the cycle, the growth is more important than the money alone...the process itself is a thing of beauty."

However, Jake encountered several obstacles along the way. He was frequently overworked due to his high academic schedule and his part-time employment. His professor had commented on the bags under his eyes, and he recalled a discussion about it.

"Jake, you're pushing yourself too hard. Is it worth it?" his professor had asked, concern lacing his voice.

Looking back, Jake recalled his own unwavering response: "Every bit of effort is a step towards something bigger. I learned that back home. After the toil comes the harvest."

Because of his perseverance, he graduated with honors and heard his name proudly announced. His focused determination was a success, not only an academic one. So far, he has been a purposeful individual seeking an unconventional position in the financial industry. He aspired to make decisions and invest in ways that reflected the principles taught to him by his parents.

This ethos was rooted in his upbringing, where he remembered his father's words on the farm, "Every crop we plant, Jake, feeds someone and brings honor in exchange for our hard work." Jake's financial career reflected this mentality, not only being profit-driven but also focusing on making a difference and contributing to the greater good. Right at that moment, Jake's phone vibrated sharply in his pocket, jolting him back to reality. The unexpected buzz momentarily broke the spell of the city's rhythm and pulled him out of his nostalgic journey down memory lane.

He glanced at the screen, his heart skipping a beat. It was a call from one of the financial firms to which he had applied. With bated breath, he answered, only to have his hopes dashed by a polite but firm rejection. The words, "We've chosen a candidate whose experience more closely aligns with our needs," echoed in his ears, leaving a sting of disappointment.

Disheartened, Jake wandered along the sidewalk, his thoughts a whirlwind of analytical replay. "Did I seem too forward during the interview? Did my lack of experience play a role in their decision?" The questions engulfed him, blurring the city's vibrancy into a dull haze. Absorbed in his turmoil, he stopped in front of a small shop. His gaze, previously clouded by his spiraling thoughts, slowly focused on the scene unfolding before him.

A group of school kids, donning crisp white karate uniforms, stood outside the shop, their faces alight with excitement. An instructor, radiating an aura of calm authority, was demonstrating a kata, his movements precise and fluid. This scene, so starkly different from the world of finance, struck a chord in Jake's heart, transporting him back to a cherished chapter of his own life.

He remembered the dojo where he had learned Uechi Ryu, a martial art he had discovered in middle school after enduring relentless bullying by a boy named Bernard Cooper. Those days in the dojo were more than just learning self-defense. They paved the path toward transformation, teaching him resilience, discipline, and the importance of inner strength. He recalled Randy, his sensei, a man whose wisdom had extended far beyond martial techniques.

One particular lesson from Randy surfaced in Jake's mind, a vivid memory that momentarily eclipsed the city's noise. He was back in the dojo, the smell of polished wood, the sound of fellow students practicing in the background, and the raw and pungent smell of sweat creating an aroma of willpower.

"Jake, remember," Randy had said, his voice firm yet encouraging, "in martial arts, as in life, you will face setbacks. But it's not the setback that defines you; it's how you respond. The transitional movements between the punches, blocks, and kicks of the kata are the most important elements because they make you stable and fluid. Every defeat and rejection is an opportunity to learn and grow stronger. Every day is an opportunity to start again."

Jake had taken those words to heart, carrying them through his journey in Uechi Ryu all the way to the state finals on the competitive circuit. Now, standing outside the shop, watching the young karate students, Randy's words echoed in his mind with renewed clarity.

Setting his phone back in his pocket, Jake absorbed the bad news from the firm with grace, also realizing that this was undoubtedly a setback, but it wasn't the end of his path. Just like in the dojo, where every fall was a lesson, this was a moment to learn, adapt, and start again. Jake continued his trek with the spirit of a warrior and the heart of a resilient dreamer.

Jake's attention then went to thoughts of his parents, Paul and Pam Stone, his foundation for tempered good sense and support. Being from upstate New York, their land had been passed down through the generations and was more than simply a place to grow food; it was a symbol of their family's love and commitment to the land.

Paul Stone, Jake's father, was a man of few words but of immense wisdom. His hands, roughened by years of tending to the fields, were a symbol of his connection to the land. Paul had inherited the farm from his father and, with Pam by his side, had turned it into not just a source of livelihood but a home that thrived on love, hard work, and the joys of simple living.

Their home revolved around Jake's mom, Pam. Jake cherished her capacity to appreciate the mundane and her infectious laughter, which resounded over the fields. Her vibrant garden was evidence that she believed in the harmony of beauty and usefulness; she could create a delectable meal with the most basic items.

Jake had his upbringing by Paul and Pam in an atmosphere where virtues such as perseverance, integrity, and diligence were not merely imparted but manifested on a daily basis. They cherished their heritage and their responsibility as guardians of the environment. This profound connection to the earth and to a life of purposeful labor profoundly influenced Jake. Deep within the expansive grasslands and cloudless regions of upstate New York, he acquired an understanding of the genuine significance of diligence and tenacity.

His parents had imparted the understanding that success should not be solely quantified monetarily but also in the gratification derived from a day's laborious effort and the recognition that one's harvest was a product of one's own hands and heart.

His parents, Paul and Pam, served as a reminder of the values and moral fortitude they instilled in their only child, which served as a compass amidst the intricacies of the urban environment for Jake. He was a man who influenced people with his unassuming and striking personality. Of average height with a lean, athletic build, he carried himself with the quiet confidence of someone who knew the value of hard work and discipline. His hair was a sandy brown, often tousled in a way that spoke of practicality over style, and his eyes, a unique shade of brown, reflected a world of dreams and determination. A faint scar on his chin, a souvenir from his days on the farm, added character to his otherwise youthful face.

Jake always had a deep admiration for his Aunt Mary, a woman whose story read like an inspiring novel. Mary, his mom Pam's sister, was a powerhouse in New York, a city where she turned her towering dreams into a breathtaking reality. Her journey from humble beginnings to becoming a self-made millionaire in real estate and banking was nothing short of remarkable. She was the one helping Jake out with the job, the move, and the shift from the quieter part of New York to the busy one.

Aunt Mary had a knack for seeing the diamond in the rough, especially in the real estate market. She could look at a dilapidated building, see a future luxury apartment complex or an empty lot, and envision a bustling shopping center. Her moves in the real estate world were bold and often unconventional but almost always spot on. In banking, she brought the same innovative mindset, understanding the ebb and flow of finances with a keen eye and a steady hand.

Her path wasn't a straight line to the top. It was littered with challenges and setbacks, the kinds that would make most people throw in the towel. With each obstacle, she just grew stronger, smarter, and more determined. She was like a phoenix, always rising from the ashes, brighter and more formidable than before.

Now, as the matriarch of a real estate and banking empire, Aunt Mary's success was undeniable. But what was even more impressive was how she remained down-to-earth despite her wealth and influence. She would often say that her success was built on a foundation of resilience and integrity, qualities she held dear from her modest upbringing.

For him, Aunt Mary wasn't just family; she was a living example of what you could achieve with hard work, determination, and a little bit of courage. Her story was a constant source of motivation for him, a beacon reminding him that no matter where you start, with the right attitude and effort, the sky's the limit.

Jake moved to New York City, surrounded by his aunt Mary and his cousin, Titiano. Growing up, they were inseparable, sharing adventures and secrets. Their bond remained strong despite distance and time. Settling into Aunt Mary's home felt natural as if part of a close-knit family circle that had expanded its boundaries. Their childhood was a tapestry of shared adventures and secrets.

The transition from the quiet, open spaces of the farm to the luxurious abode of Aunt Mary was a shift of worlds for Jake. However, he was firmly grounded in reality and understood the need to stand on his own two feet. Sure, she was providing immense help in getting ahead in his career, but Jake knew he could not rely entirely on her support. Even back in Redlands during his MBA, he found himself doing all sorts of jobs in the locality of Redlands. Jaked gazed around the streets as he neared her residence, familiarizing himself with the businesses nearby. He would have to get himself another source of distraction to stay connected to everyday people who were entirely different from the elite circle Aunt Mary navigated.

She wasn't just a silent spectator in Jake's journey. With a keen eye and a heart that genuinely wanted the best for her nephew, she saw an opportunity to help him inch closer to his dreams. She could provide for Jake in a way that she currently could not with her son. The house was empty and desolate because her son Titiano decided to forgo the life of luxury that Mary represented in favor of becoming his own man and devoting himself to social causes. Having Jake present, there was a change for the better.

She made a plan to use her connections in the business world to land him a great job at a top financial firm downtown. It just showed how much she believed in him, especially with all the new changes he was going through.

Jake was practically buzzing with excitement, like a freshman being introduced to his first beer. He turned a quick left, gripping his bags even harder. He quickened his pace. Pausing for a moment, Jake pulled out his phone to check his aunt's address. It was close by, and the weather was just perfect, so he decided to walk instead of hailing a cab.

He hadn't brought much with him to New York—just a couple of bags. Clothing was never high on his priority list; his focus was always more on books and ambitions. So, with those two bags in tow, he was every bit the picture of a bachelor, ready to take on the city streets.

Making his way to her residence, Jake couldn't help but feel a surge of gratitude. His aunt was the unsung hero in all this, the one who had opened this door for him. He could still see her on the front page of "Finance Today," prominently displayed in his new room. There she was, the second wealthiest financier around, the lone woman in a tough crowd, shining bright. That magazine cover was more than just glossy paper; it was a testament to her grit and savvy.

As Jake navigated the somewhat perplexing streets of New York, he found himself in a lane that seemed to twist and turn more than the plot of a mystery novel. He paused, looking around for a familiar landmark or sign to point him toward the main street. Noticing a man nearby, surrounded by an array of hand-painted canvases, Jake decided to ask for directions.

"Excuse me, Sir," he said, approaching the elderly painter. "Could you point me towards the main street from here?"

His hands were stained with a lifetime of colors. The painter looked up and smiled. "Sure, young man. Just go straight down this lane, then take a left. Can't miss it," he replied, his voice as textured as his paintings. Thank you, said Jake, as a familiar sound playing from a small speaker by the painter's feet caught his attention. It was Giant Steps by John Coltrane, weaving through the air like a gentle reminder of a different time. Jake's mind quickly drifted to a scene in his brain that quickly became one of the best nights of his life.

He remembered vividly the evening he and Isabella had dressed up and gone out to a jazz club right after a long night of studying. The memory was so clear: her laughter, the sparkle in her eyes, her excitement that seemed to light up the room. They had enjoyed a dinner filled with playful banter and danced as the melodies tickled their souls while every note echoed happiness. The evening had ended back at his apartment, where they reveled in each other's company, lost in their own world.

Any time thoughts of Isabella surfaced, Jake had to summon his warrior's resolve in order to suppress the longing to see her. He was again strong enough to turn nostalgia into a driving force. He compartmentalized these memories as nothing more than echoes from a time in his life that had passed and no longer constituted his identity. In the race to build a future for himself, he now sought the blueprint for success and was determined to move forward.

Still, Jake felt a rush of mixed emotions as he listened to Coltrane. He couldn't help but think about his last devastating talk with Isabella. They mutually decided to end their relationship instead of entertaining a long-distance situation that would be a distraction to igniting their respective careers. They had prioritized practicality over infatuation, and although it seemed like the right thing to do, it was painful.

After a few minutes, Jake moved on as Coltrane slowly faded into the background. With each step toward the main street, he felt more ready to take on whatever this city had in store for him. He chose to view the past as a cherished memory while the future was an exciting, unwritten adventure.

Jake had always fantasized about becoming as influential and successful as his Aunt Mary. He aspired to acquire greatness not alone for his own benefit but also to pay tribute to his parents' achievements. With a feeling of purpose and possibility, he would lie in bed every night as the clock struck twelve, peering into the blackness above. It was as if his hopes and ambitions were drawing nearer with every passing second.

However, not all members of his family shared his ambition and work ethic. Mary's son Titiano felt rather uncomfortable with the advantages of Mary's privileged lifestyle. He yearned to forge his own path, free from the looming presence of his mother's influence. He wanted to change direction in such a way that would allow him to forge his own identity.

On his way to the new residence, the same rebellious member of the family reached out to Jake. His phone buzzed with an alert—just as he was about to reach his destination. A message from Titiano popped up: "Text me when you get here; let's go hang out." Titiano had been eager to meet Jake ever since he found out his cousin was coming to the city. He wanted to be there for Jake, to welcome him into the bustling, overwhelming world of New York, a city that was now to be Jake's new home.

Titiano's message brought a smile to Jake's face. It was comforting to know that amidst the whirlwind of this new chapter, he had a familiar face waiting for him, ready to reconnect and perhaps reminisce about old times while forging new memories in the city's vibrant backdrop.

Having his own set of troubles laid out for him, Jake was well-versed in Titiano's struggle. He often observed that Titiano found himself in a reflective mood. He understood his cousin's desire for independence, yet couldn't help but feel grateful for the doors that Mary's influence had opened for him. It was a complex web of gratitude, ambition, and the quest for self-identity that each member of the family tried their best to navigate in their lives.

Titiano wanted no part of his mother's influence in his life, yet he never uttered a single syllable deterring the life choices that Jake made, for the level of respect between them was of utmost significance. Even so, they supported each other's dreams and aspirations despite their differences.

Jake finally made it to his aunt's place, lugging his two bags up to the porch. Just as he reached the steps, the main butler—a familiar face from previous visits—was already there, greeting him with a warm smile.

"Why didn't you give me a ring to pick you up from the subway?" the butler asked, a hint of concern in his voice.

With a light chuckle, Jake replied, "I figured a walk would do me good. Plus, the weather was just too nice to pass up the chance to soak in a bit of New York on foot."

After the brief exchange, Jake swiftly moved to settle into his new room. It didn't take him long to unpack his limited belongings into the neat and tidy closets. The room was something out of a storybook, richly furnished, with a touch of elegance that spoke of his aunt's taste.

It seemed strangely inviting, especially in comparison to logistics back at home or the shared room at the university. As the evening sky turned a deep shade of twilight, bringing a soothing calm to his room, Jake took a moment to freshen up and settle in. The room, with its gentle lighting and sumptuous furnishings, felt surprisingly comforting, wrapping him in a sense of luxurious contentment. He lounged with his laptop, initially intent on doing some reading, but soon his focus waned.

Jake was daydreaming as he lay in bed at midnight, the hands of the clock joining. The divergent paths that he and Titiano were following were on his mind. A sense of resolve bubbled within him—a determination to chase after his own dreams with everything he had. At the same time, he found himself hoping that Titiano, too, would carve out his own distinct path, one that wasn't overshadowed by the impressive legacy of Mary Clayton.

In the quiet of the night, with the city's heartbeat a distant murmur, Jake lay contemplating the future. It was a mix of eagerness for his own prospects and a heartfelt wish for Titiano's success in finding his unique way in the world.

Just as Jake was about to rest his head and eyes, setting his laptop aside after a long day, his phone broke the silence with a buzz. It was Titiano calling. With a stretch and a yawn, Jake reached for the phone, answering the call as he got up from the bed.

The moment he answered, Titiano's voice came through, slurred but full of joy, "Hey Jake, has the big man made it to his new abode?" In the background, Jake could hear the muffled sounds of laughter and chatter, distinctly feminine.

Jake, a bit amused and curious, asked, "What's going on there, Titi?"

Titiano, with the buzz of the bar scene behind him, reminded Jake, "Man, you were supposed to meet me, remember? Where are you at?" Realizing he had almost forgotten, Jake quickly asked, "Alright, where are you?"

"I am at The Dirty Bird Tavern, you know, that bar down by the river. It's lit here, man!" Titiano's voice was a mix of excitement and impatience.

Without a second thought, Jake grabbed his jacket, a burst of energy replacing his earlier tiredness. "Hold on, I'll be there in a bit!" he said, already halfway out the door. The thought of meeting his cousin, who was more like an old friend, and catching up over cold beers with the comforting backdrop of the cityscape was all the motivation he needed. Jake's steps quickened as he made his way to The Dirty Bird, ready to dive into the familiar warmth of Titiano's company and the promise of a good night.

Navigating through the bustling New York traffic, it took Jake nearly half an hour to reach the bar. As he pushed open the door of the bar, a wave of laughter and music hit him. Scanning the room, his eyes quickly landed on a crowd of women near the bar, their laughter rising above the tempo. Jake noticed that one of the girls had a nice ass. In the center of it all was Titiano, as charismatic as ever, holding court and clearly in his element. Jake couldn't help but smile; some things never changed.

Making his way through the crowd, Jake's phone buzzed with a message. It was from Rodney, the butler at his aunt's place, asking why he hadn't requested the car. Jake felt a twinge of annoyance—the thought of being coddled didn't sit well with him. He was about to reply when he felt a hand on his shoulder. "Already babying you, are they?" Titiano's voice broke through his thoughts, a teasing glint in his eyes.

Jake looked up, a grin spreading across his face. "Seems like it," he laughed, putting his phone away. The annoyance faded as quickly as it had come, replaced by the comfort of his cousin's familiar banter.

They clinked their beers together as the cousins and best friends had a reason to celebrate. After settling in with a few stories and laughs, Jake turned to Titiano and remarked, "Guess who got another job rejection today." He wore a forced smile.

Titiano's laughter joined Jake's, but as it faded, he caught a glimpse of something else in Jake's eyes—a flicker of disappointment quickly masked by humor. Titiano knew his cousin well enough to see beyond the facade.

"Man, the job market's brutal," Titiano said, shaking his head. "But hey, remember back in California? You were slinging drinks like a pro. Why not bartend for a bit? You know, just until you land that big corporate gig."

Jake paused, considering it. The idea hadn't crossed his mind, but now that it was out there, it didn't seem half bad. "Bartending, huh?" he mused. "I did have a knack for it, didn't I? Mixing drinks, chatting with people... it was kind of fun."

Titiano nodded enthusiastically. "Exactly! And you were good at it. Plus, it's a great way to meet people and hear stories. You never know what opportunities could come your way."

There was a moment of silence as Jake mulled over the suggestion. Then, with a decisive nod, he said, "You know what? That's not a bad idea at all. I'll start looking into it first thing tomorrow."

As they continued their evening, the gears of their conversation smoothly transitioned, but the idea Titiano had planted firmly took root in Jake's mind. The more the night progressed, filled with an easy flow of stories and laughter, the more Jake felt a sense of budding hope. The thought of bartending, which at first seemed like a mere stopgap, began to feel like a strategic step, a way to gather momentum for his future leap into the corporate world. Surrounded by the lively energy of the bar and buoyed by Titiano's unwavering support, the prospect of mixing drinks and swapping stories in a New York City bar sparked an unexpected excitement in him.

Jake had already agreed to accept his aunt's help in navigating the corporate landscape, but he was mindful of setting boundaries. He appreciated her support, yet he was determined that the crux of his success would be his own hard work and merit. The assistance was welcome, but Jake was resolute that his achievements would be the fruit of his own labor.

Chapter 2: Bartender's Gambit

In the days following his arrival in New York, Jake Stone found himself straddling two very different worlds. During the day, he was the very definition of desire and dedication as he tirelessly applied for employment and attended interviews in the business world.

Each morning, after a bracing cold shower that never failed to invigorate him, Jake would linger a little while in bed. It was his moment of quiet contemplation, a daily ritual where he steeled himself for the day ahead. Staring at the ceiling, he'd whisper a personal mantra, which was a simple yet powerful affirmation: "Today's the day. Just one step closer." It was his way of mentally gearing up, instilling a sense of hope and determination that he would, indeed, make it.

Jake's day was off to a rousing start by the time he got out of bed. He devoted his mornings to the process of refining his resumes, with each rewrite being a painstaking effort to convey his experiences and skills in the most effective manner possible. In an effort to determine where he might be most comfortable working, he conducted extensive studies on prospective employers, gaining knowledge of their business structures and cultures.

The afternoons of his life were frequently characterized by visits to the magnificent lobbies of high-rise buildings, where, as per the norm, he had to present and prove himself to be the ideal candidate for a variety of positions in the financial sector. Each interview presented him with a new opportunity to push himself closer to achieving his objective, as well as a new hurdle to overcome.

But as the sun dipped below the horizon, Jake's world transformed. As per routine, he would step into the role of a freelance bartender, a job that he picked up not just to fill his evenings but to assert his independence. Each night, he found himself in the bar, surrounded by the rhythmic pulse of music and the chatter of a new set of patrons. Every night, he focused on making the same drinks on the menu, whose recipes were ingrained in his brain. He tried to apply the same amount of precision and dedication to his interviews as well as the passion in his drinks.

A constant stream of new people and tales came through the pub each night, and Jake made sure to emerge in every tale as the bartender with a smile. With his attentive ear and welcoming manner, he rapidly became a favorite on account of his qualities. A few days into the job, he settled in and weaved his own story into the fabric of the city's nightlife, making it a point to introduce himself to as many people as you could possibly meet. In the clinking of glasses and the casual talks, he discovered joys that he had not anticipated and a sense of belonging inside the society.

Compared to his humble beginnings on a farm and his busy nights at the bars, his existence at his aunt's mansion was a striking contrast to both elements. His aunt was seldom home as her world orbited in different circles. The annoying butler, Rodney, managed the mansion in line with the luxurious lifestyle and frequently suggested that Jake take advantage of the high-end cars or the personal drivers for his job hunts.

But Jake was true to his roots and preferred the simple approach. Each time the butler proposed the idea of using one of his aunt's sleek cars or being chauffeured for interviews, Jake would decline with a lighthearted quip. "Thanks, but I think the subway is starting to grow on me," he'd say with a chuckle, or "I might get lost in all that luxury and forget where I'm heading!"

His responses were always met with a puzzled but amused look from the butler, who couldn't quite grasp Jake's preference for modesty over luxury. However, for Jake, this was a matter of principle. He was in New York to prove his mettle and build a life on his terms, and he was determined to do so with the same work ethic and self-reliance that had been instilled in him since childhood.

Jake found an unexpected sense of purpose in balancing the pursuit of his chosen career path with preserving his autonomy. Though each unfavorable response delivered via email left its mark, he discovered an unorthodox remedy among the lively patrons of the bar where his skills were appreciated. There was a comforting quality to the convivial environment, and the tales exchanged over pints helped uplift his mood. It seemed each chuckle and story shared over a drink offered a soothing message—that fulfillment in life stemmed not from the contents of his inbox alone but from human connections and experiences far beyond any rejection.

While the decisions of others remained out of his control, he took solace in the companionship and moments of levity to be found among the community he served each night. Their warmth reminded him that his worth wasn't defined by the verdicts of faceless recruiters and that life had more dimensions than the jobs he pursued.

Night after night, when he left the buzz of the bar scene and headed back to the quiet grandeur of his aunt's house, he could feel a steady surge of confidence building within him. He was slowly but surely finding his footing in the sprawling maze of New York City.

When Jake was adjusting to his new life in New York, his cousin Titiano was always just a phone call away. He made sure to check in on him on a frequent basis to ensure that he was doing well in his new environment. Titiano was always ready to offer advice or listen and offer his counsel, and their chats varied from lighthearted banter to genuine worry.

"Hey man, how's the city treating you?" Titiano's voice would come through the phone, always sounding like he was just around the corner, ready to drop by. Jake found comfort in these calls; they were a reminder of the family and familiarity he had in this vast, bustling city.

"Well, I haven't gotten lost in the subway yet, so I guess that's a win," Jake would respond with a laugh, and they'd both chuckle. Then they'd delve into deeper conversations about job hunts, life at the bar, and the latest happenings in each other's lives.

Titiano was more than just a cousin to Jake; he was a bridge to the life he'd left behind and support in the new world he was trying to conquer. Their talks often ended with Titiano saying something like, "You've got this, Jake. Just remember, we're all rooting for you back here."

These regular check-ins with Titiano were a source of strength for Jake. They reminded him that he wasn't alone, even in a city as vast and impersonal as New York could sometimes seem. He had a family, a connection to something real and tangible. The thought alone was enough to push him forward, to keep him grounded amidst the whirlwind of interviews and late-night shifts.

Jake had finally found his rhythm in the bustling profession and vibrant city nightlife during his second week as a bartender. The bar was especially active with activity because that particular night was Halloween and full of excitement. Amid the massive crowd of customers, Jake stood somewhat away and meticulously cleaned the shot glasses that were located behind the bar.

His attention was drawn to a group of young women who were dancing, and the sound of their laughter could be heard over the music. During the course of their dancing routines, it appeared as though they were sneaking looks at him, their eyes shimmering with a mixture of mischief and curiosity. After some time passed, each of them made their way from the dance floor to the bar while muffling their laughter and exchanging glances. An additional spark was added to the already lively atmosphere of the pub by their approach, which was casual yet intentional. It was a blend of fun, confidence, and real interest.

Throughout his shift that night, they flirted playfully with him, their teasing glances and light banter a welcome distraction from the routine of mixing drinks and taking orders.

"Hey, bartender, think you can concoct something special for us?" One of the girls called out, her eyes twinkling with a blend of challenge and amusement.

Jake flashed a confident smile, "I think I can whip up something you'll love. Any preferences?"

"As long as it's as charming as you," another chimed in, eliciting giggles from the group.

The night wore on with the girls lingering at the bar, engaging Jake in light, flirtatious conversations whenever he had a moment to spare. They talked about everything from their favorite music to the quirks of living in New York, their words flowing as easily as the drinks he poured.

As closing time neared, the crowd thinned out, but one of the girls from the group, who introduced herself as Mia, stayed behind. She leaned against the bar, her gaze fixed on Jake as he cleaned up.

"You know, I've always found bartenders interesting," Mia said, her voice a soft melody over the hum of the background music. "You get to meet so many people, hear so many stories."

"Yeah, it's definitely one of the perks of the job," Jake replied, stacking glasses. "Every night is a different story."

As the night progressed and the bar began to empty, Mia lingered. She perched herself at the bar, her conversation flowing effortlessly. Her words were like a melody, sweet and captivating, and Jake found himself increasingly drawn to her. There was something about the way she spoke, with a spark of humor and a touch of charm, that intrigued him.

She laughed at his jokes and paid close attention to his stories about going to New York and his hopes. By the time the bar was ready to close, the night had wrapped itself in a quiet, intimate ambiance. Mia was still there, her presence now more pronounced in the nearly empty space.

"So, what does a bartender do after closing up?" Mia asked, her voice carrying a playful lilt. As she spoke, her fingers, which had been idly tracing the rim of her glass, reached out and gently poked Jake's arm.

Caught slightly off guard, Jake raised an eyebrow in response, a hint of amusement playing across his face. Mia met his gaze with a smile, one that seemed to hold a mix of curiosity and cheekiness.

Her light and flirtatious gesture added an undercurrent of playfulness to their interaction, suggesting she was interested in more than just casual bar conversation.

In that small, seemingly insignificant moment, there was a subtle shift in the air between them, a silent acknowledgment of the chemistry that had been building throughout the night.

Jake shrugged with a smile. "Usually, I just head home, but tonight, I could make an exception."

The city was asleep as they stepped out into the quiet streets, the buzz of the bar a distant memory. They walked together, their conversation flowing as naturally as it had over the bar counter. As they reached Jake's aunt's residence, Mia paused.

"Would you like to come in for a nightcap?" Jake offered, feeling a mix of anticipation and excitement. Mia's smile in response was all the answer he needed. When she entered the residence, she marveled at the grandeur of Jake's aunt's estate. Seeing their entry on the camera, Rodney came downstairs and asked if he should prepare something for them. Mia replied, "I don't want to be any inconvenience."

Seeing Jake's companion's striking beauty, Rodney replied, "I am at your service, and it will be my pleasure." They made their way to the kitchen and talked while Rodney prepared Monte Cristos and Omelets. In comparison, he told jokes to amuse the pair. Jake saw a different side of him and appreciated the way that Rodney was trying to take care of them. After setting the table and opening a bottle of wine, Rodney decided to retire for the evening so that Jake and Mia could continue enjoying each other.

They discuss politics, movies, and relationships and tell each other jokes, keeping the fun tone set earlier by Rodney.

Unexpectedly, and at a certain point in the night, Mia leaned in for a spontaneous and exhilarating kiss. It ignited the passion that was building up between the pair as their relationship entered a new dimension. After careful contemplation, Jake commented, "Since it is so late already, you are more than welcome to stay over."

Mia looked puzzled for a second, then simply replied, "OK," after a minute.

He was in momentary disbelief, but without breaking his stride, he then said, "Let's go upstairs." It started a sequence of events that ended with them making passionate love until they both passed out from exhaustion. The next morning, as he watched the sunrise from his window, with Mia still asleep, he realized that this city was full of surprises.

The next night, Jake was found behind the bar again, immersed in the familiar rhythm of clinking glasses and background music. There was no sign of Mia, but the memory of the previous evening lingered pleasantly in his mind. The night out in the city had been a refreshing change from his usual routine, a roller coaster of emotions that left him with a subtle smile as he worked.

The bar filled with its usual blend of patrons as the night wore on. The air was thick with the sound of laughter and chatter; the atmosphere was lively and charged. Jake was in his element, serving drinks and exchanging occasional banter with the customers.

Suddenly, the mood shifted. A loud, harsh argument broke out in the Flamingo Room, shattering the bar's jovial ambiance. A few of the other patrons began to take notice as their expressions changed from enjoyment to concern.

"How dare you talk to me like that?" A muffled scream of a man emanated from the room. This caused a hush to fall over the bar as people tried to understand what was happening in the far-off room. The tension in the air was palpable. The content of the surrounding noise muffled an argument, but the aggressive tone was unmistakable.

Noticing trouble, Jake moved cautiously towards the Flamingo Room to understand what was happening and possibly defuse the situation. Hearing snippets of the argument became clearer with every step he took toward the room. The casually thrown-around words like "territory" and "deal" made Jake quicken his pace and enter the room without a second thought.

Just as he entered the brightly lit and rather questionably decorated room, his eyes darted to the cause of the yelling due to the two gentlemen being held off by the other members of the meeting. Just as he was about to speak, his attention was immediately drawn to the gentleman in a very nice suit yelling, "Do you know who I am? You are fucking with Johnny Viola." Looking back at the concerned audience of the bar, Jake proceeded to close the door to block the view of the onlookers. Two men, their faces flushed with anger, were standing toe-to-toe, voices raised in heated dispute.

Patrons began whispering among themselves, their earlier ease replaced by anxiety. Some started to edge towards the exit, not wanting to be caught in what might escalate into a dangerous altercation.

Jake, from behind closed doors, tried his best to maintain a calm demeanor and called out. "Gentlemen, please, let's settle this outside," he urged, aware that his intervention might be risky but necessary to prevent any further escalation.

But the men were too caught up in their argument to heed his words. One of them, his hand shaking with rage, knocked over a glass, causing it to shatter on the floor. The sharp sound of breaking glass was like a signal. The room erupted into chaos, with everyone starting to either exchange blows or people scrambling to get out of the way.

Watching these events unfold, Jake quickly yelled, "Guys, let's break this..." Just then, one of the elbows of the men involved in the argument hit Jake flat in the jaw, and he lost his balance and fell behind a table. A lady helped him up as she was running for the door, and then, as the tension in the bar escalated, Jake's instincts kicked in. The air changed as he heard Randy's voice briefly tell him, "Don't think, just do," as Jake recalled a Uechi technique that required him to completely turn off his brain and allow the spirit of the style to guide his movements without thought.

Moving swiftly through the audience of the Flamingo Room, Jake approached the quarreling men. The noise of the bar seemed to fade into the background as he concentrated on the situation at hand. Suddenly, one of the men, fueled by anger and perhaps too much alcohol, lunged toward Jake because he had inadvertently become a standing target.

Jake efficiently reverse-punched the opponent square in the forehead with such rhythmic force that it should have shattered his hand, but instead, the attacker fell forward with the same inertia he started with but landed flat on his face, knocked out cold. Jake then focused his attention on the center of the room, where the individual who announced himself as Johnny Viola was in a headlock. He was being punched in the face by a much larger guy.

Jake walked up as the attacker made eye contact and threw Johnny Viola to the ground hard.

Using fluid and precise movement, Jake dodged a wild and slow sucker punch from the giant and thought to himself briefly, "That would have really hurt if it had connected. Then, almost immediately, without breaking his stride, Jake threw a right cross and simultaneously executed a Uechi one-knuckle punch to the giant's temple, along with a sidekick to blow out the attacker's knee. It took one long second for the giant man to drop, but when he did, it was like a sound heard around the world.

Every single person in the room involved in the brawl stopped like they were all instantly frozen in time and stared at Jake Stone, the man with the glare of fire in his eyes and fast hands.

The room suddenly fell silent, and the patrons involved in the brawl were unexpectedly staring in disbelief. Here was their bartender, whom they had known only for his friendly service and skillful drink-mixing, revealing an unexpected side of himself. He took out the biggest guy in the room in about 7 seconds.

Jake helped Johnny Viola to his feet, which inadvertently signaled that Jake had chosen a side. The other group involved in the dispute, now seeing Jake's capability, backed down and said that it might be smarter to live and fight another day. One guy then yelled, "Did you see that? He took out Tony Rossi without even breaking a sweat. Another guy shouted, "Let's get the fuck out of here," as they helped the two men, who were knocked out cold to their feet, and started to escort them out.

As the tension dissolved and security arrived to handle the aftermath, murmurs rippled through the individuals who remained in the room. The swift yet controlled manner in which Jake handled the situation left everyone, from the mob members to the onlookers, visibly impressed. His actions spoke of a deep mastery of his art, a discipline beyond physical prowess to encompass calmness and control in the face of danger.

As the bar returned to its normal rhythm, Jake felt a sense of quiet satisfaction in the aftermath. Not only had he prevented what could have been a violent altercation, but he had also upheld the principles of Uechi Ryu—respect, restraint, and the use of skill for protection and peace. His intervention that night did more than just prevent people from getting hurt; it left a lasting impression on everyone who witnessed it. In a city where unexpected challenges lurked around every corner, Jake had shown that strength lay not just in physical ability but in the poise and control with which one faced those challenges. As he resumed his duties behind the bar, Jake knew that this night had changed the way some people saw him.

Following that rough evening, there was a change in the way the bar worked. Some of the guys who had been in the middle of the fight and contributed to the entire escalation saw how the chaotic brawl came to a halt because of Jake, yet he never talked about it or discussed what happened behind those closed doors. This created an unspoken respect.

In the days that followed, Jake got to know some of these men better. At first, they were just faces in the crowd. When they walked into the bar, they would nod to him to let him know they recognized him. They had gone from being angry to being friendly. They would sometimes make small talk, and the way they talked was a mix of careful respect and a hint of thanks.

After work one night, Jake was finishing up when a rough-looking individual walked up to him and said, "You did well the other night," in a rough but honest voice.

"You look so unassuming, yet you know how to use your skills well and aren't afraid to do so. Like a secret badass."

"Don Vincent Capoli sends his regards, you really helped us out that night when we were being ambushed by the Rossi crime syndicate."

"You tell us when you need something, kid."

The offer surprised Jake. He started to understand the kind of world these men lived in and didn't want to be a part of it. But he knew enough about New York's streets to know that this kind of offer wasn't made without real thought. For them, it was a sign of debt, proof that they respected him and saw it as a favor they owed him.

"Thanks, but I hope it doesn't come to that," Jake replied, maintaining a polite yet cautious tone. The man simply nodded, making a gesture that spoke volumes and left the bar.

This unexpected turn of events added a new layer to Jake's experience in the city. He had inadvertently found himself with allies in a sphere he never intended to be a part of. But this was perhaps not as unusual as it seemed in the city's intricate web of connections and loyalties.

As Jake worked at the bar night after night, he could feel these guys keeping an eye on him to make sure nothing bad happened. They would step in quietly if a customer got too loud or if something looked like it could get worse. There was no doubt that they would keep their word and look out for him in their own way.

Jake was still wary, though. He was thankful for the safety they gave him without saying a word, but he was careful not to get too involved. He kept a friendly but professional distance, always aware of the thin line he was walking.

Even though Jake wasn't expecting this new development, it helped him understand how complicated life is in New York City. Relationships have many sides in this setting, and partnerships can form out of the blue.

Exhausted from another long day of balancing job applications, bartending, and navigating the complex social dynamics of the bar, Jake finally collapsed into the bed. Just as he was about to drift off, his phone lit up with a message that instantly pulled him back to wakefulness. It was from Isabella, a simple yet poignant text: "Thinking of you."

The words stirred a whirlpool of emotions within him. He found himself transported back to a night that now felt like a lifetime ago. He remembered how they had gone salsa dancing, the night alive with rhythm and warmth. The way Isabella moved, her body swaying to the music with effortless grace, had captivated him completely. They had been in their own world, the dance floor their domain, where every step and turn deepened their connection.

Afterward, they returned to his place, the energy of the night still coursing through them. What followed was a night of passionate love, a physical expression of their intense bond. It was a memory that still had the power to make his heart ache, a reminder of what they had once been to each other.

Lying in bed, Jake's mind wrestled with these memories and the recent turn of events. The one-night stand he had experienced, while a moment of spontaneous connection, now cast a shadow of guilt over him. He couldn't help but compare the depth of what he had shared with Isabella to the fleeting encounter at the bar.

But then he gently reminded himself of the reality—he and Isabella were no longer together. Their lives had diverged onto different paths.

The decision to end their relationship had been mutual, a practical choice given their respective ambitions and the challenges of a long-distance relationship. Yet, understanding this didn't make the memories any less poignant or the lingering feelings any less complex.

As he lay there, Jake realized that moving on was not as straightforward as he had hoped. The text from Isabella, though simple, had reopened a chapter he thought he had closed. It was a reminder of the past but also a signal that life was moving forward, with or without the closure he sought.

As the night got darker, he could hear the sounds of the city from outside his room. Jake knew that the next part of the journey would bring more problems, more people to meet, and maybe even more sadness. On the other hand, it was a process of learning how to handle the complicated dance of past and present relationships.

The morning brought with it the familiar chime of Jake's laptop, signaling new emails. Rubbing the sleep from his eyes, he sat up, a sense of anticipation building as he opened his inbox. Two emails sat at the top, each bearing news that made his heart race. One was a job offer from Google, a prestigious Fortune 500 corporation. The second was an offer from a renowned Wall Street firm, Goldman Sachs. Jake just stared at the screen for a moment, hardly believing that his relentless pursuit was finally bearing fruit.

These offers were not merely recognitions of his efforts; they were openings to the dreams he had been cultivating for such a considerable amount of time. He envisioned himself having a fast-paced, high-flying career while studying finance, and the corporate position promised to give him that opportunity. In contrast, the Wall Street offer allowed him to enter the exhilarating world of stocks and trades, a domain that had long piqued his interest.

Nevertheless, as he sat there, a portion of him reflected on the life he was leading at the moment, being a bartender. At first, the job was a means to an end, a way to put food on the table and pay the bills. Nevertheless, as time went on, it evolved into something more. Jake discovered a slice of life that was very different from the corporate world he was working toward entering when he was working behind the bar. That was the place where he was able to recreate the carefree spirit of his college days by serving drinks, exchanging stories, and making connections with people from a wide variety of backgrounds.

In addition to that, the bar had turned into a one-time venue for him to demonstrate his skills in martial arts; it was a location where he had the opportunity to live out a dream and function as a guardian and a peacekeeper. It appealed to a different component of his mentality, specifically the warrior side of his psyche that desired adventure and the raw, often filthy sociability that came with the nightlife. Unlike the sometimes-sterile setting of corporate offices, the bar had helped him feel more grounded and connected to the ordinary realities of life. It was a stark contrast to this environment.

After receiving these two employment offers, Jake found himself in a position where he needed to make a decision. There was a way for him to achieve his professional goals, which included entering the world of business meetings and suits and the world of plans and transactions. On the other hand, there was the roughness and unpredictability of the world of bartending, with its nightly experiences and diverse assortment of customers.

The contradiction prompted Jake to engage in in-depth contemplation regarding the things that he truly desired. Was he able to commit himself totally to the role that he had been preparing for all these years, completely submerging himself in the business world that he had been studying for? Or did he cling to the aspect of his life that allowed him to maintain a connection to a more unfiltered life filled with adventure?

While he was thinking about it, the city outside started to move, and its rhythms gradually came to life. Because of the city's seemingly unlimited possibilities, New York made every decision feel significant, and every choice felt like it was a turning point in one's journey.

***

Dreams of the Past

Mystery-filled shadows filled the alleyways of Sicily, where secrets danced in the Mediterranean breeze. One of such mysteries was a man named Vincent Capoli, known simply as Vince on these ancient cobbled streets, who was a figure engraved in the undercurrents of the city's lore. Humble and unassuming, he started out in the middle of the island's bustle as a mere baker.

It was Vince's 'outside act,' as he called it. He ensured that the best goods reached his customers, causing his business and reputation to thrive.

Dozens of families struggled to make ends meet, with too many mouths to feed and no work to be found. Rather than merely handing out bread, Vince saw these men needed purpose, not pity.

He spread the word among the struggling community, offering job opportunities to anyone with the physical ability to work. Gradually, his small enterprise expanded as young men joined in, taking on tasks such as kneading dough, stocking shelves, and delivering goods. They earned money and pledged to maintain the various businesses Vince opened along the way. The trust between Vince and the families of Sicily was cultivated through his genuine efforts to keep his employees, whom he regarded as nephews, on the right path. Unlike the other families who might have employed these young men for less savory activities, Vince ensured that the jobs he offered were legitimate and imbued with a sense of community and familial responsibility.

After all, they were well taken care of. Vince made sure his employees who worked hard for him were often regarded as family, and soon, his entire group was called The Capoli Family.

In addition, his business was a symbol of integrity against the background of the environment, which could be described as full of corruption. The bakeries, run by him and other subsequent outlets, became synonymous with quality and also for their adherence to a moral code that was not common during the dealings that were associated with the Sicilian mafia. This tidiness in financial transactions was just another asset to Vince's upstanding character, who also believed and pushed for a life where he was no longer stained by crime. Vincent Capoli believed that others should be able to live a life without fear, which became a standard that others can strive for and seek Vincent's protection under. Vincent was no saint, but his organized crime structure involved him charging less protection money to the families of Sicily in order to protect them from the greater evil of the other families. Vince Started by offering protection to his nephews, including their families, and soon started to extend it to anyone who needed it.

Unlike the "protection" offered by the other families, the balancing provided by Vince's adoption was rooted in empowerment and ethics. They trusted him because he regarded his nephews as his own sons, ensuring they had jobs and careers that would open the doors to a promising future.

He was not simply a boss but a mentor guiding these young men under his hand, firm and compassionate, preventing these dangers and temptations that lurked in the darker corners of Sicilian life.

That's when trouble came knocking. Vince had attracted so much of the workforce in his region that no one wanted to work for the other organizations. Many of these other families were involved in crime and wanted to recruit Vince's men to work in their criminal enterprises. The Giovanni family had their eyes on Vince's growing success and the army of able-bodied men he had employed. The Giovanni family created a plan to pull the strings of these vulnerable men, luring them to "work" under the Giovanni family through threats both veiled and vicious.

Soon, regular faces stopped coming around the bakery, including some of Vince's most trusted. Vince knew in his gut that these employees, his nephews, had fallen prey to Giovanni's schemes. He had to act to save his community from being crushed under the fist of crime before it was too late.

Through a web of blackmail, bribery, and brute force, these criminal factions clawed their way into controlling nearly every aspect of life—the shops, the docks, and even city hall bowed to their decrees. Nothing escaped their greedy reach. Most horrific was their tactic of conscription—strong young nephews of his family plucked from impoverished homes to become expendable pawns in an endless game of criminal enterprise.

More than one mother had witnessed the death of their child in the most horrific ways upon their return from "working" for a crime family in some turf war or vendetta. The streets ran red as these fragile lives were treated as little more than ammunition. All in exchange for dreams where their realities would be filled with more money and assets than they could ever dream of, but these were all lies.

Each time he strengthened defenses or offered youth jobs away from crime's clutches, tragedy struck again. Good men fell in fields stained with virtue; families mourned needless losses.

And still, the monsters' depravity knew no bounds. Word came one grim dawn that Giovanni's newest crime plot ended in gore. Two village boys, scarce out of childhood, lay in pieces—for entertainment—because they refused to join the Giovanni crime syndicate. Vince wept bile, rage coursing his veins like molten lead as one of them was a nephew that he looked after.

The next day, Vince felt helpless as he witnessed his brother Enzo being dragged before him while he was outnumbered. He had only uttered a sentence of truce when one of Giovanni's men picked up a sharp knife and sliced through his throat like butter. Enzo gurgled blood, and the air was filled with the gut-wrenching screams of Vince, falling to his knees and screaming bloody Mary.

The blood splattered onto the cobblestone pavement as the light from Enzo's eyes drifted into the skies. At that moment, Vince also lost the joy of his life, his one and only brother. All reason fled in a storm of grieving wrath. His only brother, pride and joy, butchered like cattle in front of his eyes.

They were almost the same age, quite young, and now there was one left to grieve. Immediately, the situation made the decision for Vince to battle the Giovanni family all on his own, with no backing.

"Where is your principal now, Vince? How many more people need to die like this? You can stop this… You can easily stop this!" The main mob boss of the Giovanni family finally found a way to hurt Vince's heart as punishment for his defiance for all to see.

That was when Vincent, a man known for his principle, a young man who was figuring his life out himself, decided to take a stand for all the fallen souls.

Many hours after the Giovanni people had left and Enzo's body had bled out in the open, Vince finally rose, knees bloodied from the splatter; he uttered, "It ends today."

He went in and took out his gun from the holster, calling for the car while his brother's body lay cold on the ground.

"Today, we end this." The pulsating red veins could be seen from the madness-stricken eyes as his close followers tried to stop Vince from attempting literal suicide. He was a mere single man trying to kill off the entire Giovanni family with a single revolver gun—an impossible deed.

"You can't fight the Giovanni family alone!" One of his trusted family members tried to shout some sense into Vince, the grieving man who wailed at the sight of his dead brother with a revolver in hand.

"It is best if you leave and start over somewhere else. What about Manhattan? It is a booming place, and with the money you have, it will be easy for you to start over and save what's left of your family." The member tried to convince him again.

Fate had written a different course of action for him, one that began on a night when the sun setting in Sicily spilled scarlet and gold into the sky. Many distraught mothers looked for answers in the eyes of a man who had promised them peace. Because of the senseless killing of Enzo, Vincent will never know peace. This was all because of the Giovannis.

"What about our other kids?" A mother whose son had suffered a similar fate as Enzo screamed at Vince, holding out the cold body of his brother.

"I have two more sons; am I to expect them to be dragged away by the Giovannis as well?"

"We started to pay you for protection because we felt like you were our best chance against the Giovannis and all the other crime syndicates," another bystander yelled.

"If you cannot protect your own brother, then what are the chances that you can protect us?"

Crashing beside his brother's wasted body, Vince calmed down. He stared into the lifeless eyes of his brother and decided to get the most vulnerable families out of Sicily.

The head of the Capoli family had decided that there would be no more bloodshed of innocent souls. Vincent, driven by grief and fueled by the injustice he witnessed, made a firm decision to uphold his principles of justice and protect the innocent. With a heavy heart, he realized that merely starting over somewhere else wouldn't be enough. He couldn't stand idly by while the Giovanni family continued their reign of terror.

Vincent assembled a band of loyal followers who believed in his cause and were ready for a fight that would put his determination to the test. Standing up to the influential Giovanni family wouldn't be easy, but he was resolute in his resolve. Stopping the horrors and saving the lives of the defenseless were his primary goals, not exacting vengeance.

For the purpose of their perilous mission, Vincent and his devoted comrades set out under the cover of darkness. The infiltration of the Giovanni stronghold was accomplished with meticulous planning and resolute resolve. In order to stop the criminal empire from taking any more lives, they set out to destroy it.

In a strange and ironic way, Vincent Capoli was the definition of an antihero. His sense of justice and morality compelled him to plunge himself deeper into a world of crime in order to regulate it so that regular ordinary people would not get hurt. In order to control crime, Vincent was ready to become the darkness, the thing that ordinary men feared, and at this point, nothing could stop this transformation except death itself.

In an overnight mission, each Giovanni member and supporter fell victim to Vincent's wrath, their necks bearing the marks of their own murderous deeds. Vincent made sure that he overlooked the execution of each captured man from the Giovanni family by slicing their throat. He personally overlooked every single demise, keeping track that they were killed in the same exact way his brother Enzo was. It was a chilling display of poetic justice, a twisted mirror reflecting the pain and loss Vincent had endured. The air was thick with the scent of spilled blood, a haunting reminder of the price paid for vengeance.

Word of the confrontation quickly went through the criminal underground, where Vincent's viciousness and dogged resolve were rumored. He personified authority and power, and his name came to represent both. The once-invincible Giovanni family now lay in ruins, their power dwindling under the weight of Vincent's relentless ascent.

Fear wasn't the only thing that catapulted Vincent to fame, either. He was incredibly skilled at strategy and could always find a way to outwit his opponents. Vincent understood the delicate balance between fame and infamy, leveraging both to solidify his authority. Even the most courageous people quavered in his presence; he had become a legendary character.

***

Vince, the man who lay in his bed in New York, dreamed of his gruesome past. Sleep had taken him to a time that had changed the course of his entire life. He sighed as he sank into the soft comfort of his bed, his weary body seeking the solace of rest. But his mind, as always, was restless - plagued by memories better left forgotten.

After the massacre of Sicily, struck with grief, Vincent moved to New York with some of his businesses and made a new name here. Albeit this time, he kept his Mafia side; he used it whenever the time came to teach their opponents a taste of their own medicine. This time, he would not let others marry the principles he wished to carry in his life.

After the death of his brother and all that he had gone through, Vincent somehow managed to find himself right back on the merry-go-round of danger and intrigue he thought he'd bid farewell in Sicily. Only this time, he wasn't just along for the ride; he was back with a vengeance, determined not to let the carousel of chaos spin him around without getting a few punches in himself. His skills, honed in the streets of Sicily, became his means of survival in the competitive and often ruthless underbelly of New York. He climbed the ranks, his name becoming synonymous with power and fear, yet the dream reminded him of the innocence he had lost along the way.

From humble origins, Vince ascended to become a revered Mafia figure, now reigning power, fame, and fear in the bustling city of New York. His current status in the Mafia culture is very different from his past economic circumstances. Instead of drifting off to sleep every night as a forgotten ghost of bygone days, he woke up each morning as a man whose destiny had been shaped by the brave and clever strokes of his hand. He was an individual who had taken control of his own fate. The man who now lay at rest was someone whom nobody dared to provoke, both in Sicily and in New York.

"You are over…" The voice came back again to haunt him. It was as if he could hear the slicing of his brother's neck once again; this vivid memory jolted him awake, his breathing heavy and ragged. As awareness crept back in, he realized with dismay that the remnants of his dream still clung tenaciously to both mind and memory.

His eyes tore open with horror, and the sun's sharp rays made their unwelcome way into his eyes. Lying quietly, he strained to slow his racing pulse as unsettling emotions swirled within. Vincent, the head of the Capoli family now in New York, stirred from his troubled reverie as raised voices intruded from the hallway. The voices, charged with intensity, were unmistakably those of his son, Martin Capoli, who was a lot like Vince and Johnny Viola, his right-hand man and a close family ally.

Martin, in many ways, was a chip off the old block but with a modern twist. He had inherited his father's savvy, but his approaches and ideas were fresher and sharper. This blend of old wisdom and new perspectives made him stand out, especially in the heated discussions that were part and parcel of the Capoli family's day-to-day life.

On the other side of the argument stood Johnny Viola, whose loyalty to the Capoli's was as fiery as his personality. Johnny, a hot-headed individual by nature, wore his heart on his sleeve. This passion, though sometimes leading to clashes, was rooted in his deep-seated belief in the family's cause and principles. His outbursts were not just explosions of temper but expressions of his dedication to the family's success and well-being.

Vincent Capoli, with the measured calm of a seasoned leader, rose from his seat. Moving with deliberate steps, he approached the door and gently pressed his ear against the smooth, paneled wood. The snippets of conversation he caught revealed the heart of the matter: a tumultuous incident at The Dirty Bird Bar the previous night, which had evidently ruffled more than a few feathers and ignited tempers.

Exhaling slowly, Vincent was no stranger to the intricate dance of street business and its volatile actors. He knew all too well that when pride or profit was threatened, reason and restraint were often the first casualties. Yet, unlike others who might shy away from the heat of conflict, Vincent saw an opportunity for resolution and guidance. His years had taught him that stepping into the fray, armed with wisdom and a willingness to mediate, could transform even the fiercest disputes into bridges for stronger alliances. With this in mind, he prepared to lend his voice to the heated discussion, embodying the very essence of leadership that had long defined his tenure at the helm of the Capoli family.

The argument was getting out of hand, and Vincent knew he had to step in before the words became violent. When possible, the family would settle their differences amicably rather than resort to violence. He readied himself to play peacemaker and pulled open the door.

The walls were practically useless in keeping their voices out as Martin relayed the night's escapades with a zeal that bordered on the theatrical.

Vincent, his mind still foggy from a restless sleep, managing to shift back into this reality, asked forcefully, "What the hell is happening *now*?"

"You should've seen it, Dad." Martin, Vince's younger son, the one who had survived the massacre of Sicily, spoke to him with an air of excitement and disbelief. "We were this close to a full-blown war with the Rossi guys right there in the bar!"

That was all it took for Vincent to explode, "Great!" It wasn't the first time his son had been at the troubling end. He had been on the receiving end of such petty issues before as well and knew exactly how to deal with them.

Johnny, the loudest voice in the room with his passion flaring, suddenly fell silent as Vincent emerged, unprepared for the steely glint in his employer's eyes and the ice behind his words. He was accustomed to Vincent's usual measured tones, not this white-hot anger laid bare.

Caught off guard, Johnny took an involuntary step back, hands lifting almost of their own accord in a placating gesture. The mere glare and stance of Vincent Capoli's words were enough to calm the dispute. It all seemed futile now to the two colleagues to drag in the main boss into a matter that was usually taken care of by the handlers. For a moment, only the pounding of his heart filled the tense quiet as this realization struck; it was no small thing to incur such raw fury from a man not known to show it.

"Okay, okay," Johnny began, struggling to match the elder Capoli's scowl with a mollifying tone of his own. But his cheeks flared crimson, betraying the downplayed annoyance under that piercing stare.

Johnny's gruff voice cut in, "Yeah, but then... This bartender kid, out of nowhere, steps in our room. Handled the situation like some kind of pro. Saved our necks, honestly."

Vincent's eyebrows arched in surprise. In his years, he'd seen many things, but the idea of a bartender intervening in a mob scuffle was new.

"Who is this bartender? ... Wait, did he enter the room without consent? That bar knows not to enter when we have requested privacy unless it is absolutely necessary." Vincent's voice boomed as he stepped out of his room, immediately commanding Martin and Johnny's attention.

Martin turned to his father, his expression a mix of respect and urgency. "We don't know much about him, but he's got some serious moves. Handled big Tony Rossi like he was a rag doll. The people in the Flamingo Room were horrified. You should have seen the sheer shock on the faces of the Rossi members. They had someone just give it to them!"

Vincent pondered this information, his mind working through the implications. "And this kid, he just works at the bar? No connections to anyone?"

"As far as we know, he's clean. Just a regular guy working the bar," Johnny replied, his tone indicating that he, too, was baffled by the bartender's actions.

Vincent, leaning against the doorway, stroked his chin thoughtfully. "A regular guy doesn't just step into a mob dispute and walk away unscathed. Find out more about him. I don't want any more trouble or loose ends. If this guy proves to be trouble for us, I want to know what we are against. Although the guy saved my son's life, if he could be of use, I would love to have someone loyal and skilled next to me. The most important thing is to make sure that he is not a spy or diversion sent from one of the other families."

Martin nodded, a look of determination on his face. "We're on it, Dad. If he's got no ties, maybe we can bring him in and use those skills to our advantage. Don't worry; we have this under control."

As Martin and Johnny left to gather more information, Vincent couldn't help but feel a sense of unease. Things had finally settled down, and he did not like the sudden change in his course of plans.

"Find out more about this lad." His tone was grave but adamant.

***

Upon returning to the residence of his aunt Mary, the atmosphere was electric with excitement, which was a striking contrast to the typical peacefulness that prevailed within the beautiful home. Aunt Mary just returned from a trip, so she was already over the moon. She got even more excited when the news of Jake getting two offers at the same time got to her ears. It was not every day that one rose to such a high position so quickly.

"A celebration is in order, Jake!" Aunt Mary declared as she breezed into the living room where Jake was sitting, going over some paperwork. "We must have a party. Imagine the gathering—the city's finest, all here to celebrate your success!"

Jake looked up, a bit taken aback by her energy. "A party, Aunt Mary? That's really not necessary," he replied, slightly uncomfortable at the thought of being the center of attention among New York's elite.

"Nonsense!" she exclaimed, waving a hand dismissively. "This is a significant milestone, Jake. It's not just about the job offers; it's about you making your mark. We need to introduce you to the right people—who knows where these connections might lead."

Jake couldn't help but smile at her enthusiasm. "I appreciate it, Aunt Mary, but I'm not sure I'm ready for the socialite scene," he said, his tone light but sincere.

Aunt Mary sat down beside him, her expression softening. "I know this world can be overwhelming, Jake, but trust me, you belong here as much as anyone. You've worked hard, and you deserve to be recognized. Besides," she added with a wink, "it'll be fun. You might even meet some interesting people."

From there, Aunt Mary effortlessly shared her elaborate plans for the celebration with them, including the guest list, meal, and music. Jake was engrossed in her vision as she spoke with such fervor and detail. Her infectious enthusiasm made it difficult to remain unmoved.

During their conversation, Jake came to understand his aunt's genuine concern for his happiness and success. She wanted to express her support and share her delight in his accomplishments with the world, so she threw a spectacular celebration.

Eventually, the conversation turned to more casual topics— family gossip, updates about mutual acquaintances, and Aunt Mary's latest business ventures. Jake listened, fascinated by the world his aunt navigated with such ease and confidence—a world he was about to step into.

Settling into his chair once more, Jake sank deep in thought as Aunt Mary bustled out, eager to prepare for the celebrations ahead. Her zeal was now tinged with a shade of doubt in his mind.

This gathering, ostensibly in his honor, carried implications beyond revelry. Its true purpose, he realized slowly, was a chance to rediscover his path forward—to meet the road ahead without trepidation and claim an assured destiny once more.

Aunt Mary's unflagging optimism, though well-meant, had nearly blinded him to opportunities in his midst. But her faith, as relentless as her efforts, awakened new resolve within. Where he saw trials, she envisioned only triumph.

As Jake pondered his future over warm tea, little did he know what wheels had been set in motion beyond his perception. The events at The Dirty Bird's Flamingo Room that night held more significance than anyone could foresee. It sent ripples through complex underground networks, especially in the Rossi family. Every man who worked for the Rossi wanted to know who Jake was and what he was to the Capoli family. Word spread covertly of Jake's unforeseen deeds and how valor under fire spoke of talents beyond mixing drinks.

Intrigue grew in certain circles where discretion was doctrine. Speculation swirled around this enigma of a bartender with mystique hinting at deeper skillsets.

Comfortable in his aunt's home, Jake remained oblivious as unseen threads of interest subtly wove around his unknown and unwitting self. Without realizing it, he had become the subject of discussion in worlds where danger and opportunity danced closely. He would become the subject of research by those who lurked in the shadows.

Truly, Jake found himself in a precarious position, caught between the glittering future envisioned and murky undercurrents now edging near. As one path beckoned brightly before conscious choice, darker tides risked ensnaring the unguarded from behind. With careless steps, all it might take to fall from grace into chaos is unforeseen.

Chapter 3: Shadows of Loyalty

In a dimly lit alley, far removed from the city's bright lights, two figures stood quietly, their conversation barely disturbing the night. The first man, who had recently emerged from the comfort of a high-end car, exuded an air of luxury and refinement. His long overcoat fluttered slightly in the breeze, an odd choice for such a gritty setting. Rossi had sent his men to gather information. He needed an anonymous but experienced private investigator to look into Jake, ensuring no attention was directed back to him.

"So, what have you got on the guy and his family?" Roberto's man asked, his tone a mix of curiosity and impatience. The secluded spot heightened his eagerness to find out.

As he shifted his weight from one foot to the other, his partner, who was more comfortable in the shadows, mirrored the same movement. "Well, considering that he has only recently arrived in New York, he is pretty much a ghost. However, he is currently living with his aunt, and it appears that they have some resources," a hint of dissatisfaction in his voice due to the lack of substantial information.

"He goes by Jake, from Ithaca," he added, hoping to provide something useful.

The man in the overcoat paused his gum chewing, a habit that seemed out of sync with the seriousness of their meeting and spat it out. He took out the folder and quickly glanced through it, a smirk forming on his face. "Jake, the talented guy," he said with a heavy dose of sarcasm, his voice carrying a mixture of surprise and amusement.

Flipping through a few pages, his interest was piqued. "Well, well, looks like the Capoli family is getting creative—nerds with kung-fu skills on their side now," Rossi's man commented, half-joking yet clearly intrigued by the notion.

The private investigator continued, "I haven't found much more yet, but I'll keep digging. We need to be careful to keep this under the radar."

The man in the overcoat nodded. "Good. Keep it discreet. We don't need any unwanted attention."

The investigator melted back into the shadows, leaving the man in the overcoat to ponder the information. Rossi's orders were clear: find out everything about Jake without leaving any traces. The game was on, and they needed every advantage they could get.

The Capoli family was already in hot water with the Rossi family; tensions were already high. With Jake's interruption, the Rossi family finally found an excuse to set the wheels for their far-fetched plans into motion.

Over at Aunt Mary's grand residence, a flurry of activity buzzed through the air as preparations for the upcoming party were underway. Despite her packed schedule, Aunt Mary had entrusted Rodney with the coordination of the event. Her trust in him was implicit, yet she couldn't help but oversee the preparations, her keen eye missing nothing.

"I'm running late for today's meetings, Rodney," Aunt Mary called out, adjusting the elegant scarf draped around her shoulders, a hint of urgency in her voice. "But please, arrange a quick catch-up with the marketing team before I head out. We need to finalize the social media campaign at the earliest."

"Of course, madam, I have already readied the team to meet you right now. They are waiting for you." Rodney replied with his usual calm efficiency, moving swiftly to gather the team by the fireplace, the heart of Aunt Mary's opulent home.

As soon as Aunt Mary walked into the room, the members of the marketing team could feel the excitement in the air. Even though the room was very fancy, Aunt Mary's powerful presence was what caught everyone's attention right away. There was something about her that made even the grandest settings seem like nothing more than background noise.

"Let's make this quick. Is this all we have?" she inquired briskly, her gaze sweeping over the team with an intensity that demanded straight-to-the-point answers.

"Mary, we've been discussing how to best promote Jake's party on social media. I'm excited to share our idea for a holistic plan that includes Facebook, Instagram, TikTok, and Google advertisements," stated the marketing team leader."

He got the signal to proceed with Mary's nod.

"To reach our demographic of socialites, we want to create a string of interesting blogs and advertisements." He projected some preliminary visuals on the screen and indicated that they wanted to create an impression of exclusivity while also highlighting that the event was a captivating dinner gala.

With her curiosity aroused, Aunt Mary leaned closer. "I like where this is going. Tell me more about how you plan to use each platform. Specifics, please."

"For Facebook and Instagram, we're focusing on creating visually stunning invites peppered with teasers of what's to come. We'll use influencers to amplify our reach, ensuring that the buzz reaches far and wide," another team member chimed in, showcasing some draft posts.

"And for TikTok?" Aunt Mary wanted to know how they planned to take advantage of the unique demographic of the platform.

"TikTok will be all about creating a challenge that ties back to the party theme. We want to encourage user-generated content that not only spreads the word but also builds anticipation and a sense of community among the invitees," the social media strategist added.

Aunt Mary smiled, clearly impressed. "And Google ads?"

"We're targeting ads to appear in search results and on websites frequented by our target demographic. The focus will be on creating a sense of FOMO, ensuring that everyone who's anyone sees this as the event of the year," the digital ads manager explained.

With a nod of assent, Aunt Mary rose to her feet, her decision sealed.

"Excellent work. I want us to push forward with this plan. Let's throw Jake a party that everyone will be talking about," she mused.

"I need this team to understand something. There will be a lot of senior executives in attendance from powerful organizations. Most of the time, a lot of deals are made at these types of functions. Jake's party will be the social networking event of the year."

In less than an hour, the team, fueled by Aunt Mary's decisiveness and clear vision, had not only devised but also agreed upon a new campaign strategy. The vibrant and compelling campaign was soon splashed across various social media platforms, creating an instant buzz.

Meanwhile, Vincent was engrossed in his study at his rather expensive abode, busy signing off deals.

"These people, honestly. They come to us for help when they have their own resources to handle things," Vincent muttered, his frustration evident. He glanced at the glass of Scotch that sat untouched. All his attention was focused on the stack of papers before him. These documents were the source of his misery for the day.

His study was a sanctuary of sorts, a place where he could retreat and think. The soft rustling of papers and the occasional scratch of his pen filled the air. The room, lined with bookshelves and bathed in the mellow light of a desk lamp, was a perfect blend of tradition and modernity, reflecting the character of Vincent Capoli.

Vincent took a deep breath, trying to center himself. The demands of running a criminal empire weighed heavily on him, but he always managed to maintain an air of class and control. He picked up the glass of Scotch, savoring the rich aroma before taking a slow, measured sip. The warmth of the liquor provided a momentary respite from the chaos of his responsibilities.

Suddenly, the tranquility was broken by a rushed knocking at the door. Vincent's response, a lazy "Come in," barely concealed his annoyance at the interruption. The door swung open to reveal a man, breathless, evidently.

"Sir," he began, out of breath, as he extended his phone towards Vincent. "You need to see this. I have news regarding Jake."

"Show me this, Jake," Vincent commanded, curiosity now fully alight. Vincent wanted to see the person who had helped his family and forced the Rossi men to retreat in humiliation. The butler, adept at navigating the digital realm, quickly pulled up Jake's social media profile on the phone.

Vincent leaned back and thought to himself, "I thought that this Jake guy would be older." With the press of a button, he summoned Martin and Francesca, his children, to join him in the study.

As he scrolled through Jake's profile, Vincent's demeanor suggested a casual disinterest. Without looking away from the screen, he issued a quiet command to his butler, "Make sure we're on the guest list for Jake's party. Use whatever connections we need to." It was a clear directive from a man accustomed to leveraging his extensive network to position his family advantageously within their social and business circles.

The door opened to reveal Francesca and Martin making their entrance. In a white Sunday dress that complemented her effortless grace, Francesca looked as though she could turn heads and break them in the process. Martin, on the other hand, still bore the physical reminders of the fight at the bar. He still looked crisp and proper.

"Ah, my dear offspring." He sarcastically registered their presence. "I hope you haven't made any more issues for me to fix lately?" Just as he said this, he shot a sneering glance toward Martin, who did nothing but stare at the floor in silence.

Without wasting a moment, Vincent set his scotch aside, signaling the shift from casual observation to family business. "I have a proposition for you... well, us," he announced a statement that immediately captured his children's attention.

He continued with a hint of sarcasm that lightened the mood, "I plan to take us to a party. And we have someone rather special to thank. I want to show gratitude to the gentleman who intervened in the altercation with the Rossi group that day." The idea of attending a social event might have seemed trivial, but Vincent's tone suggested a deeper strategy at play.

"We're going to properly thank Jake for his part in saving Martin from that bar incident," Vincent revealed, laying out his intention with a clarity that brooked no argument. "That is what people with principle do."

Francesca seemed unconcerned, engrossed in her own thoughts, but Martin nodded subtly, still feeling the sting of his father's earlier words. However, the delicate nuances of family loyalty and the complex game of power and influence started to become more apparent as the topic turned to the impending celebration. Parting from his scotch for a moment, Vincent became less the thoughtful father of the family and more of a cunning tactician, keen to take advantage of the circumstances. His children were eager to side with Dad for what appeared to promise a balance between family responsibility and leisure—the remaining unity in their heterogeneous lot—despite their disparate interests and recent grievances.

Vincent, sensing the moment's potential, decided to steer the conversation in a more positive direction. "You know," he began, capturing his children's attention with a tone softer than usual, "this party isn't just a celebration. It's a way to welcome new friends and strengthen our ties with the community."

Martin looked up, his curiosity piqued despite his earlier mood. Francesca, too, seemed to forget her disinterest, glancing towards her father.

Vincent continued, "Jake has been a tremendous help to Martin, and we should acknowledge that. But this event is also an opportunity to expand our network and connect with people outside our usual circles. It's important for our family and our business." Vincent acknowledge.

Francesca, catching on to the significance of the event, nodded slowly. "So, it's not just a party. It's about building relationships and showing our support?"

"Exactly," Vincent agreed. "We honor Jake, but we also position ourselves strategically within the community. It's a chance to demonstrate our influence and make valuable connections."

"These events can often turn into networking opportunities. This could be a chance to invest some of our capital in less risky business ventures and take the family one step closer to becoming more legitimate."

Martin permitted a slight grin. "I hadn't thought about it that way. This could be a great opportunity for everyone here."

"And it gives us a chance to maybe... lighten things up a bit?" Francesca added, warming to the idea. "Especially after everything that's happened."

Vincent grinned, pleased with the shift in conversation. "Precisely. It's a time to relax and to enjoy ourselves. These moments of connection and celebration are what keep us grounded as the Capolis." The vibe in the room lightened considerably, with Vincent's children now understanding the broader purpose of the event.

***

The gentle glow of Isabella's phone screen, a lighthouse in the darkness of the evening trip, subtly interrupted her return from her cousin's lively quinceañera. A social media update flashed into view, and her heart rate spiked. The notification, tagged from Jake's account, had a unique way of making her feel a mix of excitement and suspense. It was an invitation to an upcoming celebration in his honor, planned by his aunt Mary, promising to be both big and welcoming. The sudden Direct Message sent Isabella into a tizzy of fantasies, where the colors of possibility and the unknown swirled around her.

It was during a different, fortuitous road trip when Isabella's tenuous link to Aunt Mary was woven. They had only met for a few hours, but that was enough to have them both follow each other on Instagram. Mary's charismatic presence and unexpected warmth toward Isabella left a pleasant memory of their meeting. This link notwithstanding, Isabella had second thoughts about going to the party. Although she was very comfortable with Jake, she did not know his family well enough to attend such a private party.

Suddenly, Isabella's email was graced with a personal note from Aunt Mary. Her doubts took a sharp turn. Going beyond the impersonal reach of a public post, the message extended a formal invitation to the party as a gesture of inclusion. Aunt Mary's kind words made Isabella feel more connected to the family and the event.

Given Mary's prominence in Jake's life, the invitation's thoughtfulness dispelled Isabella's doubts. It felt like an expression of friendship, hinting at her evolving feelings for Jake. She missed him, and this was a chance to do something about it.

Encouraged by Aunt Mary's direct outreach, Isabella accepted the invitation, led by a mix of curiosity and excitement. Still, as the weeks turned into days, an underlying wave of anxiety kept building up as the party day drew near. She wondered how Jake would react to her arrival. Would it evoke surprise, delight, or apathy? Her mind raced with possibilities, building anticipation with each thought.

Aunt Mary's invitation also mentioned Jake's parents, which intensified Isabella's anxiety and justified her decision to attend. Meeting Jake's family at such a personal event deepened the already intricate web of emotions she was experiencing.

She imagined herself and Jake not as distant acquaintances connected through social media but reuniting in a scene pulled from a dream. The thoughts of Jake brought memories from the past rushing forward. In seconds, she was daydreaming with a wide smile on her face. While everyone was heading to class, he grabbed her hand and rushed her away from the crowd of buzzing students. She started to remember when they both decided to skip class for a day. They ended up in a lush park, the air filled with the sounds of their laughter as they chased a soccer ball across the green expanse. The competitive edge gave way to playfulness, setting the stage for an evening that would engrave itself in her memory.

Jake made a fire as the sun dipped below the horizon, revealing a work of art composed of twilight. It was a deft performance, turning the sunset into a stage illuminated by the waltz of fire. They were drawn in closer by the warmth of the fire as it roared to life, even though the air was chilly. Jake's nonchalant gesture of putting his arm around Isabella seemed to come from nowhere; it was a subtle but powerful message of security and intimacy.

Every subject they discussed brought out new facets of their characters and the bonds they shared as their talk veered between the dream world and the actual world. A sense of closeness permeated their conversation as the shadows generated by the fire danced across their features and lit up their faces. The night air was like a web of laughter and shared tales, entangling them in a thrilling and inescapable intimacy. Voices hushed, air with a hint of romance and closeness was all the two needed.

A simple DM from her social media sparked the daydream and made Isabella relive moments that lay close to her heart. She could feel the closeness that she had experienced on that day. The fire's warmth, Jake's reassuring weight at her side, and the captivating tone of his voice – it all came back to her. It offered a glimpse of what could be, a hint of how their lives could intersect again despite their earlier decision to end things.

However, Isabella's daydream was quick to end as life had struck an unforgiving reality check, and their careers led them to make practical decisions. They had drifted apart, and she sat with an invitation that could maybe reintroduce him back into her life.

After graduation, Jake had moved on. He embraced New York life and threw himself into the vibrant city life. It didn't take long for the initial disorientation of his move started to fade, replaced by a budding sense of belonging. With its unending energy and myriad opportunities, the city began to feel less like a foreign landscape and more like a canvas on which he could start painting his future.

One evening, nestled in the modest comfort of his room at Aunt Mary's, he set up a video chat with his parents back home. The glow of the screen lit up his face as he saw their familiar expressions, a mix of curiosity and concern, wondering how their son was faring in the big city.

"It's going really well here," Jake began, his voice carrying a note of excitement that had been absent in the first few weeks of his move. "Aunt Mary has been incredible; believe it or not, she's throwing a party for me in a few days." His smile was wide infectious, a visible sign of how much he had warmed to his new life.

His parents exchanged a look with a silent communication of relief and happiness at their son's adjustment and the warm welcome he had received. "That sounds wonderful, Jake," his mother said, her voice soft but filled with joy. "We're so glad to hear you're settling in and that Mary is taking good care of you."

"Yeah, she's going all out with it," Jake continued, leaning back slightly. "It's kind of her way of introducing me to her circle here, and honestly, I'm a bit nervous but excited. New York is starting to feel like home."

As they talked, Jake shared more about his daily life, the small victories, and the challenges he faced. His parents listened, offering advice and laughter in equal measure, their conversation a bridge spanning the miles between them.

The call eventually wound down with promises of more updates and virtual visits, leaving Jake feeling anchored and loved. Turning off the video call, he sat for a moment in the quiet of his room, reflecting on the journey that had brought him to this point.

Outside, the city's sounds filtered through the window, a reminder of the bustling world awaiting him. Jake's thoughts drifted to the upcoming party, the preparations Aunt Mary was overseeing, and the curious mix of anticipation and apprehension that filled him finally came to fruition.

***

The day of the party finally arrived, and instantly, it was an absolute hit. Aunt Mary's elegant home turned into the heart of celebration overnight. The air buzzed with energy, filled with the sounds of laughter, clinking glasses, and a background hum of lively conversations. Central to it all was Jake, who, to his own surprise, found himself basking in a spotlight that seemed to particularly captivate the ladies present.

Aunt Mary, always the perfect hostess, was filled with pride as she watched Jake fit right in with the New York crowd. Seeing him make friends and charm everyone made her heart warm. But when she glanced at Vincent Capoli, she felt a bit uneasy. Vincent was charming and influential, sure, but the rumors about his shady dealings worried her.

Even though she was good at organizing these gatherings, Aunt Mary thought about how she couldn't do the same for everyone, like Titiano. It made her realize that even with all her efforts, some things were beyond her control. This made the success of tonight's party even more special to her. It wasn't just about throwing a great party; it was about keeping her family safe and connected, a delicate balance she managed to maintain amidst the complexities of their social life.

In the middle of the festivities, Jake and Titiano were locked into a spirited chatter. Their conversation was entertaining everyone within earshot. "So, Jake, have you managed to learn how to navigate the city, or are you still causing urban gridlock every time you attempt to hail a taxi?" Titiano quipped, a playful glint in his eye.

Without missing a beat, Jake retorted, his smile broadening, "Actually, I'm contemplating enrolling in flight school so I can just complete my commute by helicopter. Seems more practical than traditional methods. However, I'd hate to infringe on the turf wars of our feathered city dwellers."

Chuckles from the crowd meant the banter had so far been an absolute delight. Leaning closer as though sharing a great secret, Titiano added, "I've been toying with the idea of launching a 'Skyline Commute' initiative. How would you feel about coming on board as the Chief Officer of Ontime Helicopter Commute Inc.?"

"Count me in, but only if our official uniform includes badges. And mine needs to be particularly suited for a captain," Jake replied, the laughter evident in his voice, perfectly matching their playful tone.

Watching from the sidelines, Aunt Mary felt a wave of relief. Jake was proving he could easily navigate the social labyrinth of his new home, charming everyone from high society ladies to the city's more colorful characters.

As the night went on, Jake was the undeniable focus of attention, charming his way through conversations with a natural ease that drew people to him. Despite the fun and frivolity, Aunt Mary remained alert, her experienced gaze picking up on the complex social currents flowing through her home. Vincent Capoli's attendance and his intriguing entourage added an element of intrigue to the evening, a reminder of the complex tapestry of relationships that Jake was becoming a part of in his new life in New York.

As one would expect from a gathering of New York's elite, Aunt Mary's celebration was buzzing with anticipation and excitement. Representatives from Wall Street titans like Google and Goldman Sachs mingled among the glittering array of guests, their presence testifying to the buzz that Jake had unknowingly generated. Their attention wasn't merely focused on the extravagant party but also on Jake, the young man whose connections to the powerful self-made magnate suggested Mary's unrealized promise and potential partnerships in the future. Not only did these corporate behemoths see Jake's potential, but they also saw the opportunities and relationships abounding in Mary's network.

Aunt Mary scanned the diverse crowd, and her eyes landed on Vincent Capoli. She knew exactly who he was and knew she had to greet him.

"Interesting crowd tonight," Mary remarked to her butler, Rodney, as she subtly nodded in Vincent's direction. "Do we know how Capoli ended up here?"

Rodney glanced over and then back at Mary, his expression calm but alert. "I'll look into it, ma'am. He certainly wasn't on the original list."

"Make sure you do," Mary replied, her tone leaving no room for doubt. "I want to know who's responsible for this oversight. This might cause a controversy, don't you know? How can I, a host, not know who is coming and who's not?"

The party continued. Aunt Mary began to notice that representatives from both Google and Goldman Sachs were competing for her attention.

She turned to greet another guest, her mind already working on the next steps. "Enjoying the party?" she asked, her smile never faltering.

"Absolutely," the guest replied, noticing how the city's most notable and powerful business magnets were going out of their way to gain an audience with Mary. "You've outdone yourself once again."

"Thank you," Mary said graciously. "We aim to please."

But even as she exchanged pleasantries, her focus remained split, ensuring that the big gala event was a roaring success and introducing Jake to the higher social circles so that he would have the best chance at launching his career.

The evening was much livelier because of Jake's cousin Titiano, who was a ball of energy and comedy. With easy charisma and a sharp mind, Titiano became the party animal, effortlessly navigating the crowd and leaving a wake of mirth and laughter in his wake. The upscale party was surprisingly cozy and enjoyable, thanks to his presence.

Amidst the bustling buzz of conversation and the gentle clinking of glasses, the Capoli family found themselves truly enjoying the atmosphere of the party, with a special appreciation for the excellent assortment of food that was brought to them. Their approbation of the dishes was not a minor praise, considering that they had refined palates and were accustomed to the greatest in gourmet food.

The illustrious patriarch of the Capoli family, Vincent Capoli, who is well-known for his exquisite taste, felt that the gastronomic delights left him feeling seriously astonished. That evening, he felt compelled to share a bit of his ancestry with Jake because of the extraordinary quality of the meal that was provided.

In the nick of time, when the attention of the audience was suddenly diverted, Vincent approached Jake with a friendly smile that only partially concealed the extent of his influence with the crowd. Vincent's manner changed to one of sincerity and thankfulness as he drew Jake away from the partygoers and then moved him to a more private location, away from their prying ears.

"Jake, I wanted to take a moment to personally thank you," Vincent began, his voice carrying a warmth that contrasted with the intensity of his gaze. "Your actions in protecting my son Martin and Johnny Viola didn't go unnoticed. You've shown a great deal of courage and integrity."

Jake, taken aback by the unexpected commendation, nodded, a mixture of surprise and curiosity lighting his eyes. "Thank you, Mr. Capoli. I just did what felt right at the moment," he responded, unsure how to navigate this conversation with a man whose reputation preceded him yet whose personal acquaintance he had not made until now. Vincent clapped a hand on Jake's shoulder, a gesture of camaraderie and respect. "And it's for that reason I'd like to extend an invitation to you," he continued, his voice imbued with a blend of formality and genuine hospitality. "Come over for dinner next week. We'll prepare a traditional Italian meal for you. If you've never experienced true gourmet Italian cuisine, I assure you, you're in for a treat."

"Thank you, Mr. Capoli. I'd be honored to join you for dinner," Jake replied, recognizing the importance of this invitation and the opportunity to cement his relationship with the Capoli family further.

As Vincent nodded in approval, Jake realized the evening had taken an unexpected turn, one that would likely intertwine his path with the Capolis in ways he had not anticipated.

As the party gradually wound down and guests bid their farewells, there was a sense of contentment in the air. The night had been a whirlwind of laughter, music, and dancing, and the Capoli family's departure marked the end of a memorable evening. However, just when it seemed like the festivities were over, a surprising and unexpected guest made her grand entrance - Isabella Maria Franco.

Initially hesitant, Isabella's interest in the party was piqued when Aunt Mary reached out personally. Aware of the tender history between Isabella and Jake during their college years, Aunt Mary had a hunch that Isabella's presence would not only surprise Jake but potentially rekindle old feelings on this monumental evening for him. With a mix of matchmaking and a genuine desire to create a memorable night, Aunt Mary sent Isabella a personal invitation, subtly hinting at the possibility of reuniting with Jake.

Upon entering, Isabella's vibrant energy immediately transformed the atmosphere, her presence drawing people back to the dance floor with an almost magnetic pull. Her laughter and smiles, infectious and bright, reminded everyone of the joy at the heart of the celebration.

Jake, engaged in a conversation, froze mid-sentence as he caught sight of Isabella. His expression, a cocktail of astonishment and joy, mirrored the emotions swirling within. "Isabella? What are you... How?" he stuttered, disbelief coloring his tone.

Isabella, equally taken aback by Jake's reaction, felt a rush of excitement. "Aunt Mary invited me," she said, her voice a blend of happiness and a touch of nervousness. "She thought it would be nice for me to be here tonight."

Their exchange, initially awkward, gradually warmed as they fell into a more comfortable rhythm, reminiscing about their college days. "I can't believe you're here," Jake admitted, his initial shock giving way to a genuine smile. "It feels like no time has passed."

"Yeah, it does, doesn't it?" Isabella replied, her own smile mirroring Jake's. "Aunt Mary thought it would be a good idea. Looks like she was right."

From across the room, Aunt Mary watched the scene unfold with a satisfied smile. "I had a feeling you two needed this," she later said to Isabella, a twinkle in her eye. "Sometimes, all it takes is a little push to bring the past and present together."

Isabella glanced back at Jake, sharing a laugh over a shared memory. "Thank you, Aunt Mary. Tonight has been full of surprises."

Isabella and Aunt Mary danced the remainder of the night away, sharing stories and laughter as the music played on. It was clear to Aunt Mary that there was something special about Isabella, something that had caught Jake's attention. Throughout the evening, Aunt Mary had observed the way Jake's eyes seemed to light up whenever he was in Isabella's presence. It was in those stolen glances, in the way their laughter intertwined, that Aunt Mary sensed Isabella's significance to Jake and the connection between the two.

As the hours passed and the wine flowed freely, it became clear that Isabella might have overindulged just a bit. Aunt Mary had thoughtfully arranged a private suite for her at the Waldorf Astoria for a week, but Isabella, under the influence of merriment and too much wine, decided to stay overnight at the party.

The sun's rays gently nudged Isabella awake, bringing with them a mild headache and an invigorating sense of adventure. As she stretched, the excitement of the coming week unfolded in her mind like a well-curated itinerary; a luxurious seven days in the heart of New York, with its vibrant streets and endless possibilities, lay before her, waiting to be discovered.

As she made her way through the quiet corridors, eager to start her day, the muffled tones of a conversation halted her steps just outside the room she was about to enter. It was Jake's voice, laced with an unfamiliar earnestness, that piqued her curiosity. She paused, unintentionally eavesdropping.

"Rodney, I need you to take care of something for me," Jake was saying, his tone serious yet infused with a hint of something softer, something Isabella hadn't heard from him before.

"Of course, Mr. Jake," came the respectful reply from Rodney, the family's long-time and much-trusted butler. "What do you need?" Rodney was surprised to find Jake come to him, for he had always avoided asking for help or acknowledging the privilege that came with the house.

Jake turned to the butler, Rodney, with seriousness in his tone, "I need you to pay special attention to our guest, Isabella, this week. It's imperative she feels completely at ease, almost as if she's at home. Her stay needs to be unforgettable."

Curious, Rodney ventured, "I would love to hear the story someday of how you two met, Sir?"

Jake hesitated, a hint of color rising to his cheeks. "She's not just anyone," he admitted with a rare shyness. "Isabella is...well, she's quite special to me."

Observing Jake's uncharacteristic demeanor, Rodney couldn't resist a gentle tease, "Sir, I don't believe I've ever seen you quite so...flustered."

Jake managed a small smile, caught in the act of revealing more than he typically would. "We were...close, almost inseparable, during my time at the University of Redlands. It's where we both studied, and we dated throughout most of my tenure there."

This revelation brought a new understanding to Rodney, who nodded, now fully grasping the significance of the task at hand. He smiled, adding, "Then I shall ensure Miss Isabella's stay is as special as your history. Just don't forget, sir, even seasoned bachelors can be swept off their feet."

Jake's response was a laugh, softer and more genuine than Rodney had heard in a long time. "Well, she isn't my past anymore, but my present too, if things go well." Clearly, Isabella's visit was not just another entry in the social calendar but a meaningful reunion that he hoped would rekindle something beautiful from his past.

With her palm poised on the doorknob, Isabella remained motionless, her pulse fluttering and a flush of warmth coursing down her cheeks. She was touched and embarrassed by Jake's considerate request and detailed directions, which made her flush. Even while she knew Jake to be a lot of things, this degree of focus was shocking.

Having calmed herself, Isabella entered the room at just the right moment to give the impression that she hadn't overheard the conversation. Still, her flushed cheeks bore silent evidence of the words that had inadvertently brought them closer in her mind.

Her adventure in the city, which never sleeps, began, and it was only made better by Jake's company. The air was still tense between the two.

Despite the looming goodbye and the awareness of their separate paths, Isabella and Jake found themselves irresistibly drawn to each other. There was an undeniable chemistry between them that transcended rational thinking and commitments. It was as if fate had intervened, rekindling a fire they had once shared as a couple.

Throughout the week, their connection grew, and it seemed that their lives were interwoven in layers that were both exciting and heartfelt through the busy life of New York. Each day was full of laughter, retold memories from the past, and the excitement of discovering unexpected wonders of the city together.

But for all the bustle, the glances across the rooms that always caught each other's eyes, the light touches of fingers, and the sweetly clinging arms, it was in the quieter moments when their affection printed memories. They were irresistibly drawn to each other in such a way that each embrace felt like home. Knowing their time was limited, they both wanted to make the most of each moment.

On one such day, their adventure took an unexpected turn as they meandered through the bustling streets, lost in their bubble of flirtatious banter and laughter. Caught up in the moment, Isabella leaned in to plant a soft kiss on Jake's lips, a spontaneous and bold act.

As their lips met, the intimate moment took an unexpected turn. They were in the bar where Jake worked, a place he had wanted to show Isabella, to share a piece of his world with her. However, their tender exchange was abruptly interrupted when they collided with someone. Isabella stepped back, her cheeks a warm shade of surprise and embarrassment. "Oh, I'm so sorry!" she said, her concern genuine.

The man they had bumped into was navigating through the dimly lit bar on crutches. His leg braced a reminder of a confrontation that had occurred not long ago. Jake's heart sank as he recognized the man as a member of the Rossi family, the very same individual he had clashed with previously. Unbeknownst to Jake, that large man was none other than Tony Rossi, a mob enforcer with a reputation for violence. Tony quickly rose through the ranks of the Rossi family because he was a distant cousin to Don Roberto Rossi.

Tony Rossi fixed Jake with a sharp, evaluating stare, the tension between them palpable, overshadowing the previous warmth between Jake and Isabella. Jake instinctively moved slightly in front of Isabella, a protective gesture that spoke volumes. "Is there something you need?" he asked, his voice polite yet firm, signaling his readiness to defuse any potential escalation.

After a tense moment, Tony Rossi gave Jake a glaring death stare, then shook his head, perhaps acknowledging Jake's protective stance with a silent nod of unexpected respect. Without another word, he carefully passed them and continued his reconnaissance for the Rossi family, leaving an uneasy quiet behind.

Isabella, her initial enthusiasm dimmed by the incident, looked after him with concern. "Was that...?" she hesitated, uncertain if she wanted the question answered.

"Yeah, it was," Jake admitted, understanding immediately. "But it's okay. Let's not let this spoil our time together."

Taking her hand, Jake guided them away, determined to leave the awkwardness behind and recapture the joy of their reunion. As they moved through the bar, the unease from the encounter gradually lifted, making way once again for the warmth and affection that defined their relationship.

The morning after their encounter at the bar, Isabella and Jake found themselves in the quiet comfort of a small café, nursing cups of coffee as they enjoyed the serene start to the day. The warmth of the sun through the window mirrored the warmth between them, yet an unspoken understanding lingered in the air, like the delicate aroma of the coffee.

Isabella broke the silence, her voice soft but firm. "Jake, I have to go back tomorrow." Her words fell between them, heavy with the weight of reality.

Jake looked up, his eyes searching hers. He knew this moment was inevitable, yet he hoped they could somehow sidestep it. "And what about us?" he asked, gesturing to the space between them. "What happens to this?" With her thoughts running through the multitude of feelings and concerns, Isabella paused to take a deep breath. "Jake, we're in a different physical and metaphorical world. I love what we have, but you know as well as I do that long-distance... it's hard."

The frankness of her remarks hurt Jake, but he acknowledged their validity and nodded in agreement. "Yes, I am aware. I simply mean that... For some reason, I just have this gut feeling that we could be something special, you know?"

Isabella extended her arm across the table and took hold of his. "Hey Jake, I totally get you. But come on, we're being honest. Our lives and our careers will not magically synchronize just because we wish they would. Could we, perhaps, maintain an open-door policy? Can we still enjoy ourselves when we're together while seeing other people if the need arises?"

Jake felt a knot form in his stomach at the thought, but he couldn't deny the sense in her words. "So, kind of like a semi-open, friends-with-benefits situation until we figure things out?"

"Exactly," Isabella said, squeezing his hand. "I don't want to lose you, Jake, but I also don't want us to hold each other back. If the timing's right in the future, who knows?"

The conversation was challenging; each word was carefully chosen, but it showed their maturity and awareness of each other's needs and circumstances. Jake was happy that they had found a means to stay together, yet sad about the future.

They left the café with the decision, a painful ending to their chapter. Jake felt complex emotions whirling. He felt upset over not having Isabella with him as he wished. However, there was optimism that their strong connection would bring them back together under different circumstances.

Despite its unconventionality, this arrangement allowed them to imagine a future together without closing themselves off to the present. They took a risk, believing that if it was meant to be, they would find each other no matter what life brought.

The following week, Jake found himself at the Capoli family estate for dinner. It was an evening filled with warmth, camaraderie, and a sense of belonging. He mingled with various members of the family and got to know the staff who had been a part of the Capoli household for generations.

As the night unfolded, they shared stories, laughter, and moments of sheer joy. Traditional Italian music played in the background, creating an ambiance that felt like a journey to the heart of Italy itself. The aroma of Italian cuisine filled the air, a tribute to the same region as Vincent, the patriarch of the Capoli family.

The plan for dinner was a seven-course meal, with each plate tickling Jake's palate. With each serving, Jake thought to himself that the food could not possibly get better, but the reality was that each course was better than the last. As the night continued, the chef came out to greet everyone and introduced himself to Jake. Chef Josh Harkin had been the personal chef to the family for almost two years, and despite his youthful appearance, his culinary talents were exemplary.

Jake felt appreciated in the midst of the Capoli family, and the evening's festivities led him to a pleasant conversation with Francesca. Their exchange of introductions quickly evolved into a deep and thought-provoking discussion about a sensitive topic: the applicability of the death penalty.

Her breadth of knowledge and understanding continued to astound Jake as he continued his conversation with Francesca. With an enchanting blend of clarity and eloquence, Francesca possessed extensive knowledge and a deep understanding of the intricacies of politics and the law. She referenced a book called "Navigating Through Space" that explored the intrinsic value and resiliency of the human soul. Sometimes, your true self is not what you see on the outside. With a seasoned debater's deftness and a storyteller's kindness, she brought even the most intractable topics to light.

Her position surrounding the death penalty stemmed from an innate belief that life itself was something guaranteed to every living creature and that no human being had the right or moral fortitude to take away a life, no matter what the circumstances.

Francesca believed that the punishment should fit the crime, but only up to the point where death was considered a choice.

They had an instant rapport based on mutual regard and understanding, which showed in the ease of their discourse. Their conversation was fun and illuminating because they were both open-minded, which helped them navigate the complicated issues at hand.

Jake's position, on the other hand, was quite different. He believed that the world operated on an unspoken warrior's code. If the law failed to uphold the principles of justice, then an individual who was powerful enough could settle an account by their own hand, which could lead to a death.

At one point, Francesca's eyes sparkled with pride as she turned toward her father, Vincent. "You know, it's Dad's unwavering adherence to principle that inspires us to strive harder in both our personal endeavors and our business dealings," she said, her voice imbued with admiration. "His example is the reason we never shy away from challenges, always pushing ourselves to excel."

Vincent, who had been following the conversation with a mixture of pride and interest, nodded appreciatively at his daughter's words. His philosophy of integrity and hard work had always been central to the family's ethos, and hearing Francesca articulate it so passionately was a clear sign of its impact.

He did not agree with her view on the death penalty but appreciated her fiery disposition and presence of mind as she defended her view. Vincent also thought that the topic was a bit ironic because he had been forced to plunge deeper into crime as a way to regulate and control it in order to keep himself and those around him safe. Vincent's view aligned closer with Jake's regarding death sometimes being necessary in the pursuit of justice.

The conversation took a subtle turn when Francesca, caught up in the moment, began to steer towards a more sensitive topic—the reality surrounding Enzo.

Her words started to tread into territory that was perhaps not meant for public disclosure, her enthusiasm momentarily overshadowing her discretion.

Vincent saw the conversation was going in a certain direction and made a small but noticeable motion to change the course. A delicate but forceful reminder was given when he firmly set his whiskey glass on the table, making a loud sound to grab Francesca's attention without frightening anybody else. After first looking very engaged, Francesca's countenance calmed down, and she lowered her head slightly to show that she understood her father's nonverbal warning.

Jake, witnessing this exchange, felt a flicker of confusion. The sudden shift in the atmosphere, the unspoken communication between father and daughter, hinted at layers and undercurrents within the family that he was not privy to. The moment was fleeting, but it left him with a sense of intrigue about the complexities of the Capoli family dynamics.

"Sorry, I guess I got a bit carried away," Francesca apologized, smiling sheepishly at Jake. Her ability to gracefully navigate the delicate balance of personal conviction and familial respect was impressive.

"No problem at all," Jake assured her, his curiosity piqued but his tone remaining light. "It's clear your family holds some powerful values. It's really admirable."

The conversation gradually resumed its earlier, more general flow, but Jake couldn't help but feel intrigued by the brief glimpse he'd received into the Capoli family's internal world.

Before the night ended, they exchanged social media contacts, a modern-day way of staying connected. Jake couldn't help but notice a hint of flirtation in Franchesca's demeanor, adding an exciting layer to their newfound connection.

Jake's life took an unexpected turn after a fascinating evening at the Capoli family home, revealing the mob's mysterious world. In this world, he encountered several memorable individuals, like Johnny Viola and Knuckles McGee.

Johnny Viola had a knack for stirring the pot and pushing people to their limits just to show their true mettle. His chaotic nature, along with his dramatic flair, brought a sense of excitement to social gatherings, making them unpredictable and always interesting. You never knew what would happen when Johnny was around, but one thing was certain: it would never be boring.

Knuckles McGee, the mob's enforcer, was huge and famous. He was eager to test Jake's resolve and reputation, reflecting the underworld's brutal yet honest nature.

In the middle of the ongoing chatter, Vincent Capoli, the esteemed head of the Capoli family, looked at Jake, who was immersed in listening to an interesting story. He patted Jake's shoulder and solemnly uttered. "Jake," he started, his words were a blend of sincerity, "I want to share a bit about what happened in the Flamingo Room at The Dirty Bird. It's a complicated world we navigate, and understanding these dynamics can be crucial."

Vincent's recounting was purposefully vague, offering just enough insight to sketch the outlines of the incident without delving into the depths of mob politics. This deliberate choice reflected Vincent's awareness of the burdens his world carried and his reluctance to involve Jake unnecessarily.

"I appreciate the insight, Vincent. It's a complex world indeed," Jake responded, his mind piecing together the fragments of the story.

Looking at Jake with a soft but stern seriousness in his gaze, Vincent Capoli spoke, "In our world, trust is the cornerstone. We protect our own and hold loyalty in the highest regard." His tone carried an undercurrent of intimidation, making it clear that Jake needed to understand the weight of these words."

Jake replied, "Loyalty is key. I understand that."

He was forever changed by their little discussion. He took Vincent's statements as a deeper understanding of the Capoli family's principles. Jake made a personal decision based on this understanding and the Flamingo Room brawl details. If Francesca or Martin were in danger, he would try to help them. Jake's honesty and respect for the Capoli family drove this decision. He pledged his silent support based on his newfound ties and the complicated tapestry of loyalty and trust that defined his entrée into the Capoli's World.

Chapter 4: The FBI's Chessboard

The skyline of New York stretched before the office of the FBI task force. Absorbed in the continuous sound of phones ringing and people running from one door to another, Agent Maurice Jackson leaned back in his chair and gazed at the sky. He had a steaming cup of Earl Grey tea in hand as he sat listening to a confession of a criminal in a recording.

"Oh, he is done. That is a minimum of 25 years at least."

Agent Jackson had greyed his hair, working for the task force. He knew this city, a concrete jungle with more secrets than a high school locker room. Every skyscraper, every crowded street corner, felt like it held its breath, hiding something just out of sight. He was a grizzled old warhorse in the fight against crime and understood the city's rhythm. He knew the jungle of concrete and steel that hid secrets was a complex web and knew that only someone with his experience could begin to unravel it.

Jackson wasn't born into the gleaming world of the FBI. He came from a different kind of battlefield—the unforgiving heat and grit of the military. Under the relentless desert sun, he honed his skills in intel gathering and recon. He learned to become a ghost, a silent observer, a master of extracting secrets from the shadows. Those skills became his calling card when he transitioned to the Bureau.

His baptism by fire came in a sprawling narcotics investigation that stretched across state lines. He was a rookie back then but did not shy away from embedding himself deep undercover. For months, he navigated the treacherous world of drug lords and traffickers, all while feeding intel back to his team. The sting operation's success became a legend within the Bureau, and

Jackson's name became synonymous with focus and nerves of steel. He emerged from the operation as a changed man, hardened by the experience, but his moral compass was even truer.

Word of his exploits spread like wildfire. When the task force targeting the city's organized crime syndicate was formed, there was no question who would be leading the surveillance wing. Jackson was their secret weapon, a man who could vanish into the bustling crowds yet pick out a pre-arranged signal from a block away. He could analyze grainy security footage and spot a flicker of recognition in a criminal's eye, a detail others might miss. His intel was gold, his judgment even more valuable. He wasn't just the most skilled; he was the most trusted. In the murky world they were about to delve into, trust was a currency worth more than any badge or gun.

Taking a sip of his tea, he savored the warmth and the brief respite it offered from the never-ending cycle of cases that filled his days. His phone buzzed, snapping him back to the reality of his job. Maurice picked it up, glancing at the caller ID before answering with a practiced tone of neutrality, "Jackson here."

"Sir, it's Lina," came the voice of his assistant from the other end, always efficient and to the point. "Do you need anything for the briefing later today?"

"Yes, Lina, please bring files on the top five families active in New York, as I had set aside earlier for you. It's time we updated our strategy based on the latest intel," Maurice requested, setting his tea down and preparing for the work ahead.

A short time later, there was a knock on the door, and Lina came in with files that showed the dark side of the city's rich and powerful. She put them on his desk—a mix of possible leads and information about some of New York's most infamous families.

"As requested, sir. Everything from the Capolis to the Rossi's and beyond. There's been some movement in the Capoli family that might interest you. A newcomer named Jake has been drawing some attention. A lot of Rossi men were looking into this guy," Lina reported, her voice carrying a hint of curiosity.

Maurice raised an eyebrow, picking up the file labeled 'Capoli.' "Jake, you say? Let's see what makes him so interesting to our friends in the underworld." His fingers flipped through the pages, each document a piece of the puzzle he was determined to solve.

"Keep an eye on any developments, Lina. These families are like a hydra; cut off one head, and two more spring up in its place. It's Jake today; it could be someone else tomorrow. We need to stay ahead," Maurice mused, his gaze fixed on the photographs and reports that sprawled across his desk.

"Will do, sir. Anything else you need from me?" Lina asked, ready to assist with whatever her boss required.

"For now, just ensure we have surveillance on this party the Capolis are setting up. It might just be the break we need to get closer. Oh, and Lina," Maurice added, his voice taking on a lighter tone, "do keep me posted on the status of the coffee machine repair, will you? I'm starting to think this tea could be used as a new interrogation technique."

Lina couldn't help but smile at the comment. "Will do, sir. I'll personally see to it that you're the first to know once it's up and running. We can't have you torturing yourself with this tea any longer."

As Lina exited the office, Maurice Jackson took another sip of his tea, grimacing slightly at the taste but appreciating the moment of levity they had shared. His thoughts swiftly shifted back to the task at hand. It had been 12 years to him in this office, and he had seen hundreds of people come and go.

He gazed at the wall where his old picture hung. There used to be many agents, friends, and even family. Many of his close ones had lost their lives to the task force. He waved his tea to the picture and whispered, "You guys would have gone ballistic had you tasted this rubbish."

Agent Jackson was well-liked around the office for his unique blend of dedication and humor. His ability to defuse the high-stress environment with a timely joke, like his quip about tea, endeared him to his colleagues.

Agent Maurice Jackson walked slowly to the briefing room as if he knew how important the talks that were about to happen were. The room was usually busy with the low chatter of agents sharing information and news, but when he walked in, there was a hush of anticipation. Jackson laughed immediately and asked, "What, did I wear my invisible suit today?" A ripple of laughter broke the tension.

As the laughter subsided, Jackson took his place at the head of the table, signaling the start of the briefing. "Alright, team, let's dive into our current strategies for infiltrating the major mafia families of New York. We've had some progress, but there's a lot more ground to cover."

Agent Collins began the discussion, outlining the latest updates and their systematic approach to gathering intelligence. The conversation was precise and focused, reflecting the team's dedication to their mission.

The topic soon shifted to a more specific case. "The FBI has successfully placed Chef Josh Harkin within the Capoli family's culinary team," Jackson announced, capturing his team's full attention. "Josh recently reported an incident involving a kid who unexpectedly intervened in a potentially violent meeting between the Rossi and Capoli families. Following the altercation, it seems Vincent Capoli has taken a particular interest in this individual."

An agent pointed out that both the Rossi and Capoli families seemed to be investigating the same individual, which was unusual. Jackson leaned back in his chair, eyes scanning the detailed report Josh had sent in. The room's attention was fixed on him as he contemplated the situation.

After a moment, he spoke up, addressing a colleague's suggestion that Jake might not be affiliated with either family. "While it's possible Jake isn't directly connected to either family, the interest from both sides is peculiar. We can't dismiss the possibility of him playing a more significant role."

Several voices rose in opposition, suggesting that Jake was indeed working with one of the families, citing the unusual attention he had garnered.

Jackson listened carefully to each argument, his expression thoughtful. "It's essential we keep an open mind and consider all possibilities. Jake's involvement, whether as an ally or a pawn, could be pivotal in understanding the dynamics between these families. Let's focus on gathering more concrete evidence before jumping to conclusions."

As the briefing unfolded, diving into the depths of strategy and potential moves, Jackson's insight into Jake's situation seemed to pivot their approach. The atmosphere in the room shifted, charged with a renewed sense of purpose. Every agent there was acutely conscious of the fine line they walked in their mission to penetrate the hidden layers of New York's formidable crime families.

"We'll keep tabs on Jake as well," Jackson added, his statement resonating with a room full of seasoned agents. His proposals, met with enthusiastic nods and murmurs of agreement, showcased the respect and trust he had cultivated over the years. The team was ready to follow his lead, their confidence in his judgment unwavering.

Lina caught everyone off guard as the meeting began to wind down, with agents gathering their notes and preparing to tackle their assignments. With a mischievous grin, she placed a steaming cup of coffee in front of Jackson.

"Looks like the interrogation techniques can take a backseat now," Jackson quipped, his joy at the sight of real coffee palpable.

"Sir, we couldn't let our best agent feel down," Lina answered. "But know this is instant coffee. The machine is still down." Apology trailed her expressions.

"You guys are killing me." He buried his face in his hands and chuckled. Lina smiled as he thanked her.

***

Even though it had only been a few days since Jake had started his new work, his pulse was pounding in his chest as he neared the towering glass skyscraper of Goldman Sachs. When he approached the building, it felt like he was approaching it for the millionth time. The magnificence of the structure, which reflected the sun in the early morning in a thousand sparkling hues, served as a constant reminder of the world that he was about to enter, a world in which his aspirations and dreams were at stake.

Walking through the revolving doors, Jake felt a mix of excitement and trepidation. He was determined to impress his finance production managers and prove that he was more than just a newcomer but a valuable asset to the team. His initial days were filled with an onslaught of information, and he quickly absorbed the training materials, eager to master the complexities of his role.

Despite his efforts, Jake was keenly aware of the steep learning curve ahead, especially concerning the advanced AI in decision analysis systems that Goldman Sachs relied on heavily. He knew mastering this technology was crucial for his success and securing a positive review before the year's end.

One afternoon, after a particularly grueling training session, his manager, Mr. Simmons, called him aside. Jake braced himself, hoping his nerves didn't show too much.

"Jake, I've been watching your progress over these past few days," Mr. Simmons began, his tone serious but encouraging. "You've shown an impressive ability to grasp the training material quickly. Your dedication hasn't gone unnoticed."

Jake's face flushed; he waited for the famous "but" to come. "Have I done something wrong?"

"Hahaha, no, no," his manager chuckled.

Jake felt a rush of gratitude and relief. "Thank you, sir. I'm really trying to give it my all. I know there's a lot to learn, and I'm up for the challenge."

Mr. Simmons nodded, a hint of a smile on his face. "I'm glad to hear that because there's one area where you're going to need to focus your efforts significantly—our AI decision analysis systems. They're at the core of what we do here, and becoming proficient in them is not just beneficial; it's essential."

Jake's pulse quickened at the mention of the AI systems. Given their prevalence in the training modules and discussions around the office, he had suspected as much.

"I understand, sir. I've been fascinated by the potential of AI in finance. I'll admit, it's a bit daunting, but I'm eager to learn more and become adept at using the technology," Jake responded, his determination shining through his initial nervousness.

Mr. Simmons's expression softened, clearly pleased with Jake's response. "That's the spirit I was hoping for. It's going to be challenging, no doubt. But I've seen your work ethic, and I believe you have what it takes to excel. We'll ensure you have access to additional resources and support to get you up to speed."

As they continued to discuss Jake's training plan and the specific goals for mastering the AI systems, Jake felt a mix of fear and excitement. The path ahead would not be easy, but the challenge invigorated him. He was ready to dive deep into the world of AI to demystify its complexities and harness its power for his role at Goldman Sachs.

Jake's steps echoed purposefully down the polished hallway as he returned to his desk. Mr. Simmons' words echoed in his mind, a validation of his skills that ignited a renewed sense of purpose. The road ahead was a steep climb, a mountain of data and algorithms waiting to be conquered. But a thrill of determination surged through him. He wasn't naive to the challenge, but the anxieties of the first few days were morphing into a burgeoning confidence.

A determined click of the laptop lid echoed in the quiet. The screen flickered on, revealing a complex arsenal of tools and AI decision analysis systems—his gateway to the uncharted territory where finance and technology converged. He was ready to conquer this new frontier.

Just then, his phone buzzed a discordant note in the focused silence. A jolt of electricity shot through him as he saw the message notification—Isabella's name glowing on the screen. He unlocked his phone with a flourish, a grin already spreading across his face. The message read, "Heyy, I bet you look amazing in that button-down today."

The playful jab sent a wave of giddiness washing over him. The day had been good, productive even. A successful meeting with Mr. Simmons and a newfound sense of purpose were clicking into place. In a burst of euphoria, he spun around in his chair, the joy bubbling over.

He whipped out his phone again to capture a quick selfie. With a mischievous glint in his eye, he posted it on Instagram, tagging Isabella with the cheeky caption, "Posted this because someone wanted to see me in a button-down."

There was a digital tether that connected Isabella and Jake despite the fact that they were separated by a great distance. Emojis, which are essentially winking and blushing substitutes for human expressions, were dancing over their screens. Each one of them was like a playful poke that sent a tingle down Isabella's spine while she was watching them.

A steady stream of likes poured down on them like confetti, serving as a constant validation of their relationship. Isabella's recollection was filled with reverberations of New York, a metropolis that constantly throbbed with an unrelenting energy that reflected the spark that existed between them.

In comparison to the snatched minutes with Jake, the brilliant lights and the rush of sensations were nothing more than a minor inconvenience. He laughed, and the way his eyes wrinkled at the corners when he smiled—these were the mementos that she treasured the most, and she kept them hidden away in the recesses of her heart.

Recently, Isabella stepped into an exciting new chapter of her life. Fresh from her graduation from the University of Redlands, where she majored in Physics and Mathematics, she was offered a position as a Senior Data Analyst at the prestigious Jet Propulsion Laboratory (JPL) in Pasadena, California. The opportunity was a dream come true for Isabella, a chance to delve deep into the realms of space exploration and contribute to humanity's understanding of the cosmos. Her role at JPL was to analyze vast datasets, decipher the secrets of distant galaxies, and craft algorithms that might one day unlock the mysteries of the universe.

One evening, as the Californian sunset painted the sky in orange and pink hues, Isabella recounted her recent achievements and the whirlwind of changes to Jake over a video call.

"I still can't believe I'm here, Jake," Isabella said, her eyes sparkling with excitement. "JPL is incredible, and the work we're doing is mind-blowing. But I'll admit, it's a bit surreal. I keep expecting to wake up and find it's all a dream."

Jake's face lit up with pride as he listened to her. "Isabella, that's amazing! I knew you'd do great things. And hey, if it feels like a dream, it's because you're living the dream. Just promise you'll send me a postcard from Mars, okay?"

Isabella laughed, a sound that Jake wished he could bottle up and keep. "It's a deal. But only if you promise to show me around Wall Street when I come back to New York. It seems you're making quite the name for yourself at Goldman Sachs."

Their conversation meandered through topics of work, dreams, and the occasional reminiscence of their time together. It was clear that despite the physical distance, the connection between them was as strong as ever, perhaps even strengthened by the challenges they each faced in their respective careers.

As their call came to a close, Isabella couldn't help but feel a mix of happiness and a tinge of longing. "Jake, I'm really glad we're staying in touch like this. New York was unforgettable, thanks to you. And now, with everything happening here at JPL... It feels like life is moving so fast."

Jake nodded, his expression softening. "I feel the same way, Isabella. And no matter where or what we're doing, I'm just a call away. Remember that."

The screen eventually went dark as they said their goodbyes, but the warmth of their conversation lingered. Isabella sat back, her mind racing with thoughts of distant planets and the infinite possibilities that lay ahead.

***

In the quiet hum of their office late into the night, Agent Maurice Jackson and his partner, Agent Collins, huddled over a cluster of files and photographs scattered across the table. The dim light from the desk lamp cast long shadows, giving the room an intense, almost cinematic quality. It was here, amidst cups of stale coffee and the soft whir of a malfunctioning air conditioner, that they pieced together a plan that could change the course of their investigation.

"Jackson, look at this," Collins said, pushing a photograph across the table. It was Jake, captured in a candid moment, laughing with some members of the Capoli family at a recent event. "He's got their trust. It's rare to see someone from the outside get this close to the Capoli circle."

He leaned forward, his eyes narrowing as he considered the image. "You're right. And it's not just the Capolis. If our intel is correct, he's on Rossi's radar too. He's uniquely positioned, Collins. If we could bring him on board, he could be invaluable."

The agents spent hours debating the moral and ethical implications of recruiting Jake, a civilian, into their web of espionage and surveillance. Finally, they agreed that the potential benefits outweighed the risks. They needed someone on the inside, someone unsuspected by both the Capoli and Rossi families. Jake was their best shot.

"But how do we approach him? We can't just show up and ask him to spy for us," Collins pointed out, her forehead creasing with concern.

"We'll need to be subtle, offer him protection, and maybe even appeal to his sense of justice. We need to make him see the bigger picture—that he could help us save lives by stopping whatever war might brew between these families," Jackson replied, his voice firm with conviction.

The plan was set. They would monitor Jake closely, looking for an opportunity to approach him discreetly. They would outline the risks and the stakes involved, making it clear that his safety would be their top priority.

Weeks passed, and the perfect moment finally arrived. Jake was alone at a coffee shop, looking more contemplative than usual, gazing out the window at the bustling city. Jackson and Collins, dressed in plain clothes to blend in, took the adjacent table.

After a few moments of tense silence, Jackson cleared his throat and turned to Jake. "Excuse me, are you Jake? I've heard a lot about you. Mind if we have a word?"

Jake looked up, his initial surprise quickly replaced by a cautious curiosity. "Sure, I guess. Do I know you?"

"Not yet, but we've closely followed your interactions with the Capoli and Rossi families. We believe you could help us with an important matter," Collins chimed in, his tone friendly yet serious.

As FBI agents, Jackson and Collins took the time to explain their jobs and the nature of the investigation. It was said that innocent lives were frequently caught in the crossfire as a result of the families' risky game. They said Jake may be vital in stopping the bloodshed because of his insider knowledge and fresh viewpoint.

As the conversation drew to a close, Jake leaned back, his expression unreadable. "I need to think about this," he finally said. "It's not something I can decide on the spot."

Jackson nodded, exchanging a glance with Collins. "Of course. Take your time. We'll be in touch."

The agents left the coffee shop, stepping back into the night, leaving Jake with his thoughts. The city around him felt different now, charged with a sense of purpose and danger. The game had changed, and he was now at its center, holding the potential to tilt the balance in a long-standing feud.

Sitting alone in the coffee shop, Jake felt a sense of unease wash over him. He had finally landed a job, a step forward he had been eagerly awaiting, yet here he was, faced with uncertainties that seemed to dwarf his recent achievements. The thought of diving into another complex situation, especially one fraught with potential danger and moral ambiguity, was the last thing he wanted.

Though presented with a veneer of civility and concern, the conversation with the agents left him wrestling with a dilemma he felt ill-prepared to tackle. "Why me?" he thought, a mix of frustration and apprehension clouding his thoughts. The world of high finance was challenging enough; stepping into a role that could embroil him in a conflict between two notorious families was not what he had envisioned when dreaming of making his mark in New York.

Jake's mind raced as he tried to reconcile the opportunity to contribute to something meaningful with the risk of getting tangled in a mess that could have unforeseen consequences. The allure of a simple, straightforward life, focusing on his career and personal growth, seemed increasingly attractive compared to the murky waters the FBI agents were inviting him to wade into.

As he left the coffee shop, the city's vibrant energy around him felt slightly muted, overshadowed by the weight of the decision that lay before him.

***

The busy city of New York had a flair for vices and people who were ready to revel in violence. Even the files in the task force were arranged with severity. The Rossi and Capoli families, out of all the others, both deeply entrenched in the city's underbelly, vied for control, their ambitions set against the backdrop of Manhattan's sleepless nights and endless opportunities.

Roberto Rossi, the American-born head of the Rossi crime family, was a figure steeped in contradiction. Raised on the streets of New York, he possessed a charisma that belied the ruthlessness of his intentions. His empire, built on the shadows of evil vices such as drugs, prostitution, and human trafficking, stood in stark contrast to the somewhat more honorable dealings of the Capoli family. Where the Rossis delved into the exploitation of human misery, the Capolis, albeit still on the wrong side of the law, engaged in enterprises like casinos, gambling, and high-stakes digital crimes—ventures that harmed wallets but not bodies.

The heart of their conflict lay in control. To Roberto, New York was not just a city; it was the ultimate prize, a throne from which to oversee an empire that fed on vice and fear. The Capolis, under the guise of their "victimless" crimes, posed the only significant threat to his dominion.

One night, Roberto sat across from his trusted advisors in a dark room that was shrouded in secret. His dark eyes were filled with anger and determination. "The Capolis think they can hurt us with their moralistic talk about honor and crimes that don't hurt anyone." They forget how this jungle works. In New York, people with power don't care about morals.

His advisors nodded, their expressions a mixture of admiration and fear. They knew all too well the lengths to which Roberto would go to secure his reign over New York. The streets whispered of the Rossi's cruelty, tales of vanished enemies, and shattered lives—a testament to the dark legacy Roberto was crafting in his quest for control.

"We need to make a move and quickly. They will never know what hit 'em," Roberto declared, his voice cutting through the room's tension like a knife. "The Capolis have grown too comfortable. It's time they're reminded of who truly owns the streets of this city."

As the meeting adjourned, the air was thick with the anticipation of the impending conflict. The Rossi family mobilized, their operations tightening like a noose around the areas still under the Capoli's influence. For Roberto, this was more than a battle for territory; it was a declaration of his supremacy, a message to all who dared to challenge his rule.

Meanwhile, the Capoli family, led by the astute Vincent Capoli, prepared for the inevitable clash. Unlike Roberto, Vincent preferred the shadows to the spotlight, his strategies woven with precision and foresight. The Capolis knew the Rossis were coming, and they intended to meet force with cunning. The clash between the Rossi and Capoli families was not just a fight for control but a struggle to define the soul of the city's darkest corners.

***

The next meeting was in the same coffee shop. While Jake made up his mind, Agent Jackson stood up, announcing he was going to grab a coffee. "This might take a while; I never can decide what I want," he said with a wink, leaving Jake and the other agent at the table engulfed in an awkward silence.

The coffee shop buzzed around them, but the table felt like a small island of silence. Jake shifted in his seat, exchanging a hesitant glance with the agent, who offered a shrug as if to say, "What can you do?"

Meanwhile, at the counter, Jackson's interaction with the cashier turned into a funny moment. "What's good today? Actually, it surprised me. No, wait—do you have that new caramel thing?" he bantered, the cashier laughing along. "Make those two, and let's hope my colleagues don't fall asleep while I make up my mind here."

Back at the table, Jake attempted to break the ice with the other agent. "So, do all FBI agents take their coffee orders this seriously?" He joked, trying to ease the tension.

The agent cracked a smile, replying, "Only the ones who've been undercover too long. They develop a taste for... drama."

Their lighthearted exchange was cut short as Jackson returned, a triumphant smile on his face, carrying the coffees. "Hope you guys didn't miss me too much. This, my friends, is what I call a coffee worth waiting for."

The reality of Jake's situation was far more complex than the black-and-white scenarios of his childhood fantasies. The Capoli family had shown him kindness and trust, pulling him into their fold in ways he hadn't anticipated when he first arrived in New York. To betray that trust now, even in the name of justice, felt like crossing a line he wasn't prepared to cross.

"I understand the position you're putting me in, and I'm not saying I don't want to help," Jake started, his voice steady despite the turmoil inside him. "But the Capolis... they've been good to me. I can't just turn my back on them without solid proof that they're the villains you're making them out to be."

Agent Jackson leaned forward, his expression earnest. "Jake, we wouldn't ask this of you if we didn't believe you could make a real difference. You've seen the underbelly of their operations, even if indirectly. You know what's at stake here."

Jake sighed, the weight of the decision pressing down on him. "I always thought if I had the chance to make a difference, to do something meaningful, I'd take it. But this... it's not as simple as right and wrong, is it? There are shades of gray everywhere, and I'm right in the middle of them."

The agents exchanged glances, understanding the conflict raging within Jake. They had seen it before—the moral quandary that came with delving too deep into the complexities of organized crime.

"We know it's a difficult decision," Agent Collins chimed in, her voice softer. "But remember, Jake, sometimes doing the right thing means making the hard choices. We'll be here, whatever you decide."

As the meeting drew to a close, Jake was left alone with his thoughts, the clamor of the coffee shop fading into the background. He was aware of the FBI's interest in him, and the realization that he was now a person of interest to both the law and the mob weighed heavily on his mind.

The moral dilemma of choosing between right and wrong, between loyalty to the Capolis and his innate desire for justice, was not one he could resolve easily. Jake knew the decision he made would define his path forward, for better or worse. Jake understood that no matter what choice he made, he would have to live with the consequences. The idealistic child who dreamed of being an FBI agent was now a man caught in a web of loyalty, morality, and survival.

Jake's weekends were still dedicated to the familiar hustle of bartending, a job he cherished for the joy and spontaneity it brought into his life. During one of these weekends, he struck up a friendship with Rodney, the Butler, and Titiano, whose camaraderie had become a surprising yet welcome addition to his life in New York. In a spur-of-the-moment decision, Jake suggested they go bowling one night, seeking a break from the usual routine. The evening was filled with laughter, competitive banter, and a couple of beers, a perfect escape for the trio.

As the night wore on, their paths unexpectedly crossed with Mia's, a friend that Jake met shortly after moving to New York. Her excitement at seeing him again was palpable, her intentions clear—she wanted to reconnect. But Jake, whose heart had been gently reoccupied by Isabella, found himself in a predicament. Despite the warmth of their connection and good times, he knew he had to keep Mia at arm's length, and his commitment to Isabella was a silent vow he was determined to uphold.

The encounter left Jake contemplative, his mind wandering back to the offer from the FBI that he had declined. The thought of saying no, of stepping away from a chance to contribute to something bigger than himself, still lingered in the back of his mind, casting a shadow over his decisions.

It wasn't long after that night when Titiano called him up. Their conversation started with the usual pleasantries, and Titiano quickly steered the topic towards Isabella. "So, how are things with the lovely Isabella? Has she swept you off your feet yet?" he teased, his voice laced with humor.

Jake offered a non-committal laugh. "Things are good, Titi. We're just taking things one day at a time." But his mind was elsewhere, tangled in thoughts of Mia, the FBI, and the complex web of decisions that seemed to be his constant companion.

Titiano picked up on Jake's distracted tone. "You alright there, buddy? You seem a bit out of it today. Anything on your mind?"

With his recent experiences and choices weighing heavily on him, Jake hesitated. "Really, it's not much. Simply put, I've been reflecting a bit regarding everything."

"Ah, the burden of profound contemplation," Titiano quipped, trying to lighten the mood. "Remember, Jake, whatever it is, you're not alone. We've got your back."

The reassurance from Titiano was a small comfort, but the turmoil inside Jake refused to settle. He brushed off the subject, not ready to dive into the depths of his thoughts, especially not about the lingering possibility of involvement with the FBI.

As they wrapped up their conversation with plans to meet again soon, Jake couldn't help but feel the weight of his silence. The night out bowling, the unexpected meeting with Mia, and the constant reminder of the path not taken with the FBI wove a complex tapestry of emotions and decisions in Jake's mind.

He was caught in the middle of a life that was moving forward yet tethered by the threads of what-ifs and maybes, a constant battle between moving on and looking back.

Chapter 5: Deceptive Allegiances

It was a new day in the headquarters of the task force, and the ecosystem was filled with the typical sense of urgency that permeated the atmosphere. When his phone rang, Agent Maurice Jackson was sorting through the avalanche of reports that had arrived that morning. When he took a quick glance at the caller ID, he noticed that it was Wendy, the station clerk for the department. Wendy, who was a crucial but frequently overlooked cog in the massive machinery of the FBI, had been working covertly for the team for years, accumulating snippets of information that frequently proved to be essential.

"Jackson, got a minute?" Wendy's voice crackled through the phone, a mix of urgency and secrecy hinting at the importance of the call.

"Always for you, Wendy. And remember, you still owe me lunch for that tip last month," Jackson replied, lightening the moment with a joke, a small reminder of the camaraderie they shared despite the seriousness of their work.

Wendy chuckled, "One of these days, Jackson. Anyway, listen. My informants in the Rossi camp picked up the chatter. Seems like they're not too happy about Jake's intervention at the bar. They're talking revenge."

Jackson's mood shifted at the mention of the Rossi's interest in Jake. He knew the Rossi family's reputation for brutal retribution all too well. "Thanks, Wendy. This is big. Let's keep this under wraps for now. I'll bring it up in the briefing."

Hanging up, Jackson gathered his team for an urgent briefing.

The room fell silent as he relayed Wendy's message, his tone somber. "The Rossi's have Jake in their sights. We know their history—how they've dealt with opposition. It's never pretty. We lost a good agent to them, someone like family to us."

The team nodded, the gravity of the situation sinking in. Past encounters with the Rossi family had left deep scars, memories of fallen comrades a stark reminder of the stakes involved.

At that moment, the FBI bureau chief, Sean Brady, stepped into the room, his presence commanding immediate attention. A former Police Commissioner, Brady was known for his no-nonsense approach to law enforcement. Jackson, who usually kept the mood light, knew better than to crack jokes in Brady's presence.

Brady addressed the team, his voice firm. "We have an opportunity here. The Rossi's interest in Jake could be our leverage. We protect him and bring him into the fold; in return, he gives us insight into the Capoli family. It's time we get ahead of this."

The plan was clear, but the ethical implications weighed heavily on the team. Using Jake as bait against the Capoli family was a risky maneuver that could put him in even greater danger.

As the briefing concluded, Jackson and his team were left to ponder the difficult path ahead. The line between right and wrong blurred further with each decision, the battle against the city's underworld a constant test of their morals and resolve.

The task group wasted little time in keeping tabs on the Rossi family in the days that followed, all in an attempt to keep Jake safe. The moral conundrum of contacting Jake again with a suggestion that might alter the course of the young man's life was weighing heavily on Jackson's mind. In the dark nooks of the city lay not just the criminal underworld's secrets but also the unseen struggles of its protectors. The struggle was far from done for Agent Jackson and his team; seeking justice would be an eternal odyssey into the depths of evil.

***

Jake's desk at Goldman Sachs reflected his rapid ascent in his career and the relentless demands of his position. An abundance of files and an inbox brimming with tasks competed for his attention, each vying to claim victory in consuming his time. Despite the overwhelming workload, Jake thrived, relentlessly pushing himself to excel in the fast-paced realm of high-level finance. He not only kept pace with the demands but also strategically charted a course for advancement, setting his sights on a substantial account that held the potential to propel him to a highly deserved position.

The clock struck noon, and the office gradually emptied as his colleagues headed out for their lunch break. Jake, however, remained glued to his chair, determined to plow through another report. Then, his manager, Mr. Simmons, passed by, pausing at the sight of Jake's cluttered workspace.

"Planning to build a fort with those files, Jake?" Mr. Simmons joked, a light-hearted smile on his face.

Jake chuckled, rubbing the back of his neck. "Feels like it, sir. But no, just trying to stay ahead of the game."

"I admire the dedication, but remember, even the best needs a break," Mr. Simmons advised warmly before walking away.

To Jake's surprise, a junior staffer appeared at his desk a short while later, delivering a croissant and a coffee with Mr. Simmons' compliments. The small gesture brought a genuine smile to Jake's face, a much-needed break in his hectic day.

As he sipped his coffee, Jake's phone rang. It was Francesca. "Hey, Jake! I hope I'm not interrupting. I just wanted to personally invite you to my birthday bash at the Rumpus Room in East Village. We've got the whole venue for the night. It's going to be epic, and I'd love for you to come."

Jake's eyes lit up at the invitation. "That sounds amazing, Francesca. Count me in. And if it's alright with you, I'd like to bring Titiano along. He's been a great friend since I moved here."

"Absolutely! The more, the merrier. I can't wait to see you guys there. It's going to be a night to remember," Francesca said excitedly before they said their goodbyes.

Energized by the upcoming event, Jake quickly shot a message to Titiano detailing the plans for Francesca's birthday party. "Hey, Titi, gear up for an epic night at the Rumpus Room this weekend. Francesca's birthday. You in?"

Titiano's response was almost instantaneous, his enthusiasm matching Jake's. "Wouldn't miss it for the world. Let's make it a night to remember."

***

A groan escaped Jake's lips before he even fumbled for his keys. The office had been a battlefield today, and he felt like a war-weary soldier trudging home. As he unlocked the door, a wave of what smelled suspiciously like freshly baked cookies hit him. He braced himself.

"Jake, darling! How was your day? Tell me everything!" she bubbled, her eyes sparkling with genuine interest as she maneuvered around the living room, straightening cushions and fluffing pillows; her movements matched that of a ballet of domestic efficiency.

The exhaustion of the day's labor melted away under her watchful eyes, and Jake couldn't help but smile. You were right, Aunt Mary. Not bad, just busy. There's a major project I'm working on that has the potential to revolutionize the company.

With her focus squarely on Jake, Aunt Mary halted. So, you're saying it's serious? The air of secrecy about her words suggested she might have the key to her success; she spoke as though about to reveal it.

Curious, Jake leaned in and took a seat. "Oh? So, what exactly is that?"

Aunt Mary joined him at the table, her eyes sparkling with delight. "An investment fund is run by one of my clients. Quite the influential person, and they're always on the hunt for new and exciting projects. I've raved about your intelligence and diligence to them. Meeting you would pique their attention, Jake.

Jake couldn't believe it. It was shocking that Aunt Mary would do all that she could to be of great assistance to him. "That is just amazing, Aunt Mary. You must be kidding me. Please don't give me your time; I am only starting out."

"Nonsense!" Aunt Mary exclaimed, her voice firm yet full of warmth. "You're not wasting anyone's time. You're exactly the kind of talent they're looking to support. This could be your big break, my dear."

The conversation flowed into the evening, with Aunt Mary offering advice and encouragement. She detailed her client's background and what Jake could expect from the meeting. The prospect of such a connection was exciting but daunting. Yet, with

Aunt Mary's life in him as the guiding light, Jake felt ready to take on the challenge.

As he prepared for bed that night, Jake reflected on his life since moving to New York. From the uncertainty of his early days to the promising opportunities unfolding before him, it was a journey marked by unexpected twists and turns. And through it all, Aunt Mary had been his constant support.

Lying in the darkness, Jake felt a deep sense of gratitude. The path ahead was uncertain, but with Aunt Mary's guidance and the prospect of new ventures on the horizon, he felt a renewed sense of purpose and determination.

As Jake left work, his phone buzzed with an unexpected call. It was Agent Jackson, his voice casual but firm, requesting a meeting at the local diner for a "chit chat." Jake's stomach tightened with anxiety. Meetings with the FBI were never just casual.

As Jake approached the diner, he noticed Agents Jackson and Flanagan already outside, leaning against their car, scanning the area with casual vigilance. The sight did little to ease the knot of anxiety in Jake's stomach. The agents spotted him and pushed him out of the car, their expressions hard to read.

"Hey, Jake," Jackson greeted him with a nod. "Glad you could make it. But you know what? We've been thinking—this place has gotten some terrible reviews lately. How about we head to a better joint, we know? Their pie is edible," he added with a grin, trying to inject a bit of levity into the situation.

Flanagan chimed in with a smirk, "Yeah, unless you're in the mood for a side of food poisoning with your coffee."

Despite the seriousness of the meeting, Jake couldn't help but chuckle at their attempt to lighten the mood. "Lead the way," he said, feeling a reprieve from his apprehension.

The agents directed him to their car, and they set off for the new location. The atmosphere inside the vehicle was tense, yet Jackson and Flanagan's occasional banter offered brief moments of normalcy on the drive.

Upon arriving at a more secluded spot, one which Jake did not know, the semblance of casualness evaporated as they entered a nondescript building. Jake turned around to gauge the area; just then, Agent Flanagan held his shoulder and suggested that, for fun, he keep walking.

"Don't be afraid, kid. You are literally with the good guys."

Jake's pulse raced, the steady thump in his chest a loud counterpoint to the tense silence that had fallen over the room. The air felt thick, charged with an unspoken ultimatum, as he sat cornered by the two agents. The precarious balance of the conversation shifted dramatically when Agent Flanagan's patience snapped like a frayed rope.

"You listen here, Jake!" Flanagan bellowed, slamming his hand down on the table with a force that made the cutlery jump. "You think you can just waltz around, playing both sides? No, you're in this now. And if you don't cooperate or give us something substantial on the Rossi family, you'll be looking at jail time before you can say 'misunderstanding'!"

The abrupt hostility sliced through the mist of Jake's uncertainty, and he drew back. Looking surprised and disapproving, Agent Jackson's brows knit together across the table, suggesting that even he was taken aback by Flanagan's outburst. They had planned to start a careful operation with Jake, but this escalation was out of character and could have derailed the whole thing.

"Patrick," Jackson intervened, his voice steady but laced with a stern warning, "that's enough." He turned to Jake, attempting to mend the frayed edges of their conversation with a hint of humor. "You'll have to excuse my partner; he takes his coffee way too seriously."

The joke landed in the tense air like a lead balloon, doing nothing to lighten the mood. Still reeling from the threat, Jake struggled to find his footing in the conversation. Jackson, realizing the futility of his attempt at humor, adopted a more serious demeanor.

"Jake," he said, leaning in, the earnestness in his voice clear, "we're not here to make threats. But you need to understand the gravity of the situation. The Rossi family... they're dangerous. And their interest in you isn't just passing curiosity. They're known for ruthless retribution against those they perceive as threats."

The room fell silent as the weight of Jackson's words settled over them. Jake's thoughts raced, and the fear of entanglement with the Rossi family became tangible in the room.

"I... I just wanted to keep things simple," Jake stammered, his voice barely above a whisper. "I didn't sign up for any of this."

"We know, Jake," Jackson replied, his tone softening. "And we're not asking you to play the hero. Just keep your eyes open. Let us know if you see or hear something that could help us. We can protect you."

The promise of protection was a small comfort against the backdrop of Flanagan's earlier threat and the looming shadow of the Rossi family. Jake nodded, a mute acknowledgment of the uneasy truce they had reached. As the meeting drew to a close, the agents reiterated their offer of protection, their expressions serious.

The drive home left Jake lost in thought, the city lights streaking past him a blur of color and motion. He was no longer just a bystander in the intricate dance between the FBI and the city's underworld; he was now an unwilling participant, caught in the crossfire of a war he had never wanted to join. The path ahead was fraught with danger and uncertainty, and Jake could only hope that he had made the right choice in the face of overwhelming odds.

Jake stared at the blinking cursor on his phone, the warmth from the conversation with Aunt Mary fading as reality flooded back. The good news about the course and the potential investor hung in the air, a bright spot in the growing storm brewing around him. The Rossis, the Capolis, the FBI – it felt like he was caught in the crosshairs of a movie he didn't want to be in. Every win at work seemed overshadowed by the ever-present danger.

He needed an escape, a friendly voice not clouded by suspicion or threats. With a sigh, he typed out a message to Isabella, his fingers flying across the screen.

Isabella: "Hey Jake! Just aced a big project at work. 🚀 How's the city treating you?"

Jake: "That's amazing, Isa! 💥 The city's the same: busy and bustling. Makes me miss our quiet moments."

Isabella: "Speaking of quiet moments, I've been thinking... maybe I need some New York chaos in my life again soon. 😌"

Jake's heart warmed at the thought, a smile spreading across his face as he typed.

Jake: "New York, or someone in it? 😄 Either way, the city and I can't wait to have you back."

Isabella: "Definitely someone in it. 💝 Also, did some special shopping today... something I think you'd like to see."

The flirtatious turn of their conversation sent a thrill through Jake, igniting a spark of anticipation for her visit.

Jake: "Oh really? Now you've got me curious. New York or not, I'm looking forward to that show. 😌"

Isabella: "Patience, Mr. New York. It'll be worth the wait. Promise. 💋 But seriously, I can't wait to escape here for a bit and fly over to you."

A smile tugged at the corner of Jake's lips. Maybe, just maybe, a little normalcy, a stolen weekend with Isabella, was exactly what he needed to face the storm head-on.

***

The night of Francesca's party finally came, a bright spot of joy in Jake's otherwise chaotic life. While he was getting ready for the night, the battle that had grown inside him was reflected in the mirror. The weight of the lies he now held made every step he took into the fancy world of the Capoli family feel heavier. He was caught up in a web of lies, which was very different from the simple life he had imagined for himself in New York.

While Jake was dressed appropriately for the event, he tried to shrug off the anxiety he was experiencing and instead focused on the promise of an evening filled with laughing and light-hearted talks. However, just as he was ready to depart, his phone rang, and the caller ID displayed the name Vincent Capoli. It served as a reminder of the complicated dance he was now a part of.

"Jake, my boy," Vincent's voice came through, warm yet undeniably commanding. "I wanted to thank you personally for attending Francesca's birthday party. It means a lot to her and us. Don't be a stranger, you hear? Our doors are always open to you."

The call, though brief, left a lingering impact on Jake. The offer extended by Vincent Capoli, which was dripping with politeness, highlighted the complexities of his position. Jake couldn't help but feel the draw of two worlds as he went out into the night and headed towards the location of Francesca's party. One was of normalcy and camaraderie, and the other was a murky domain of alliances and dangers. Jake couldn't help but feel the pull at the same time.

Jake stood in front of his mirror, adjusting his shirt and smoothing out any wrinkles. The anticipation for Francesca's party was tinged with a thread of nervous energy, making his hands shake slightly as he tried to perfect his look. The night promised to be an escape, a chance to step away from the shadows that had begun to crowd his life.

Just as he was contemplating whether to wear a tie, his phone rang, cutting through the silence of his 800-square-foot bedroom. "Titiano," the screen flashed, and Jake couldn't help but smile as he answered.

"Hey, Jake! Man, I'm downstairs, but listen, I'm not stepping one foot inside. If Ma sees me, she'll have me moving back in by the end of the night," Titiano's voice boomed through the phone, filled with mock horror.

Jake laughed, grabbing his keys and heading for the door. "Understood, I'm coming down. Wouldn't want to unleash that fate on you."

Rushing down, Jake found Titiano waiting, his ever-present charisma undimmed by the chill of the evening. Together, they decided it wasn't just the two of them making an appearance at the party; they would bring Rodney along for the ride, turning the evening into an adventure for the unlikely trio.

The Rumpus Room in Manhattan's Lower East Side was a grand display of wealth and power straight out of a mafia film. As they approached, the sight of personalized DJs setting the night on fire with music, armed guards stationed discreetly yet visibly around the venue, and extravagant decorations set the scene for a night to remember.

"Wow, look at this place," Rodney whispered, his usual composure slipping in awe at the spectacle before them.

Titiano whistled lowly, "Talk about living the high life. This is next-level."

"You could live the same life, too, man, if you just agree to live with your mother and give in to her desires." Letting out a throaty laugh, Jake teased Titiano.

Titiano chuckled, shaking his head. "No way, man. I'd rather keep my freedom."

Jake grinned, feeling the energy of the place seep into his bones. "Well, let's make the most of tonight. Looks like it's going to be unforgettable."

The trio walked into the venue, the vibrant atmosphere wrapping around them. The Rumpus Room was buzzing with excitement, the perfect backdrop for Francesca's grand celebration. There, they saw the biggest cake they had ever seen, which became the night's centerpiece. It was surrounded by endless streams of free drinks and an immaculate ice sculpture, a testament to the Capoli family's lavish lifestyle. The Rumpus Room itself was sprawling, with opulence on full display, and luxurious art spoke of wealth and influence.

"Seriously, having your DJ is next-level," Jake remarked, raising his glass with a grin.

Titiano, always ready with a retort, replied, "Well, when you throw my birthday bash, don't forget the DJ, Jake. Guest of honor, remember?"

"And maybe dial down on the armed decor?" Rodney added, the corner of his mouth twitching in amusement.

Their trio was about to become a duo as a young woman danced her way over to Titiano, her movements to the music deliberate and inviting. She cast a seductive glance his way, and in the blink of an eye, Titiano was captivatingly drawn to her like a moth to a flame. With a smooth step, Titiano joined her, their bodies moving in sync with the rhythm. Jake watched, amusement twinkling in his eyes, as his friend effortlessly shifted from bantering companion to charming dancer.

"Looks like you're always looking for trouble, Titi," Jake called over the music, his voice laced with humor.

Titiano, caught mid-twirl with the girl, shot back, "Women want me, Jake. What can I do, after all?" The cheeky grin plastered on his face was visible even under the pulsating lights of the dance floor.

Jake laughed, shaking his head at his cousin's unabashed confidence. As Jake watched Titiano get swept away in the dance, he couldn't help but smile at his cousin's antics. Turning around, his gaze found Rodney standing somewhat apart from the celebration, observing the scene with an amused detachment. Jake made his way over, preferring the butler's quiet company to the boisterous energy of the party.

"You should be out there, having fun," Rodney remarked, a slight smile playing on his lips as he caught sight of Jake approaching.

"I'm perfectly fine here," Jake responded, settling in next to him. "Actually, I wanted to have a chat with you."

Rodney chuckled, glancing back at the dance floor where Titiano was now fully engrossed in his dance partner's company. "I see Titiano found himself a beautiful distraction," he joked, the corners of his eyes crinkling with mirth.

The sight of Titiano having fun was always entertaining, so Jake could only shake his head and laugh. Titiano has a rare talent. He always knows exactly what to do to bring a party to life.

Their banter demonstrated how comfortable they were with their newly found connection, and the talk flowed freely as a result. After what seemed like an eternity, Rodney's face relaxed, and his eyes became serious. He inquired, "So, Jake, are you missing Isabella?" with sincere curiosity.

The question caught Jake off guard, and the mention of Isabella's name sent a pang of longing through him. He hadn't realized how much he missed her until that moment, her presence a missing piece in the evening's festivities.

"Yeah, I guess I am," Jake admitted, his smile fading slightly. "It's strange. Everything's so lively and fun here, but... talking about her just now made me realize how much I wish she was here, too."

Rodney nodded, understanding the sentiment. "She sounds like a special person. It's the ones who make us miss them in the middle of a party that really have a place in our hearts, isn't it?"

As Jake and Rodney were lost in their conversation, a familiar, slightly slurred voice pierced through the din of the party. "Jakeeeeee, there you are!" Francesca, clearly having enjoyed the party to its fullest, beamed as she stumbled slightly towards them, two shots too deep but glowing with happiness.

Both Francesca and Martin made Jake and his companions feel incredibly welcome. They kept asking them if they were having fun. Francesca has to be controlled by Martin more than once because she almost tipped over the food on Jake's shirt.

Their hospitality and warmth showed the inner workings of the Capoli family. To Jake, they seemed to be the people who preferred family ties over anything else.

Amidst the celebration, Martin took a moment to give a speech about his older sister. His words were heartfelt and tinged with humor, painting Francesca as the formidable yet loving sibling she was.

"And here's to Francesca," Martin announced, raising his glass high, "the only person I know who can simultaneously run a business meeting and a marathon, all while planning this insane party. Cheers to you, sis!"

Right after his toast, TItiano made his entry. His timing, impeccable as ever, added an extra layer of excitement to the already vibrant celebration.

"Did someone mention a party without shots?" Titiano announced, brandishing a tray of shots like a trophy, his eyes sparkling with mischief. Francesca, never one to back down from a challenge, especially on her birthday, met his gaze with a triumphant smile.

"Oh, you're on, Titi," she declared, her confidence unshaken. "But be warned, I'm undefeated."

The crowd around them grew, drawn by the promise of a showdown that was sure to be memorable. Jake, Rodney, and the rest of the Capoli clan gathered, forming a tight circle around Francesca and Titiano. The air was electric with anticipation, everyone eager to see who would come out on top.

The rules were simple: back-to-back shots until one conceded defeat. As the game commenced, Jake found himself cheering on Francesca, swept up in the crowd's infectious energy. Shot after shot, the two competitors matched each other, neither willing to give in. But to no one's surprise, especially those who knew her well, Francesca emerged victorious, her smile wide and triumphant as Titiano conceded with good-natured grace.

"I have to hand it to you, Francesca," Titiano said, loud enough for the crowd to hear, "You really can hold your liquor. I'm not sure whether to be impressed or terrified."

As the laughter continued, Jake turned around and caught sight of Vince Capoli, smiling warmly at the scene before him. From his table, Vince clapped for Francesca, his pride in his family members evident in his eyes. Jake watched as Vince's gaze swept over the gathered family and friends, the smile on his face reflecting a rare and deeply genuine contentment. In that moment, Jake saw a different side of the Capoli family: fiercely loyal and unabashedly loving.

The celebration continued, with the crowd dispersing back into the rhythm of the party. Jake couldn't help but feel a sense of belonging. For a few hours, the complexities of Jake's life faded into the background, replaced by the simple joy of being part of something bigger than himself—a family celebration where everyone, regardless of their background or future paths, came together to honor one of their own.

As the night wore on, Jake found himself bumping into none other than Johnny Viola and Knuckles McGee. The encounter could have been tense, given their reputations, but the mood of the party seemed to keep everything light-hearted.

"Ah, Jake, enjoying the party?" Johnny asked, a sly smile playing on his lips. His presence was commanding, yet he seemed to be genuinely inquiring.

"Absolutely," Jake replied, deciding to keep things friendly. "It's not every day you get to see such an... extravagant celebration."

Knuckles McGee, standing in a silent fortress beside Johnny, let out a low chuckle. "Francesca knows how to throw a party. Makes our usual gatherings look like quiet nights in."

The conversation veered into the lighter sides of their lives, with Johnny sharing anecdotes that had the group laughing. Even Knuckles, usually so stoic, joined in with a story or two, showing a surprisingly humorous side.

The complex personalities among the Capoli circle were evident to Jake. However, these incidents exposed a different side to them. One centered around family, loyalty, and humor beneath the intimidating exterior of these formidable leaders in New York's underground.

The party continued to unravel around them, a whirlwind of music, laughter, and shared stories. For Jake, the night was a vivid tapestry of interactions, each conversation with the Capoli associates deepening his understanding of the complex world he'd found himself intertwined with. Despite the undercurrents of power and tension that ran beneath the surface, tonight, it was all about celebrating Francesca, and in doing so, Jake found himself more entwined in the fabric of their world, a place of contrasts where danger and warmth coexisted in close quarters.

As the party rode on, Rodney came through the crowd. He clapped Jake on the shoulder, a wide grin splitting his face. "Alright, son, looks like this party's still rolling. I'm going to head out and let you youngsters have some fun. Remember, moderation!" he winked, then shuffled towards the exit.

"You know I am going to head out too." He mentioned. The thought of Isabella was making him gloomy in the rather exquisite affair.

Jake watched him go to grab the car, then scanned the room to wish Francesca a happy birthday before leaving for home. Titiano was in the corner making out with the same blonde woman. With the way they were plastered to the wall, he thought it was best to leave him a text, which he would probably see in the morning. It was a sea of bobbing heads and flashing lights. The music pulsed through the air, making it difficult to hear anything over the din. He couldn't see Martin, Titiano, or Johnny anywhere, lost in the throng. He decided to grab another drink and find Francesca, hoping to share the good news about the course.

A commotion caught his eye as he weaved his way through the crowd. In a corner near the makeshift photo booth, a group of three guys were huddled around Francesca. They all wore matching neon Hawaiian shirts, a stark contrast to Francesca's simple black dress. At first, it looked like they were just taking selfies, their arms draped playfully around her shoulders.

But something felt off. The guys were loud, their laughter bordering on obnoxiousness. Their hands lingered too long on Francesca's back, venturing lower towards her hips. She wasn't smiling, her body stiff and uncomfortable.

One of the guys, a lanky fellow with a scraggly beard, held up his phone, recording the whole scene. He leaned in towards Francesca, his breath reeking of cheap beer, and tried to plant a kiss on her cheek.

Jake's blood ran cold. This wasn't a friendly selfie session; it was harassment. He pushed through the crowd, his temper simmering. Just then, he saw another guy grab a hold of her ass with force.

"Hey, move!" Francesca's back was to Jake, and he sped up his pace to get to Francesca.

Just then, the third guy held her firmly while the lanky guy who felt up her butt stole a kiss. "There, there, birdy. You are the birthday girl; I want to make you feel special." He breathed onto her neck, which made her repulsed even more. He grabbed her dress and started yanking it up. "Let's take you on a ride, sweetie."

Unable to see Francesca's face and the many heads in between, Jake remained unaware of the severity of the situation.

Moving swiftly toward them, Jake thought that a direct approach might escalate things, and with no Martin or Johnny in sight, subtlety was his best bet.

He sidled up to the group with a mischievous grin, channeling his inner party animal.

"Whoa, whoa, whoa!" he exclaimed, throwing his hands up in mock horror. "Hey there, beautiful lady! What's with the sad face? Don't these fine gentlemen know how to treat a lady right?"

Francesca looked up, startled, and then a flicker of relief crossed her face as she recognized Jake. "Jake! Hi," she said, her voice strained.

The guys, momentarily taken aback, turned to him.

Unfortunately, the playful charade couldn't last. Just as Jake offered to escort Francesca out of the corner, the mood shifted. The three neon-clad guys puffed out their chests, their earlier nervousness replaced by misplaced bravado.

"Hey!" the bearded one snarled, stepping between them. "We were talking to her."

"Yeah," the shorter one added, trying to sound tough but his voice cracking slightly. "We weren't done here."

Jake sighed internally. Playtime was over. He straightened his posture, a steely glint entering his eyes. "Look," he said, his voice calm yet firm, "it's clear you're not getting the picture. Why don't we all just walk away, pretend this never happened?"

The bearded guy scoffed. "Or what?"

"Or," Jake continued, his voice dropping a notch, "you could learn the valuable lesson of respecting personal space the hard way."

The air crackled with tension. Before anyone could react, the bearded dude took a clumsy swing at Jake. It was telegraphed like a slow-motion movie scene, giving Jake ample time to duck. Jake connected with the guy's jaw with a well-placed elbow, sending him sprawling to the floor with a resounding thud.

The other two guys stood frozen for a moment, clearly not expecting such a swift response. Then, the shorter one lunged at Jake, aiming for a wild punch. At this moment, Jake realized that he had practiced the very same scenario dozens of times in the dojo. Jake instinctively pivoted and executed a Uechi circle block that allowed him to grab his elbow while simultaneously blowing out his knee. Jake then followed up with a solid reverse punch square in the forehead and watched as his opponent fell forward into unconsciousness.

The confusion was complete. The third guy, a round fellow with a bewildered expression, just stood there blinking, unsure of what to do next. He looked like a lost puppy caught in a dogfight. He then reached into his jacket, pulled out what seemed to be a pistol, and raised it squarely in the air.

Jake, observing everything, instantly leaped across the table and tackled the man, resulting in a chokehold, which caused him to drop the gun. The impact caused a loud thud. Those who were close could hear Jake whisper now it's time to go to sleep, asshole as he cut off the assailant's air supply, and he quickly passed out.

The music seemed to fade away as everyone stared at the unexpected hero. Jake stood up, panting slightly but otherwise unscathed, holding the gun aloft like a trophy. "Seems like someone forgot the cardinal rule of club etiquette: no weapons!"

The room erupted in a cacophony of cheers and gasps. But the celebration was cut short. Out of the corner of his eye, Jake saw a flicker of movement. A fourth guy, one he hadn't noticed before, emerged from the dancing crowd. A glint of metal caught the flashing lights – a pistol pointed straight at Jake.

Adrenaline surged through him as time seemed to slow down. In that split second, he saw Rodney react with lightning speed. With a powerful lunge, Rodney launched himself at the armed man like a human battering ram. They collided in a heap, a tangle of limbs and flailing bodies.

A loud crack echoed through the air, followed by a pained yelp. Rodney had managed to tackle the gunman to the ground, effectively disarming him in the process. But the force of the impact wasn't without consequence. A sickening crunch resonated as Rodney landed on the guy's arm, likely breaking it in the struggle.

Finally alerted by the commotion, security guards and the Capoli family's staff pushed their way through the crowd. The police were called, and the night took a sharp turn towards officialdom. Relief washed over Jake as he watched the officers take the instigators of the fight into custody. One by one, the three neon-clad guys and the surprise gunman were escorted out, their earlier bravado replaced by a mixture of dejection and pain.

Jake released his hold on the groaning figure at his feet. He stood there momentarily, stunned, his heart still pounding in his chest. He looked at Rodney, who was gingerly flexing his hand, likely nursing a sore arm from his takedown. Then he looked at Francesca, whose eyes were wide with a mixture of fear and relief. It certainly wasn't the "real dance" he'd promised, but somehow, it felt like a different kind of victory. They had faced danger together and emerged on the other side, shaken but unharmed.

A gruff voice boomed over the stunned crowd as the dust settled from the brawl. It was Knuckles McGee, the Capoli family's head of security. "Alright folks, the party's over!" he declared, his voice leaving no room for argument. Security guards swarmed the area, their presence a stark contrast to the earlier carefree atmosphere.

With a sigh, Knuckles turned to Johnny Viola and said, "Hurry and get the Capoli kids home safe and sound. No arguments." Johnny nodded curtly, his mind still in shock about the night's events suddenly replaced by a weary concern for his boss's kids. He ushered a shaken Francesca and a sheepish-looking Martin out of the club, stealing a sympathetic glance at Jake as they passed.

Later, as the news of the night spread through the city's underbelly, a revelation sent shockwaves through the criminal underworld. It turned out the three goons who accosted Francesca weren't random barflies. They were hired muscle planted by the Rossi family. Their goal was to humiliate Francesca and send a clear message to Vincent Capoli – no one, not even his children, was safe from their reach.

***

Across town, in a lavishly furnished mansion, the Rossi family was fuming. The aging patriarch, Don Rossi, slammed his fist on the mahogany table, scattering expensive cigars and crystal ashtrays.

"Those imbecilic goons!" he roared, his voice trembling with rage. "Not only did they fail to complete the mission, but now we have to bail them out of jail! We look like a bunch of bumbling amateurs!"

His son, Marco, a man with steely eyes and a cruel smirk, leaned back in his chair, steepling his fingers. "Agreed, Father. This whole thing has been a disaster, and this Jake character...he's becoming a problem."

Don Rossi scowled. "Indeed. This is the second time that he has interfered with our plans, and now I am starting to think that it is not just merely by chance." "He has clearly aligned himself with the Capoli outfit, but his choosing a side now makes him a target. Don't worry; we will find a way to deal with him."

Jake and Titiano were in the back seat of the Rolls Royce recounting the night's events. Titiano, still drunk, blurted out, "I was very close to getting lucky tonight, but at least I got her number. Good things come to those who wait." Jake replied, "How can you joke at a time like this?" Then he turned his attention to Johnny. "I had no idea you could fight like that," Rodney replied. "Touche, Sir."

Titiano suddenly became serious, "Guys, I was only joking before, and I'm really glad that you guys stepped up to help Francesca tonight. Going into this party, I did not realize I would be rolling with a real-life Batman and Robin. I do not think we should tell Mom about this because she would worry, and even worse, she may try to get involved with tonight's events to make sure that we are safe. It seemed like the police handled things."

After a period of silence, Rodney responded, "I agree, Sir, the Madam should not have to be burdened with such things."

Jake finally spoke up and said, "I agree as well; whatever happens tonight stays between us." At that moment, the trio became formally united in brotherhood and secrecy.

Rodney sarcastically added, "I am the Batman, and he is the Robin," and the car exploded in laughter.

News of the botched operation also reached Vincent Capoli's opulent office. He listened to his capo, a wiry man named Sal, recount the details with a stony expression. When Sal finished, a dangerous glint flickered in Vincent's eyes.

"They crossed a line," Vincent said, his voice low and cold. "They attacked my children. That's a violation of the code, an act of war." After a moment, he whispered, "The Rossi's have no respect; they do not even know what honor means."

Sal nodded grimly. "Absolutely. They need to be dealt with."

Vincent leaned back in his chair, a steely resolve hardening his features. "Then let's send them a message they won't forget. It's time to go on the offensive. And this time," he added, his voice becoming impossibly more serious, "We make sure that they face our judgment."

The fragile peace that had held the city's criminal factions in check was shattered. The night's events had ignited a spark, and a war was brewing on the horizon. And in the middle of it all stood Jake, a reluctant hero caught in a dangerous game of power and revenge.

Chapter 6: Intricate Maneuvers

Tensions were high at the Capoli mansion after the attack on Francesca at her birthday party. The grand house was a symbol of normal, solemn, and peaceful air most of the time. However, since the turn of events at her birthday, the halls of this massive mansion were riddled with security teams. Someone had dared to threaten the Capoli family publicly.

Many meetings were held with each of its members to ensure there were no loopholes in the entire ordeal and that the children of the Capoli family stayed safe and sound. Hurried footsteps and the radio's static through the receivers echoed through the vast corridors whenever a member of the Capoli family decided to go on out about their day.

In the basement, Vincent Capoli took it upon himself to hold meetings with the security leads and other business cooperators to determine who was explicitly involved in making his daughter's life unsafe.

In the center of the crowded room, a group of men clutched their cigars tightly between their teeth as they shook their heads in exasperation. The tension was palpable as they watched the unfolding events with growing concern. Vincent Capoli sat there with the utmost grace, right at the head of the table. He sat on an oversized leather chair by the fireplace, swirling a glass of 25-year-old single malt whiskey between his fingers. The liquid glinted amber in the firelight, and he savored the smooth, smoky flavor with each sip. He leaned forward, and the flames from the nearby fireplace cast shadows of his mangled past. Everyone saw his features as he mulled over his family and business issues.

Vincent's usually stoic demeanor cracked, revealing a simmering rage burning in his eyes. How he looked around the room mirrored his troubled mind, which was planning vengeance with each sip. He was haunted by the ghosts of his past and tinged with the acrid bitterness of his current struggles. Despite the quiet luxury of his opulent home, an underlying tension gnawed at him, threatening to boil over at any moment. All eyes were on him; his family and his closest associates looked at him for the next turn of events. Even with everything going wrong, he sat there calmly, instructing everyone with authority and poise. Vincent Capoli was not a man you could shake easily.

Knuckles McGee growled, his voice low and dangerous. "I ain't never seen him this angry before. Time to get our hands dirty," he mentioned to one of his men who stood by his side. His brow furrowed in concern over the amount of liquor Vincent was taking in. However, he seemed the most sober of the lot.

Everyone awaited his guidance; they were all hanging on the decisions that would come from this introspective moment by the fire. He had gone through the same road before, where his family had come under attack. He had lost his brother under similar conditions. Vincent knew there might come a day when his family and business would end in the blink of an eye if he wasn't careful. The boss man motioned for McGee to approach, his voice low and thick. "Any update from Martin?"

Knuckles answered in a strained tone, "Not yet. But he'll be back soon." He was surprised to see Vincent so leveled in his speech and his manner.

Martin, Vincent's son, was still out having meetings at the site where the incident had occurred. He had sent his own son to talk to the head of security about where it all went wrong. Martin had seen the look of fear on his sister's face that night and wanted to take an active role in keeping the family safe. Vincent Capoli had decided to take control of all meetings concerning this business directly to show leadership and direction.

While he listened to the reports of his advisors, he kept an eye on one of the men at the end of the table. He was busy on a phone call. The moment he sat the receiver down, Vincent asked him loudly, "So what became of the implanted thugs? Were they granted freedom through bail, or will Roberto go for the classic slash of throats inside the discreet prison walls?"

"They just got bailed, sir," the man answered in a small voice.

Nothing came out of Vincent apart from a small muffled chuckle. He shook his head at the classic Roberto move. Everyone could sense something was being cooked in his brain. The air was riddled with anticipation about how the boss would answer the rather blatant declaration of war to his enemies.

Vincent Capoli became utterly preoccupied with altering his organization's strategy days after the mayhem at Francesca's birthday celebration. The episode served as a huge blow to his reputation as the intimidating Mafia leader. The events had reflected it to be an unmistakable indication of the Rossi family's objectives. Being the master strategist he was, Vince had an air of urgency around him. He knew he had to be clever in making the next move.

Vincent knew he had to aggressively fortify their defenses and prepare to face the Rossi family after meticulous planning. The daring attempt on his empire had struck a significant blow. Vincent was not going to let that go, especially with his direct family involved.

Roberto Rossi's criminal empire was built on the most immoral activities imaginable—drugs, prostitution, human trafficking, smash-and-grab robberies, and extortion. Rossi had no moral compass, which made him a dangerous and ruthless adversary who would stop at nothing to expand his power.

The never-ending concern for his daughter continued to take precedence in Vincent's strategic plans. He checked on Francesca often to make sure she was doing okay after the party. Whenever they briefly crossed paths, he would inquire, "Are you sure you're okay, Francesca?" His voice always betrayed his true concern.

Martin Capoli took his position as a brother as well very seriously. He was on high alert and kept a tight eye on who came near his sister and how she was spending her time; Martin was doing more than just checking in on her.

Given the seriousness of his family's role in the criminal underground, his care for Francesca went beyond simple brotherly affection and became a duty. His mission was now to prevent anyone with the faintest suspicion from approaching her. He had assigned Knuckles McGee, a reliable enforcer renowned for his dogged devotion and keen intuition, to keep him apprised of everything happening around his sister in order to achieve this goal.

From inside the estate and beyond, Knuckles had a network of informants and eyes that could detect and neutralize any danger before it reached Francesca. Martin kept his sister safe and gave her the illusion of normalcy in her daily existence by taking preventative measures for her security.

Right when he left for his meetings with the bar owners and the security teams, he had called on Knuckles McGee to come and talk to him in his office.

"Knuckles, I need a full update on Francesca's movements and her interactions," Martin began, his voice low but commanding.

Knuckles agreed and handed over a small notebook that was full of thorough notes. "Mainly clear. We have added more patrols to where she usually hangs out, and I've doubled the checks on anyone who enters those areas."

"Good, keep it tight. I don't want any surprises," Martin responded, flipping through the notebook. "And the new faces at the club she visits, any word on them?"

"They're clean as far as we can tell. New in town, just trying to make a name, not connected to anyone on our radar," Knuckles reported.

Martin closed the notebook and met Knuckles' gaze. "Stay on it. If you see anything out of the ordinary, I want to know immediately."

"Understood, boss," Knuckles affirmed with a nod.

Martin put the notepad in his jacket and got ready for his next appointment, content with his work. His movements were deliberate, as if he were always planning ahead, just like his father. As the head of his family's security operations, Martin Capoli had the weighty responsibility of protecting his family, too.

Since the tragic passing of his brother many years ago, nothing had unsettled Vincent as much as the recent episode. After making certain that the immediate danger was gone on the night of the party, Vincent had drawn Francesca into a tight embrace. His arms enveloped her in a rare display of unfiltered emotion - a mixture of comfort and evident terror of almost losing her. Those who were present witnessed a side of Vincent rarely seen - the worried parent who feared for his daughter's safety.

Johnny Viola, who was accustomed to the harshness of their world, later spoke to Martin about that specific exchange. "I have never seen your father like that," Johnny confessed as they stood in his room at the luxurious Capoli estate. "When he embraced Francesca... it was as if he was holding onto something he could not bear to lose. It reminded me of the stories I heard about when he lost his brother."

Nodding solemnly, Martin continued. "Well, they threatened his authority. My father is not okay with such disrespect. I was also frightened by it. The stakes are so high when you see him like that. It has more to do with family than with power."

The Capoli family members, who were previously driven by unspoken devotion and the unwritten link of their business, now felt a greater calling to their positions. They were standing together as a family in the face of an oppressive adversary, and it wasn't simply a business they were safeguarding.

Even though Vincent's schedule was full of meetings and planning, the incident at Francesca's party remained a constant reminder of the threats they were up against as he continued to prepare. With all the present Capoli family behind him, Vincent was prepared to do whatever it took to protect their interests and cement their place in the underworld's hierarchy of the city.

With the Rossi family's danger growing, Vincent Capoli felt he needed to bring in Timothy Scott, whose experience went well beyond the boardrooms of corporations. He was his wild card, the one who would give him the extra edge in this fight. Not only was the African-American attorney, Timothy, a major player on the board of directors for one of the Capoli family's businesses, but his significant impact went unrecognized in many fields. As the criminal underworld's gloom deepened, Timothy shifted into his alternate role as Vincent's Senior Counsel and confidant. His feedback on Vincent's cleverly thought strategies was highly needed by the Capoli family.

He had Vincent's undeterred confidence. The foundation of their long-standing friendship was mutual respect and an awareness of the fine line that separated their lawful business dealings from their covert ones. Knowing that his knowledge was more needed than ever, Timothy wasted no time responding to Vincent's summons.

Vincent met Timothy in his spacious study upon his arrival at the Capoli home. The space was filled with the aroma of old leather and the gentle crackle of the fireplace. There was tension in the air, but being with Timothy made everyone feel better.

"Tim, I really appreciate you showing up so quickly," Vincent started, his voice solemn as he gestured for Timothy to sit down.

"Sure thing, Vincent." Sitting in the plush leather chair across from Vincent, Timothy responded, "I know the situation is bad. His expression remained level as he mentally prepared for any possible actions or countermoves they could contemplate.

Vincent did not dally in describing the difficulties they encountered. "Because the Rossi's are acting so fucking crazy, our standard strategies may not work at this time. To safeguard our interests and prepare ourselves to confront their assault, we require a comprehensive strategy."

In his analytical state, Timothy nodded in agreement. "We need to fortify our defenses, certainly," he said. "More significantly, though, we need to make it plain that the Capoli family will not stand for any kind of hostility. It's about more than simply staying alive, Vincent; it's about keeping control and making sure everything stays stable."

Using Timothy's knowledge of the law and Vincent's insight into the inner workings of the criminal underground, the two men spent hours debating potential strategies. In order to protect their operations, Timothy proposed several defensive moves and advised them on the possible legal ramifications of such maneuvers. He said to keep ahead of the Rossi family, "It was critical to use their vast network for intelligence gathering."

A feeling of assurance washed over Vincent as the meeting progressed. Timothy's advice was priceless because it gave us direction and clarity in the midst of all the chaos. During his most critical moments, Vincent could rely on his systematic and exacting approach.

"Tim, I highly value your guidance for the upcoming weeks," Vincent acknowledged with gratitude in his tone. "Your ability to navigate these treacherous waters while keeping us within the bounds of our code is why I trust you so *implicitly*."

Realizing the gravity of the situation, Timothy nodded slightly. "I am here for you, Vincent. As we always have, we will weather this storm together."

The room was bathed in lengthy shadows generated by the fire's flickering light as Timothy departed from the study, leaving Vincent to sit back in his chair. With Timothy Scott at his side, he was prepared to confront any obstacles the Rossi family may throw his way, even though the road ahead was treacherous. Their bond, formed through hardship, had endured and would now be needed to safeguard the Capoli family's history and future.

***

Jake was completely absorbed in his work at Goldman Sachs, where he was serving as the project lead for an experimental artificial intelligence decision analysis learning machine. This cutting-edge technology had the potential to transform the way financial projections and calculations were produced, potentially decreasing the amount of time necessary for these operations to a fraction of what the teams that were now in place required. Every day, Jake worked relentlessly to bring in new clients and methodically fine-tuned every project component. He ensured that every detail was up to the high standards that Goldman Sachs had set for itself.

Jake was a major member of an investment team, and he worked on the artificial intelligence project during his time there. In this function, which was effectively a sales job, he was entrusted with persuading prospective customers that letting Goldman Sachs handle their assets and securities was the most effective method for them to keep or expand their wealth. His workdays frequently lasted far into the evening because of the dual responsibilities he was accountable for, which kept him incredibly busy.

After a particularly long day, he checked his phone one evening and saw that he had missed a call from Isabella. He was saddened by this realization. Earlier in the day, she sent him a text message to catch up with him and discuss the specifics of her upcoming trip to New York. Jake had entirely forgotten to respond because he was so preoccupied with the pressure of his assignments.

Several hours had elapsed since Isabella's first message, and by the time Jake checked his phone, a second notification awaited him. Unlike the first, this one was tinged with annoyance due to his delayed response.

Isabella: "Guess you're too busy to even send a quick reply now... I understand you're swamped, but a simple acknowledgment doesn't take that long, Jake."

Feeling guilty, Jake immediately apologized.

Jake: "Isa, I'm really sorry. Work is just overwhelming right now, and I have completely lost track of time. Let's set a time this weekend to catch up properly; I will make it up to you. ☺"

As he sent the message, Jake made a mental note to manage his time more effectively, ensuring that his career ambitions did not jeopardize his personal connections.

***

Roberto Rossi, the Mafia Don and the regenerator of all the problems that the Capoli family was about to face, was born in the United States and spent a lot of time and effort to present himself to the outside world as a legitimate businessman. Rossi gave everyone who was peering in the impression of being a successful business leader, diligently supervising a network of legitimate companies. This facade, on the other hand, was a deliberate cover designed to conceal the darker and more ruthless realities of his genuine objectives.

In spite of the fact that Rossi presented himself as a respectable individual among the masses, he was intimately involved in the criminal underground, and no one could pin it on him in broad daylight. His courage in embracing the dark side of organized crime with no accountability or conscience had managed to make him take advantage of the most ominous parts of this world.

In contrast to some of his colleagues, who might have avoided engaging in particular illegal actions, Rossi committed himself wholeheartedly to any endeavor that promised high rewards, regardless of how morally repulsive it might have been.

Reputable businesses, such as drug trafficking and people smuggling, as well as the coordinated smash-and-grab robberies of high-end jewelry stores and department stores, served as the basis upon which his empire was constructed. As part of his repertory, he also engaged in activities like extortion, blackmail, and financial fraud. Each of these activities contributed to his fortune and expanded his power within the shadowy corners of the city.

It was common knowledge among Rossi's contemporaries and subordinates that he was a brutal individual, and terror was a tactic he utilized to effectively maintain control and loyalty. Even in New York, the instances of his wrath and absurd punishments to his opposers made the Law Enforcement think twice. Because with Rossi, it wasn't just about having a rivalry. It was about taking your opponent and everything they held dear and dragging them through the dirt. His main source of entertainment was to ensure that his opponents and the next generations did not live long to see the light of the day. For the borrowed time they were on this Earth, he would make sure to make every breath a tormented one.

It was not just a source of enrichment for him to engage in illicit activities; they were also expressions of his confidence in his own invincibility and the authority to govern over his territory with an iron hand. Roberto Rossi had despised the Capoli family's move to New York as he witnessed his territories and Iron Hand rule dissipate. As a consequence of the Capoli's coming to New

York, crime and profits had been organically divided and shared between the two families.

Over the years, he had always hated how the Capoli family, who constantly underestimated him, had taken over the dark streets of New York.

For Rossi, he did not live by principles, which was a practice introduced into the Mafia by Vincent Capoli.

"These Italians, them and their principles. Do I need to be a principled criminal to survive now or revel in its obscurity?" He would often spit distasteful comments whenever he heard of the family.

"I should have killed them when his family was just starting out. I should have nipped the bud in time. If Vincent Capoli was not enough, he has unleashed his ever-so-calculated son on the underworld. The fool does not know he is making a mistake trying to enforce rules in a place where havoc thrives."

Rossi's calculated chaos at Francesca's party was the most painful dart the Capoli family received so far in the ongoing war. This wasn't just the proof of a disruption – it was a clear challenge dressed up in the outer appearance of entertainment. The way Rossi engaged the Capoli family that night was specifically intended not just to embarrass them. Their main aim was to strike at the mainstay of their affairs, ripple defiance on them and through the entire criminal underworld and the audiences of the high-profile guests around them. He knew all you needed to do was spoil their leaders' image, which immediately weakened their hold on their operations and strengthened his resisting actions.

Vincent Capoli was literally pierced in the heart by this perfidy in its raw sense. The chance was a personal insult, a dazzle in front of his family business and his honor. Standing there, it was quite a challenge for him to suppress the emotions of anger and calculation that were forming in his heart. He sat there, witnessing his daughter's birthday, a time that was supposed to be glowing with joy. Instead, it became one of chaos and sadness, which woke up a part of him that he had long forgotten about. Through this conversation, Roberto Rossi was sending a clear message; the Capolis were just as vulnerable to his schemes in instances like this and with ease.

After his initial discussions with his advisor, Tim Scott, Vincent had to rethink his strategies. In addition to the traditional motives such as territories or profits, this time was seen as mainly the contest of the old and powerful family vs the lawless and merciless enemy. Vincent had long heard rumors about the Rossi family wanting to take over his gambling business. Rossi's actions of starting a war could be the first step in trying to acquire a business that Vincent built, not through making a legitimate offer but through force.

He was aware that he must have countered the opponent's cunning and aggression in his own way. Every move from then on required a considerable amount of time and effort, and there was no room for blunders. Rossi, with his blunt attack, challenged Vincent. This came as a surprise to the latter, but he never left guard, realizing his family's future was with his next move.

Roberto Rossi was a master of the art of living a double life. To the general public, he was a model citizen and a successful businessman, always seen with a charming smile at charity events, generously giving donations, and deeply involved in community projects. But behind this carefully crafted facade lay a completely different persona - that of a cunning criminal mastermind.

Shrouded in the darkness of the underworld, he orchestrated a vast web of forbidden deeds. His empire thrived on deceit and cunning, hidden from the judgmental gaze of society.

Rossi worked hard with his minions. He had very calmly planned out ruthless crimes, hiding his dark intentions behind a friendly smile. He had been in the process of recruiting henchmen for the pending conflict. The elaborate plan he had created, which resulted in attacking Francesca at the party, was just the beginning. Roberto needed manpower to provoke the Capoli's into full-scale battle by putting them in a tough position. He had the money and resources to not just instigate but also sustain this conflict.

He believed that by getting a greater number of people on his side, he would be able to push the Capoli's resources and concentration to their limits, leaving them susceptible to attacks from the outside and collapsing their infrastructure from within. Each and every action he took was a measured step toward achieving his ultimate objective, which was to have complete control over the criminal underworld in the city.

Roberto Rossi was a man who never doubted his own power and had big dreams. As things were getting tense with the Capoli family, he was ready to step up his game. He wanted everyone, whether friend or enemy, to always feel a mix of fear and respect when they heard his name. It was like he was playing a serious game of chess, willing to sacrifice anything to win. The more cruel his tactics became, the more he enjoyed the challenge. It was clear that there was a huge gap between the image he showed the world and the darker truth hidden inside him.

***

Jake felt a mix of relief and joy as Isabella finally picked up his call after several attempts. It's been a long time since he heard her voice.

"Isa, I'm so sorry for not getting back to you earlier," Jake started, his words tumbling out in his eagerness to make things right. "Work's been crazy, but that's no excuse. I've missed talking to you."

Her voice was warm and forgiving, coming through the line. "I understand you're swamped. Just try not to forget me completely, okay?"

The sound of Jake's laughter was light and genuine. "Forget about you? That's *impossible*. How about I make up for what I've done? You and I are going to spend a week together touring the upstate region of New York. Only the two of us, along with the open road?"

Isabella responded with a voice that was filled with joy and said, "That sounds absolutely incredible. Do you know what? I have been waiting for a chance to see you again."

Playfully hiding his smirk, his intentions clear. "We could go to some charming little towns, eat way too much local food, and maybe even go on a couple of hikes," he said.

The phone rang with Isabella's laughter as she responded, "I'll pack my hiking boots, but you're buying all the snacks." Isabella's laughing rang through the phone. After the laughter faded, she whispered under her breath, "I really miss you; I wish you were here right now. I would have planted a kiss on your cheek."

"I really need time to go by quickly now," Jake laughed. "I really like the direction of these thoughts, ma'am. More of this, please."

Both of their emotions were filled with a sense of anticipation and a slight sense of lightness as they made preparations for their approaching road trip. Isabella also shared some great news regarding her work. "What do you think? At the Jet Propulsion Laboratory in Pasadena, CA, I've joined a specialized team tasked with such an exciting project. We are analyzing thousands of objects orbiting within our solar system that pose a potential threat of colliding with Earth. Our goal is to determine the composition and origin of this space debris to better understand and mitigate any risks they might present." She chimed gleefully.

"That's incredible, Isa! You're turning into a real-life space detective, I see," Jake responded, admiration evident in his voice.

"Yeah, it's pretty cool," Isabella admitted, blushing a little. "I can't wait to tell you all about it when I see you up close, you know." This made Jake chuckle.

After a long day of work, this small call was enough to make Jake feel at ease. He, once again, promised to clear his schedule and take some time off from work, wanting to ensure that their week together was as perfect as possible. After hanging up, he immediately went to talk to his Aunt Mary and Rodney.

"Aunt Mary, I'm planning to take a little vacation next week with Isabella. We're thinking of exploring upstate New York," Jake announced, hoping for her blessing.

Mary smiled warmly, her eyes twinkling with approval. "That sounds wonderful, Jake. You both deserve some time to relax and enjoy each other's company."

"And Rodney, could you help make sure everything's set here while I'm gone?" Jake asked, knowing how reliable he was.

"Of course, Jake. Enjoy your time away," Rodney responded, giving him a supportive nod.

Jake let out a deep breath as he finally felt a sense of calm wash over him. The recent chaos at the bar fight and Francesca's party had been intense, even for someone as seasoned in handling pressure as him. Now, with everything settling down, all Jake needed to completely unwind was to hear Isabella's voice on the other end of the phone.

***

As agents, assistants, and staff members navigated the controlled pandemonium of a crucial department meeting, the Federal Bureau of Investigation (FBI) operations center was bustling with activity. The room was filled with the low hum of many conversations, the clacking of keyboards, and the shuffling of papers because of the sheer volume of the noise. The voices of the two agents were laced with a sense of urgency as they discussed the most effective way to proceed in light of the impending deadlines that were being discussed in one of the corners. In the vicinity, Agent Jackson's assistant was attempting to expedite the delivery of certain essential files that had not yet come with the revised reports. She spoke on the phone in a tone that was authoritative.

An oasis of tranquility amidst the chaos was Agent Maurice Jackson, who reclined in his chair, coffee cup in hand. Listening to Patrick Flanagan, he made light of the situation and joked, "You know, amidst all this chaos, as long as I've got my cup of Joe, I might as well be on vacation."

Patrick chuckled, appreciating the moment of levity. "Yeah, if only these briefings were as relaxing as a day at the beach."

The meeting was about to go into full swing as Bureau Chief Sean Brady and Special FBI Task Force Lead Agent Susan Collins prepared to give a detailed briefing. Agent Collins adjusted her glasses and cleared her throat, signaling the room to settle down. "Thank you, everyone. Let's bring this to order. We need to discuss our next moves concerning the Capoli and Rossi situation and evaluate our recent interaction with Jake."

Agent Jackson took the opportunity to summarize their meeting with Jake, detailing their approach and his responses. "We met with Jake as planned. We laid out the stakes clearly and tried to nudge him towards cooperating more actively. He's cautious, understandably, given his position, but I believe he's starting to see the reality of his situation and the potential danger he's in."

FBI Agent Collins carefully nodded and took some notes. "Excellent work, Jackson. This relationship needs to keep growing. We have the best chance to learn about how the Capoli's work with Jake. Our plan must include a way to keep him safe while also getting the most information from him."

Superintendent Brady spoke up, his voice strong but reassuring. "Let's also make sure we know what the Rossi family plans to do in advance. Their behavior is hard to predict, and it's clear that things are getting worse after the party stunt. Is there any new information on that?"

"Their known friends are watching them, and we have some information on their financial activities that could reveal future plans," said Agent Collins. Our team is working hard on a thorough report about that."

Discussions about allocating resources, possible risks, and backup plans continued during the meeting. As the briefing went on, the room's energy changed from loud and chaotic to focused, with each agent adding to the group's work to handle the tricky and dangerous dance of stopping organized crime.

Agent Susan Collins directed the conversation toward the latest intelligence reports coming in from their informants embedded within both organizations.

"We've got eyes and ears in place," Agent Collins explained, pointing to the digital map on the screen showing various points of interest. "Our insiders have been crucial in providing us updates on both families' movements. It's clear from the recent events at Francesca's party that the Rossi family is aggressively pushing the Capoli's, testing their boundaries."

"The party stunt wasn't an arbitrary act of disturbance," Agent Jackson clarified. The Rossi group took this strategic step to loosen the Capoli family's control over their business. Based on historical trends, the Capolis' response could be just as forceful; therefore, we must be ready for it.

The room nodded in agreement, understanding the potential for this tension to escalate into something more significant.

Chief Brady weighed in, his voice steady but concerned. "We need to stay one step ahead. It isn't just about monitoring their actions anymore. We need to find leverage points that could help us dismantle their operations. Whether it's financial, operational, or through their personal connections, we need actionable intelligence."

Agent Flanagan glanced up from his dossier review. It appears that both dynasties are also attempting to forge partnerships with other minor figures in the city. The power dynamics may become more complex, and new chances for intervention may arise.

"The trick here," Agent Collins cut in, "is to quietly throw a wrench into their plans. We may not have the resources for an all-out street fight, but we can surely try to sow discord and suspicion among them. They may end up taking care of each other if we time it correctly, and then we'll be left to cope with what's left.

The agents deliberated possible plans to penetrate the organizations further, utilizing their existing intelligence to anticipate and counteract the actions of both families. From stepping up monitoring of important individuals to eavesdropping on their communications to learn their next move, many ideas were discussed.

With the meeting coming to a conclusion, every agent was aware that the days ahead would demand laser-like concentration and pinpoint accuracy. A single slip-up could tip the scales of power, and the position was precarious. As they ventured into the perilous realm of organized criminal intervention, they would be guided by the concepts of preparedness and attentiveness.

***

In a dimly lit room, Vincent Capoli sat alone with his glass of whiskey, sipping it with a grace like no other. His eyes were glued to the television, where a news report unfolded, carrying the weight of a young girl's fate. In front of him, the harsh reality of human trafficking was taking place—an activity Vincent Capoli and his family strongly avoided. Vincent was no saint, but he ran his criminal operations differently, focusing on things like gambling, corporate ransomware, and credit card fraud that didn't directly harm people. He made it clear to his team that trafficking humans was a line they should never cross.

He hated the thought of even considering this option, but it was a focused business interest for Roberto. This was a solid way to provoke the man who had made the mistake of attacking his daughter into an all-out fight.

A 14-year-old Mexican girl, her innocence stolen and her life hanging in the balance, was hurriedly being escorted through a crowded airport by an older white man. They maneuvered through the bustling crowds, their faces filled with desperation and fear, their every step filled with urgency.

Time seemed to stand still as they reached the security checkpoint, with their anxiety reaching new limits on every turn. However, fate had a different plan. Just as they stood in line, a surge of airport security personnel swooped in with a predetermined purpose. In a swift motion, they seized the older man who worked for Roberto Rossi and freed the young girl from his grip.

Vincent Capoli, who always seemed to be one step ahead, had managed to involve the media perfectly. He understood the influence of public opinion and cleverly informed the Channel 6 news team anonymously about a human trafficking operation connected to the Rossi empire. Everything went as planned, with cameras showing up just in time to capture law enforcement's intense rescue efforts. The broadcast was happening live, making sure that people in the city and beyond witnessed the exposure of the darkest secrets of Roberto Rossi. This move wasn't just an attack on his rivals; it was a well-thought-out strategy to damage their reputation and reveal their ethical flaws to the world. Capoli orchestrated it all to offensively divert and undermine the Rossi family's attempt at control.

Vincent felt a slight easing of the weight on his shoulders. This was only the first move in an all-out war against the notorious Roberto Rossi and his vile human trafficking ring. He understood that exposing their despicable operations required careful planning and cunning tactics.

Vincent, always keen to maintain control and order within his domain, grabbed his phone and called the chief of the airport security detail. "Well done, my friend," he said, expressing his satisfaction. "Your team's swift response today saved a life, and we will ensure that your payment is promptly processed."

One of Vincent's employees sprinted into the room, with expressions filled with anticipation, as the call came to a close. In an excited voice that threatened to break their voice, they walked up to Vincent and said, "Boss, you won't believe it!" The local news station we were in touch with was able to help us out. "They broadcasted the whole rescue, bringing Rossi's dark web to the world's attention."

Vincent smiled as he savored the taste of an initial victory. The revelation that the older gentleman was working for Roberto Rossi was a clever strategy and the first step to unraveling the intricate threads of the Rossi criminal empire. Vincent's plan was set in motion, and the first blow had been struck.

"Now, Roberto," Vincent whispered to himself, his voice filled with determination, "you're about to witness the full force of the Capoli family. No darkness will remain hidden; no life will be left shattered. It is just the beginning of our relentless pursuit of justice."

As the room fell silent, Vincent's mind raced with thoughts of the battles ahead. He knew that the war against the Rossi human trafficking ring would be arduous, filled with danger and sacrifice. But he was ready to give it his all for the sake of every innocent soul trapped in the clutches of this vile trade.

With a resolute gaze, he raised his glass and silently toasted to the young girl, now safe from harm and to the countless others still awaiting their freedom. At that moment, he vowed to ensure Roberto had nothing left. As the battle lines were drawn and the war raged, Vincent Capoli and the Capoli family embarked on their noble quest to dismantle Roberto Rossi's empire.

***

Martin and Francesca Capoli decided to host a lively game night at the prestigious Capoli estate. They invited Jake, along with a group of their close friends, to enjoy an evening of laughter, friendly competition, and a few drinks. The atmosphere was warm and inviting, with the sound of cheerful conversation filling the air.

As the night progressed, Jake's friendly and outgoing nature shone through. He effortlessly took over as the interim bartender, showcasing his impressive mixology skills. Martin and Francesca's friends were captivated by Jake's talent, marveling at his ability to craft exquisite cocktails.

Francesca's eyes were sparkling with admiration as they approached Jake. "You truly have a gift, Jake! These drinks are sensational. It's like you've been doing this for years!"

He was humbled by the praise and blushed at the comment. "Thank you, Francesca. I've always had a passion for mixology, and it's a pleasure to share it with all of you tonight."

As the night wore on, the jovial atmosphere filled every corner of the Capoli estate. Conversations flowed, and laughter echoed through the halls. It felt like a genuine bonding experience, and Jake relished in the company of Martin and Francesca's friends.

Before bidding farewell, Jake made his way to Vincent, who stood in a corner, discerningly observing the festivities. Vincent's presence exuded both power and wisdom, and Jake felt a mixture of respect and curiosity in his presence.

"Vincent," Jake said, extending his hand, "I wanted to thank you for the invitation tonight. It's been a wonderful evening, and the company of your family and friends is truly remarkable."

Vincent's eyes met Jake's with a hint of intrigue. "You've made quite an impression, young man. Your bartending skills are remarkable, but there's more to you than meets the eye."

Jake chuckled; a touch of modesty rang in his voice. "Well, Vincent, I guess we all have our hidden talents. It's been an honor to be here tonight, among such esteemed company."

Just as Jake prepared to leave, he noticed two familiar faces in the crowd—Johnny Viola and Knuckles McGee. They stood there talking to each other as if they were waiting for someone. Curiosity piqued, he approached them, eager to exchange greetings.

The two stood arguing over some matter, not knowing they could be heard by their visitors. "Well, it's true that they got him at the airport right in time. The girl would not have been tracked if it were not for our reconnaissance team. The shitshow who got arrested belonged to the Wonderland Gentlemen's Club. Turns out, he was a handler for the Rossi family."

Jake's eyes widened with a mixture of shock and intrigue filling his expression. "Hey, Johnny! Knuckles! It's great to see you both here," overhearing their conversation. Jake's interest was piqued, and he approached them to say hello.

Johnny's eyes darted briefly towards Knuckles, a silent signal passing between them. "Hey, Jake. We're glad you could make it. It's been a night of surprises, hasn't it?"

"Surprises? What do you mean?" Jake had stopped in his tracks. His interest was piqued.

Knuckles interjected, his voice low and guarded. "We were just discussing this case. It is no big deal." He smiled at Jake with a satisfied stare. "I hope you had fun?" He asked Jake.

"Oh… yes! I did!" Jake noticed the change in his tone and demeanor as Knuckles and Johny tried to change the topic. "Seems like you are dealing with something serious." Jake chuckled and waited for them to respond. He could not help but get curious. "I heard the Rossi family? That's... that's heavy stuff. You guys must be involved in something big."

Johnny nodded with a subtlety in his gaze. "You have *no* idea, Jake." He tried to laugh it off.

Knuckles added, "We're fighting a war against these criminals, trying to dismantle their operations piece by piece." But he was abruptly cut off by Johny, "It's just business. You know how it can get, haha…" Just like that, Johny brushed off the topic completely.

It's dangerous work, but someone has to do it."

As the conversation ended, Jake left the Capoli estate with a sense of purpose and a deeper bond. In his heart, Jake knew that he had his concerns for being acquainted with the lot. He had made great friends, but his intuitions were hinting at a darker time ahead.

Although he was glad to be of help with the bar fight and maintain his job, he had to remain unscathed with the happenings of their affairs with the Rossi for now. His days at the company were finally turning for the better, and continuing with this was too big of a risk.

***

Aunt Mary had set her sights on a prominent building nestled in Manhattan's bustling downtown financial district. The plan was to acquire the corporation that owned the building and then sell portions to interested parties, reaping a substantial profit.

While taking a journey to get something to eat, Jake happens to cross paths with Rodney, their butler, who is rapidly becoming more of a friend. At the Maman café in downtown Manhattan, which was close by, they decided to have lunch and catch up. While they took their seats, Rodney, who is often quiet, revealed something unexpected.

"You know, Jake, I was a member of a highly trained special forces unit in the Brazilian military before I found my way to serving Aunt Mary," Rodney revealed, his voice quiet but slightly proud.

Jake was taken aback and made no effort to conceal his amazement. "I can't believe it, Rodney. I was unaware of your past. What made you leave all that behind for a butler's life?"

After much thought, he responded, "Life has a way of throwing you curveballs you never expect," while his eyes gleamed. "A chain reaction began after my service and ended with me here. My experience and training in the military have not diminished my skill set. They're just beneath the surface, part of who I am."

His admiration for Rodney became stronger. There's usually a whole lot more going on with people than what you can see at first glance. That is truly admirable, Rodney. It reveals that your trip is rich and complex.

They went beyond the usual employer-employee relationship as their chat progressed, forming closer bonds. As they bid farewell to one another and finished their supper, Jake gained a deeper respect for Rodney's complicated history and the nuanced strength he brought to his present position.

As Jake left the café, his mind raced with thoughts. He glanced over and saw Agent Jackson and Patrick Flanagan seated at the table next to him. The moment their gazes locked, a shiver went down his spine; their very existence had startled him. Evidently, they had been following him, and the unexpected meeting made him wary while simultaneously making him wonder what they were up to.

"Agent Jackson, Patrick..." Jake said suspiciously as he gingerly made his way to their booth. "Are you here for some reason? And what gives it away is that you seem to have been anticipating my arrival.?"

Jake was the center of Agent Jackson's intense gaze as he wore a severe face. "We've been closely monitoring the situation, Jake. You could be in harm's way if you become involved in the impending conflict between the Capoli and Rossi families."

With a low and anxious voice, Patrick leaned in. "Jake... please share any knowledge you may have with us. Tell it like it is. We are concerned for your safety."

Their comments were like a heavy burden, and Jake could feel it growing heavier by the second. It appeared like denying would do nothing; he wanted to do something to make sure they would stop bothering him. His words were heavy with caution, and he spoke with a measured breath, "I... I did hear something. The person who was caught. The older gentleman who was caught with the underaged Mexican girl. Well, that gentleman was a member of the Wonderland gentlemen's club. So, that is all that I can tell you."

Jake was highly uncomfortable with the way the two gentlemen were after him. He was unsure about his trust in them.

Nodding firmly, Agent Jackson's gaze sharpened. "Jake, I need your **help** on this. We have had our eye on the Wonderland club for some time, but we require any and all information you can give us."

"Agent Jackson, I really wish that you would not drag me into this. Is it really that easy for you to endanger my life by trying to make me your informant? I really do not appreciate two fine gentlemen sinking to such levels, and right about now, I am too mad to be scared of you. Why don't you try to do your own research rather than get intel from a damn bartender? Are your own detective skills really that horrible that you need me to do your job for you? If so, I really doubt the abilities of your department." The dangerous actions of the FBI agents annoyed him because they were putting him in danger, and he really wanted them off his back.

"Easy there, boy…" Patrick growled at the young man's audacity.

"Listen, you really need to understand what I am saying; I will not be your spy. Neither am I going to do the JOB for you. This is something left for professionals to handle and stop putting me and the people around me at risk. What the fuck are my tax dollars paying for if the FBI cannot handle organized crime with all those damn resources?" He let out a sarcastic sigh. Jake hesitated for a moment, his mind racing. His frustration with the two had led him to say too much.

He needed to sever ties with these agents to protect himself from the dangerous world encroaching upon his peaceful existence. With a determined gaze, he met their eyes. "That's all I have to offer, and I will not tell you anything else."

Patrick, holding his glazed doughnut, was about to pounce on Jake. Agent Jackson saw his partner close to crossing the line. They could easily get in trouble for forcing someone to make a statement.

"From this point forward, I want no further involvement. Leave me the fuck alone." Jake's voice quivered a little, but he had to tell the detectives decisively. "Agent Jackson, Patrick. It's time for me to distance myself from this crazy fucking situation."

Patrick had silenced himself because of Jackson. However, the crimson on his face clearly reflected his desire to shove the food in his hand down Jake's throat.

The silence in between an intense eye contact was finally broken by Agent Jackson. "Oookay, I think I have lost my appetite. Let's *LEAVE* Patrick." He patted Agent Patrick's back and urged him to get out of the booth.

The Agents exchanged a knowing glance as the weight of their gaze lingered upon Jake.

"Very well, Jake. We'll respect your decision. But remember, the world you've stepped into can be unforgiving. Stay vigilant." Agent Jackson spoke to Jake with an air of disappointment. He held onto Patrick as if his hold was keeping him from saying or doing something rather obnoxious.

Departing, they left Jake with a whirlwind of emotions; he couldn't help but feel a sense of relief mingled with lingering apprehension. His affection for the Capoli family angered him.

They appeared to be respectable people. Jake couldn't understand why the agents were adamant about finding something fishy from their side.

The events of the day had thrust him into a realm of danger and intrigue, forcing him to confront the shadows lurking beneath the surface of his seemingly ordinary life.

A few days later, the news of the successful FBI raid on the Wonderland Gentlemen's Club spread like wildfire through the law enforcement community. The revelation that the establishment, owned by a shell company indirectly linked to Roberto Rossi, had been operating as a hub for underage trafficking sent shockwaves across the nation. The TV was on blast as he got ready for the office one morning when the words from the news TV reporter tore through the room.

"Another day, another raid, and this time, the Rossi family are under severe criticism. However, the question remains: Will they be held accountable, or will a slap at the wrist be the most common thing that will come out of this situation?" Jake knew he had to make sure to keep to himself more and reduce his affiliation with the Capoli family.

"A group of terrified, missing adolescent girls were rescued by the strike team headed by Agents Jackson and Flanagan, with Special Agent Susan Collins providing invaluable support. The captive girls, who had been kept in a complex subterranean cellar, were freed." As they told the story of their captivity and the horrific things that happened to them, the media attention grew exponentially. The FBI's quick response demonstrated the agency's steadfast dedication to solving terrible crimes and became one of the main talking points of this nationwide story.

When Roberto Rossi learned of the raid, his wrath was uncontrollable. He was overwhelmed by rage and wondered aloud how his operation had been revealed as he sat in the center of his lavish estate. There was an underlying sense of suspicion that the Capoli family was involved in this catastrophic setback for his criminal empire, and he couldn't put it out of his mind.

Roberto summoned his most reliable Cappo, Antonio, who was a trustworthy confidant who had stood by Roberto through good times and bad. Almost fearing for his safety, Antonio slowly made his way into the room. "Roberto, I have some news to share regarding the raid on the Wonderland club," Antonio started, his voice betraying his nerves. "It appears the FBI orchestrated a successful operation, rescuing the girls and dealing a severe blow to our interests."

Rossi's venomous voice matched the narrowness of his gaze. To what extent is this feasible, Antonio? How were they informed? Who turned against us?"

With his eyes locked on the floor, Antonio paused. "Roberto, I've heard whispers. Rumor has it that someone in the Capoli family was involved. Their actions against us have grown, and now they appear to have delivered a crushing blow."

As Rossi clenched his fists at his sides, his scowl revealed his level of irritation. "I know this was the Capolis. Are they taking a risk by trying to come after me? This betrayal will cost them! Antonio, gather as much information as you can. Whoever planned this assault on us, please tell me."

Antonio gave a sad nod, clearly understanding the seriousness of the issue. "Roberto, I consider it done. I will investigate every possible avenue. We will find out what happened and hold the guilty accountable."

Irritated and frustrated, Rossi let out a raging tantrum as Antonio stormed out of the room. He now considered the Capoli family his mortal foes despite their past as friendly rivals. His revenge would be so fierce that it would rock their world to its core, he swore.

Furthermore, among the most elite members of the FBI, the agency's standing had been greatly enhanced by the raid on the Wonderland club. A significant triumph in the struggle against organized crime was achieved with the rescue of the trafficked girls after their discovery. Fear gripped anyone brave enough to partake in such heinous deeds as the FBI dealt a crushing blow to Roberto Rossi's criminal organization.

In spite of all the praise they were receiving, Special Agent Susan Collins, Agent Flanagan, and Agent Jackson knew that their fight against the Rossi family was far from done. A perilous dance had begun between the Capoli and Rossi families, with their deeds caught in a web of justice, vengeance, and power.

As the raid came to a close, the Capolis and Rossis battle heated up, with both sides getting ready for the impending showdown. Everything would be shattered, relationships would be put to the test, and loyalty and honor would be shredded.

Jake stood inherently in the middle of the storm, swept up in a tempest he hadn't seen coming. As his bond with the Capoli family deepened and peril hung heavy in the air, he would soon be confronted with decisions that would determine the outcome of this struggle.

He had no idea that the road he had begun would take him more into the shadows, where courage and selflessness would be his constant companions. As the conflict progressed, Jake learned the value of devotion, the burden of duty, and his strength.

A showdown that would decide the destiny of countless lives was about to unfold, with the battle lines drawn and the stage prepared. The conflict between the Capolis and the Rossis had just started when it would have far-reaching consequences, bringing devastation, salvation, and the unbreakable will of those who battled to save the defenseless.

Chapter 7: Casualty of Secrets

The open road stretched out before them, an invitation to adventure. Isabella's eyes sparkled with excitement as she turned to Jake. They had come such a long way since college.

Looking at his face, she thought of the time away from him and shuddered at the thought of not being together. In her heart and mind, they belonged to each other.

She leaned in as he drove and planted a small kiss on his cheek, "Are you ready for this?" she asked, her hand finding him across the center console.

Jake grinned, his fingers interlacing with hers. "You bet. Just you, me, and the open highway. This is going to be epic."

They reached a small town first. Seeing a lot of tourists heading to a nearby market, they got to know of a small fare happening down the road.

"We have to make a stop!" Isabella squealed in delight. Jake saw the kiddish smile on her face and knew he had to say yes to her.

"It is so easy to make you happy." He chuckled, grabbed her hand, and gave her a small kiss on her knuckles.

The main street was lined with quirky shops and mom-and-pop diners. Isabella dragged Jake into a vintage clothing store, her competitive spirit shining through as she challenged him to a thrift store fashion show.

"How do I look?" Jake asked, emerging from the dressing room in an oversized cowboy hat, the brim nearly swallowing his face.

Isabella doubled over with laughter, snapping a photo. "You're a natural-born cowboy, that's for sure."

As the sun began to set, they stumbled upon the lively county fair everyone was talking about. Hand in hand, they strolled through the bustling fairgrounds, sampling local delicacies and trying their luck at the carnival games.

"Ooh, the ring toss! I bet I can win you a prize," Isabella said, determination etched on her features.

True to her word, she clinched the win, proudly presenting Jake with a massive stuffed bear. "My hero," he teased, kissing her cheek.

The next day, they ventured into the heart of the countryside, winding through lush forests and sprawling farmlands. Isabella marveled at the stunning vistas, her fingers tracing the contours of Jake's hand as he drove. When they stumbled upon a secluded waterfall, they couldn't resist the temptation to explore.

"Race you to the top!?" Isabella called; just as she said these words, Jake was the first to get out of the car. He had parked the vehicle hastily by the side of the road and had sprinted right out.

"The last one to get there will be buying dinner!" he shouted over his shoulder as he sped up.

"Jake!!! You are *such* a cheater!" She screamed from behind. Getting out of the car, she stumbled a little but gained her pace shortly after.

Jake was wearing cotton shorts and a slight see-through. Isabella saw his sculpted figure from behind and thought about a playful yet manipulative plan.

Her eyes sparkled with mischief as she sprinted towards the cascading waterfall. Jake chuckled and quickened his pace. Just then, "Ouch!" she let out a small scream and posed to fall to the ground.

"Hey, wait…Are you okay?" Jake turned and worried, he started to run towards her. "Isabella!"

Just as he reached her and tried to help her up, she mischievously pushed him and made a run for the base of the fall.

Giggling on her way over, she shouted back at him, "Gotcha!!"

Jake sat on the floor, shaking his head in disbelief. "So, you are in for a game, huh, miss? He checked her out, and she ran as fast as she could, holding her heels in hand.

"Be careful!" Jake couldn't help but still worry a little. The woman had decided to take on a rocky road with bare feet.

As they reached the base of the falls, Isabella turned to him, a playful grin on her lips. "Think you can keep up, hotshot?" she teased, already beginning to scale the rocky terrain.

"Wouldn't dream of falling behind," Jake replied, his gaze locked on her every movement. He followed closely, admiring the way her muscles flexed beneath her sun-kissed skin.

When they reached the top, Isabella turned to face him, her chest heaving from the exertion. "Looks like I win," she panted, her hand reaching out to trace his jawline.

Jake's breath caught in his throat at her touch. "Guess that means I owe you a prize," he murmured, his arms snaking around her waist and pulling her close.

She rose on her toes to meet his height until her lips were inches from his. "I can think of a few things I'd like," she whispered, her fingers tangling in his hair.

Their kiss was soft and lingering, as if time stood still and the world stopped existing just for them. They became one floating in the air with no worries and no care in the world. Hurried water and a light touch of wind were nothing at all, just a white noise in the background. Only they were the true center of attention.

"Don't you want to meet my parents? Or do you have other plans?" Jake planted small kisses, and he went down her neck.

"I think we have made them wait long enough." She giggled and pushed him away.

"Come on, let's go."

Getting into the car, Jake told Isabella all the funny stories of his childhood, all the pranks he used to pull on his father.

"At one point, Mom was ready to leave the house; she was so sick and tired of us pulling pranks. She once came in between them, and well, there was the event of her wiping off the salsa from the ceiling of the kitchen. I think it would be best if she told you the story herself."

Isabelle laughed her heart out. "You devil! What did you make the poor woman do?"

"Hey, according to my schemes, it was Dad who had to go in the kitchen. I didn't know she would be home early and straight for the stove now, did I? I am telling you; she tells the story way better than I do."

Of all the things that made Isabella fall head over heels in love with Jake, the way his eyes crinkled when he smiled, and his hand would find hers at the same time. She tried to find his. They were completely smitten with one another. There was an invisible thread that held them tied to each other at the hip.

Jake had promised to bring Isabella for dinner, and their little rendezvous near the falls had already put them behind an hour.

They finally reached the house, and Isabella had nothing but nice compliments to say about the homey exterior.

A small but lovingly maintained house tucked away at the end of their farm—Jake's childhood home—was finally reached. Anxieties gripped Isabella as they entered the driveway. Meeting Jake's parents was a huge step, but she had faith in him and was eager to find out his family history.

When Paul and Pam, Jake's parents, threw wide the front door, they welcomed them with open arms and boundless energy. "Welcome home, son!" As he embraced Jake tightly, Paul spoke. Pam saw Isabella standing behind; she was quite shy.

"I'm glad you brought your friend." Pam gave a motherly smile to Isabella.

"Jake has told us so much about you. He said you studied together! I am grateful that he had you with him as a friend during his studies," she welcomed Isabella in.

The discussion was easygoing as they enjoyed a home-cooked meal. Paul and Pam's love and pride shone through as they told Isabella tales of Jake's youth. A feeling of belonging washed over her as she beheld the solid background that had molded her friend.

The way Isabella looked at Jake did not go unnoticed by Jake's parents. There was an air of unsaid understanding between the two, and Jake's mother saw through it clearly. Pam regaled them with stories of Jake's childhood, from his mischievous antics as a young boy to the day he brought home his first A+ report card.

"He's always been such a kind, hardworking boy," Pam said, reaching across the table to give Isabella's hand a gentle squeeze. "And now, seeing the wonderful young man he's become, well, it's all we could have hoped for."

Paul gave a satisfied nod. A grin grew across his face as he expressed his agreement. "Well, young lady, we have you to thank as well. He has been very happy to have you there with him as a friend. I am sure you two support each other, given you two are both working now. He looked down at the cup of tea as he tried his best to phrase that sentence. Getting approval from his father would not have been easy. But things had turned out to be just fine. The words "Jake is the special one" came out of her mouth as she gazed at him with immense admiration. She then realized where she was and quickly regained her composure.

As the evening was drawing to a close, Jake and Isabella were finishing the dishes in the kitchen. "You guys will leave in two days, yes?" Pam asked as she smiled sweetly at Isabella.

"Yes, we will leave for New York, I guess," Jake answered absentmindedly to his mom.

"Well, how about we girls go for a walk and then grab some coffee on the way?" Pam grabbed the set of plates Isabella had set aside after drying.

"Sure! I would love to!" Isabella smiled so wide her eyes disappeared.

"What? Where is my invitation? Why am I not going?" Jake asked, shaking off some water drops on Isabella in a playful way.

"Well, you can stay home and help your father fix the car. It's a girl's outing only, sir. You cannot crash our party," she winked at Isabella, and both of them started laughing. She ruffled Jake's hair and then bid both of them a good night.

The next two days were filled with joy and laughter. In these two days, Jake's father also opened up a little and started conversing with Isabella. He never had a daughter, so his ways were always a little awkward.

During their stay, Pam made sure to make the kids eat their hearts out. She had gone above and beyond to make the heartiest of meals—a fact that Paul was clearly too happy about.

"Watch it with the meat, hon, your cholesterol!" Pam swatted her husband's hand away from grabbing another chicken leg from the roast. Jake and Isabella couldn't help but giggle over this.

Blushing flush red in the cheeks, Jake's father complained like a little child. "But my son is visiting; I am allowed to sway a little from the restrictions, aren't I?"

Jake's father had a stoic air around him, but in front of his wife, he turned more toward his playful side.

When the time came to leave, Pam quickly whispered in Jake's ear. "Don't let this one get away, sweetie! We're counting on you."

Isabella couldn't help but giggle at the playful message she had heard.

Jake laughed and simply winked at his mom in reassurance.

***

"*MAN*, that was an IMPRESSIVE slam dunk, folks! The opposing team really needs to think of a strategy if they are to survive this game. The voice on the speakers blared through the crowd, and with it, people erupted with joy. The screams echoed through the cavernous arena, the air electric with the frenetic energy of the basketball game unfolding on the court below. From his perch in the exclusive skybox, Vincent Capoli leaned back in his plush leather chair, his eyes trained on the action with a detached intensity.

Around him, a group of his most trusted advisors were gathered, engaged in a hushed discussion. Capoli's gaze flickered between the game and the men, his keen mind processing the information they were sharing.

"So, the initial assault on the Rossi camp was a success?" he asked, his voice low and measured.

Tim Scott, who was Vincent's friend and wartime counsel, was always on top of his game. He nodded. "Yes, sir. Our men were able to draw the FBI in, just as you predicted. They raided the Wonderland club and uncovered the trafficking operation."

At this, Vince smiled; his demeanor reflected an air of satisfaction. "Excellent, and what of our young friend, Jake Stone? Did he take the bait as we expected?"

Scott glanced down at the notes in his hand. "It seems so, sir. The FBI made several attempts to recruit him, and he ultimately agreed to assist them in their investigation."

A soft chuckle escaped Vince. "I knew that boy would prove useful." Vincent was a mastermind, and his plan of using Jake to tip off the FBI had worked perfectly.

The crowd erupted in a deafening roar as the Knicks scored a crucial basket, the pulsing energy of the game washing over the skybox. Vincent sat back, his gaze unflinching as he surveyed his lieutenants.

"Gentlemen, I believe it's time we take this conflict to the next level. The Rossi family has been a thorn in our side for far too long. Things have already been set in motion, and I intend to put an end to their reign of terror once and for all."

His advisors exchanged a series of uneasy glances, the weight of Vince's words settling over them like a heavy blanket.

"Sir, are you sure a full-scale assault is wise? The Rossi clan is not to be underestimated, and such a move could plunge the city into all-out war," one of the men cautioned.

Vince's expression hardened, his eyes narrowing. "I'm well aware of the risks, but the potential rewards far outweigh them. The time has come to strike decisively, to show the Rossi's that no one challenges the Capoli family and lives to tell the tale."

He leaned forward, his fingers steepled as he spoke. "We've carefully orchestrated this entire scenario, from the FBI's involvement to recruiting our young Mr. Stone. Now, we must capitalize on the momentum we've built."

The crowd roared again, the sound of the game fading into the background as Vincent's advisors absorbed his words. The man sat with an air of grace and power, his every movement exuding a sense of control and confidence.

As the discussion continued, Vince seemed satisfied with the outcome. He knew, all along, about the FBI's attempts to recruit Jake Stone, and he had used that knowledge to his advantage. The young man had been an unknowing pawn in his carefully crafted plan, a tool to be wielded against the Rossi crime family.

"I must commend you all on your excellent work," Vince said, his gaze sweeping across the group. "Thanks to your efforts, we are now poised to strike a decisive blow against our adversaries. The Rossi clan will never see this coming."

He leaned back in his chair, his fingers drumming against the armrest. "The next step is a full-frontal assault on their remaining businesses and strongholds. We'll hit them hard and fast, leaving no room for retaliation."

The advisors nodded, the weight of the task ahead evident in their expressions. Vince's calm demeanor.

As the game drew to a close and the crowd erupted in thunderous applause, Vince rose from his seat, straightening his impeccable suit. "Gentlemen, let's adjourn for the evening. I trust you all know what needs to be done. Keep me informed of any developments."

With a nod, he strode towards the exit of the skybox, his presence commanding the attention of all who crossed his path. It was clear that this was a man who wielded immense power, a true master of his domain.

***

The open road stretched out before them, the miles melting away as Jake and Isabella made their way back to the city. The windows were down, the warm breeze tousling their hair as they sang along to the radio, their laughter and playful banter filling the car.

"You know, this trip has been the perfect blend of adventure and relaxation," Isabella mused, her hand finding Jake's across the center console. "I'm going to miss it when we're back home."

Jake squeezed her fingers, his gaze flicking between the road and her radiant face. "Who says the adventure has to end?" he asked, a mischievous glint in his eye. "I was thinking we could make this whole 'us' thing a little more official. What do you say, partner? Ready to take the next step?"

Her heart skipped a beat. A dazzling smile spread across her face. "I thought you'd never ask," she murmured, leaning in to press a tender kiss to his lips.

"Does that make me your boyfriend now?" Jake asked flirtatiously,

"I believe it does." She looked deep into his eyes and caressed his nose.

As the minutes ticked by, they decided to stop for a leisurely lunch, eager to savor a few more moments of uninterrupted bliss before the demands of their everyday lives came crashing back. The restaurant they chose was a charming little place, its rustic decor and cozy ambiance inviting them to linger.

Seated at a secluded table, they pored over the menu, their playful banter and flirtatious remarks punctuating the conversation. When the waitress arrived, they placed their orders, their eyes lingering on each other as they did so.

"I have to say, this trip has been absolutely perfect," Isabella said, her hand reaching across the table to intertwine with Jake's. "So, is this considered our first date since we are again boyfriend and girlfriend?" she traced small circles on his arm.

Jake nodded shyly, his thumb gently caressing her knuckles. "Me too. I can't imagine going through all of this with anyone else by my side."

As their meals arrived, they dove in with gusto, their appetites fueled by the long drive and the excitement of their newfound commitment. But just as Isabella was about to take another bite, her expression suddenly shifted, a look of discomfort crossing her features.

"Excuse me," she murmured, pushing back from the table and hurrying towards the restroom.

"Are you okay?" Jake asked worriedly.

"Yes … No, I feel rather nauseous. Let me come back from the ladies room. It may have been the food," she answered, waving him off and not to be concerned.

Jake watched her go, a frown of concern etched on his face. He waited patiently. Then, opening his phone to pass the time, he watched random reels on TikTok. When a good half hour passed, that was when he started to get a little worried. Pulling out his phone, he sent a quick text: "Hey, are you okay in there? Should I come to check on you?"

But there was no immediate response, and Jake's unease began to build after ten more minutes passed. Glancing around the restaurant, he saw that the other patrons were engrossed in their own meals and conversations, oblivious to his growing concern. After fifteen minutes more, he got up from the seat and looked around the restaurant just in case she had run into someone and was busy chatting. Still, there was no sign. A waitress passed by, and Jake asked her to check the washroom to see if Isabella was okay. When the waitress came back, she informed him that there was no one in the stalls. He asked all the restaurant waiters and waitresses, but they refused to see something out of the blue.

"Excuse me, ma'am, have you seen a woman with dark hair and brown eyes in there?" Jake asked a random woman who was seated near their table, his voice tinged with worry.

The woman shook her head. "No, I'm sorry. I haven't seen anyone in there for a while." Jake felt this sense of bewilderment, his fingers tightening around his phone as he tried to resist the urge to panic. He quickly fired off another message to Isabella, his fingers moving like lightning.

"Where are you? I'm starting to get worried."

Still, there was no response, and Jake could start to feel a knot of anxiety tightening in the pit of his stomach. Retracing his steps, he scanned the restaurant, his gaze sweeping over the familiar faces, searching for any sign of Isabella.

But she was nowhere to be seen.

Striding back to their table, he snatched up his jacket and keys, his mind racing. "Excuse me, ma'am," he called out to the waitress, "have you seen the woman I was dining with? She went to the restroom a while ago and hasn't come back."

The waitress frowned, her brow creasing with concern. "I'm afraid I haven't, sir. The other waitress also checked the ones on the first floor; no one saw a woman with your description."

Jake nodded, his fingers drumming against the tabletop as he waited, the seconds ticking by like hours. When the manager emerged, shaking his head regretfully, Jake felt his heart sink. He opened his phone and tried to check her location, but her location was not showing at the restaurant anymore.

His mind was spinning with a thousand terrible scenarios, and Jake's fingers were shaking as he grasped his phone. In what location was Isabella? What may have possibly resulted in her leaving? Simply considering the possibility that his companion was in any type of danger was enough to cause his heart to tighten up with unbridled terror.

With a solemn expression on his face, the manager hurriedly returned. "Sir, I have asked the cleaners, too, and they also reported the same to us. She could have just gone home. Have you tried on any other number? If you are certain about her being in danger, we can call the cops for you."

Jake nodded, his gaze never wavering from the restroom door. "Thank you," he managed, his voice barely above a whisper. "Her location is different," he mumbled.

"You can take further matters with the police; it would be suitable for them to intervene if that is the case." He nodded to one of the waiters and asked them to fetch Jake a glass of water and calm Jake down. The rest were asked to resume work. With one final nod, he went back to the mundane chores of the day.

Pulling up her contact on his phone, Jake's thumb hovered over the call button, his mind racing with unhealthy scenarios. He just wanted to hear her voice, to know she was alright. But with each unanswered call, his panic only grew.

After nearly two hours, the sound of sirens was finally heard in the distance. Jake went straight to the entrance, and he flagged down the responding officers, his words spewing out much faster than his normal cadence.

"My friend, she went to the restroom and never came back. I've tried calling her, but she's not answering. Please, you have to find her. I know… I can feel that she is in trouble!"

The officers exchanged a grim look, one of them placing a reassuring hand on Jake's shoulder. "We'll do everything we can, sir. Can you tell us what she was wearing and when you last saw her?"

Jake's mind raced as he tried to recall the details. His memory was clouded by the overwhelming fear coursing through him. "She was wearing a blue blouse and jeans. It's been, but at this point, I don't know how long. "

The officers nodded, their expressions grim. "Alright, we'll start our search here. I suggest you stay close by in case she returns or contacts you."

With a heavy heart, Jake watched the officers disappear into the restaurant, their footsteps echoing in the now-silent dining room. He paced the floor, his gut racing with panic. *Where could she be? What if something terrible had happened to her?*

His mind conjured up horrific images, and he had to fight the urge to be sick. Isabella, the love of his life, defied the odds and found her way back to him, and this time, they would both be happy. But what if he never saw her again?

Sinking back into his chair, Jake buried his face in his hands, a strangled sob escaping his lips. "Please, Isabella," he whispered, his voice thick with anguish. "Please be okay. I need you to be okay and well."

The minutes ticked by, each one feeling like an eternity. Jake's gaze fixed on the restroom door, his heart pounding in his chest. He had to find her, had to bring her home safe.

Whatever it took, he would move heaven and earth to bring his partner Isabella back.

***

Vincent was seated in the back seat of his Black Escalade, with a calm expression as he looked out the tinted windows. It wasn't just that his mind was recreating the delights of the Knicks game that he had just enjoyed; it was also involved in the planning that he had undertaken with his counselors.

Vincent was returning home, and as they neared the Capoli estate, the driver slowed down at the front gate. The grand wrought-iron gates stood tall, a formidable barrier protecting the luxurious property. The security guard approached the vehicle with a stern but respectful expression. He handed over his identification and waved for them to get done checking and opening the gates. The Escalade glided forward and moved up a long, winding drive toward the main house, its bullet-resistant windows reflecting the moonlight.

The man at the gate was busy scrutinizing the documents for a moment before waving them through. Just then, two vehicles materialized on either side of the Escalade, boxing it in. Before the driver could even react, the windows on both sides started to roll down, and Vincent felt a cold chill run down his spine.

The driver had noticed several individuals on his side brandishing weapons. His eyes widened in horror, and he immediately hit a concealed button, causing the windows on all sides of the Escalade to roll up instantly. "This is a gift from Roberto Rossi," a voice bellowed from the vehicle on the driver's side, the words barely registering in Vincent's mind before a hail of bullets pierced the Escalade's sleek exterior. These were no pistols; whoever had decided to attack was using heavy-duty military-grade rifles.

Despite his quick reflexes, it was too late. A single bullet had already penetrated the window before it fully closed, striking the driver. The force of the impact caused him to jerk violently and made his head slam into the steering wheel. He slumped forward, unconscious, as the armored vehicle's automatic defenses continued to engage, attempting to protect Vincent from further harm.

Vincent tried to remain calm, knowing that he was close to the main house. The time it was under fire, the bullets hammered into the glass and metal of the Escalade, causing the car to rock and shake violently. The intensity was so overwhelming that it seemed like the Escalade would not be able to hold off the attack at certain points.

The sound of the assault was deafening inside the confines of the vehicle. He covered his ears and battled to maintain his calm; he could feel the adrenaline running through his veins and his heart beating in his ears. Throughout the ordeal, Vincent was able to control his emotions through almost a warrior's resolve. He instinctively controlled his breathing, focused his mind, and braced himself.

Any bullet could be his last. Any breath could be his final one.

Vince reached down to the floorboard of the Escalade and pulled open the lid of a hidden compartment, which was barely big enough for him to fit inside, but he lay there curled in a ball, grabbed a thick, immaculate blanket, and wrapped it over his body and head.

It was imperative that he seek assistance. He dialed the number of one of his most trusted lieutenants. "This is Vince," he yelled into the receiver, his voice barely audible over the sound of the assault. "We are coming under attack. I am in desperate need of assistance right now!"

The voice on the other end of the line was filled with a sense of urgency, and the response came right away. "Sir, we are on our way. Stay safe. We will get there as fast as we can."

The gates started to close, and the attackers withdrew back from the main gate. It meant that someone was controlling the main gate, Vincent's reinforcements were on their way, and the attackers had only moments to make their escape. Vincent clenched his fists around the phone, and his knuckles turned white with focused anger.

"Somebody fucking come already!" He shouted from within the enclosed floorboard compartment while making sure that the Immaculate blanket was still covering every part of his body.

A shudder ran down his spine as the Escalade lurched and shook, and the sound of shattered glass and twisted metal sent echoes throughout the world.

Vincent was meticulously waiting for a way out of this situation and wondered if his men would be lucky enough to capture any of the assailants. He could hear noises in the distance of the attackers fleeing while his men were coming to the rescue from the main house.

"Damn you, Rossi," he said out loud, "You will pay for this with your own blood."

***

Over at the restaurant, the police were still conducting their search while trying to calm Jake down. One of the officers on the scene informed Jake that a person normally needs to be missing for 24 hours, but since they had come to the location, they would do a quick search in the area to see if this could be easily solved.

His mind raced with a thousand horrific scenarios, each one more terrifying than the last. What if she had been taken? What if she was hurt or worse? The thought of her in danger sent a wave of sheer panic and anger coursing through him.

Pulling out his phone, he dialed his cousin, Titiano. He needed to hear a reasonable viewpoint on what was happening.

"Jake? What's wrong, man?" Titiano's tone was laced with concern, and Jake was glad to hear his cousin's voice.

"Titi, something's happened. Isabella, she... she disappeared." Jake's voice cracked, the words stumbling out in a desperate rush.

There was a moment of stunned silence on the other end of the line and then Titiano's voice, low and urgent. "What do you mean, disappeared? Did you guys have a fight? Tell me what happened."

Jake spent the next few minutes filling Titi in on the events that happened before and during Isabella's disappearance. "In some ways, it's like she just vanished out of thin air," Jake explained. Titiano tells Jake to calm down and finish with the police so he can head straight home. He will wait for them to figure out their next move in order to find Isabella. "Don't worry, man, no matter what... I am with you," Titiano says reassuringly before he hangs up. His words were laced with a determined calm, and Jake felt a small measure of relief.

Jake closed his eyes for a moment as if he was conducting a silent prayer, then took a deep breath, his gaze sweeping the restaurant as if Isabella might suddenly materialize before his eyes.

After the officers had surveyed the entire location, Jake went down and had a conversation about what they would do to find her. He reiterated everything to them again about her GPS, and one officer took access to his phone, reviewed the Find Me app, and walked back to the car. "Hello, Dispatch. This is Unit 3; I have a location. Can you send a patrol unit to see the location shared? A person has gone missing, but we have their active location. This is urgent, and I need any patrol units nearby to respond!" The officer called out on his radio, sat in his car, and drove away.

The officer standing with Jake was busy speaking on his radio. He looked at Jake and asked, "Hey, do you have any more details apart from the description of the girl? Did you guys have a dispute or anything?"

Jake shook his head with his anxiety clear out in the open. "No dispute. We were just talking, and then she disappeared. Something's wrong. I can feel it."

The officer nodded, processing the information. "Alright, come to the station with us. We need to get a full report before we can start a full investigation."

Jake agreed. He was relieved to be doing something. They asked him to stay calm, go home, and let them do their job after filing the report. But Jake wasn't about to just sit and wait.

At the police station, Jake found himself in a frustrating back-and-forth with the front desk officer. They asked him to go home and wait for their call. After much frustration and fros, his voice started rising. It was enough to draw the attention of others in the station. "I need to speak to someone higher up! This is urgent!"

The front desk officer sighed, clearly used to dealing with anxious individuals, but finally relented and called for a more senior officer. After a few tense minutes, a lieutenant approached. "What seems to be the problem?"

Jake took a deep breath and tried to steady his nerves. "My girlfriend Isabella disappeared. I know something happened to her. She wouldn't just vanish like this."

The lieutenant listened, his expression serious but constrained by protocol. "We understand your concern, but department regulations state that a person must be missing for 24 hours before we can officially take action."

Jake's frustration boiled over. "24 hours? She could be in serious danger right now! Waiting could cost her life!"

The lieutenant remained calm but firm. "I understand your concern, sir, but those are the rules. We can't launch a full-scale investigation until the time frame is met."

Jake pleaded, his desperation evident. "Please, there has to be something you can do now. She's not safe. I can feel it."

The lieutenant shook his head. "I'm sorry, sir. We're bound by these regulations. There are procedures we have to follow."

The heated exchange continued for a few more minutes, with Jake refusing to back down. After going a few rounds, the lieutenant did not budge. Finally, the officer who had initially referred Jake to the station stepped forward. His face softened with sympathy as he handed Jake his card.

"Look, I know this isn't what you wanted to hear," the officer said quietly. "But I promise you, as soon as those 24 hours are up, I will personally jump on this case. Keep my card, and call me the moment you hit that mark. We'll do everything we can."

Jake took the card as the feeling mixed with anger and helplessness washed over him. "Thank you," he managed to say, though the words felt hollow. He knew waiting wasn't an option, but he was out of moves.

Walking out of the station, Jake's mind raced. He had to figure out something in the meantime. He couldn't just sit and do nothing. He started praying almost out loud for Isabella to be safe wherever she was.

While driving back to his aunt's estate, Jake tried to calm down but found it impossible. His phone was glued to his hand, counting down the minutes until he could call the officer and get the investigation started. He replayed their last conversation over and over in his head. He tried to search for any clue that he might have missed. The uncertainty gnawed at him, making every second feel like an eternity.

***

Jake got into his vehicle and started the long journey home that he had started with Isabella, but now he is ending it alone. He had roughly 250 miles to go before he made it back to New York City, but he decided that the open road would give him clarity in terms of planning his next move. He was playing in his mind the last instances where they were together and happy. Isabella had started to eat, and after taking a few bites, she suddenly felt nauseous and went to the bathroom. There was nothing abnormal and absolutely no warning about what was going to happen.

It took nearly five hours before Jake reached home. When he reached his aunt's residence, it was nearly 1:00 AM, and he rushed inside, leaving everything in his car. Jake's frantically searched his room until he found Agent Jackson's card. He paused for a half second, thinking about the last time they had an exchange and how, finally, he was adamant about not having anything to do with the FBI, but now things have changed.

He hoped this person wouldn't let him down.

The call immediately went to voicemail. "Agent Jackson? It's Jake. I need your help. My girlfriend Isabella is missing, and the cops asked me to wait. Her location was live on GoFindMe, but that ended up being a dead end. Please let me know if we can meet, and I will wait for your call."

***

The Capoli estate was in a state of frantic chaos as Vincent's security team rushed to the front gate, their faces etched with a mixture of horror and determination. The sight that greeted them was nothing short of a nightmare – the driver, his dead body slumped over the steering wheel, a gaping wound in his head. In his hand was a 9mm in hand, unused.

"Hell, No!" the man who first opened the door muttered in disgust.

Vincent was tucked away in the floorboard compartment of the Escalade. His body lay still, waiting for the next moment. An immaculate cloth was draped over his entire form, covering his head down to his feet, rendering him nearly invisible in the dim light. Each breath he took was shallow and rapid. The commanding mob boss now seemed invulnerable, considering all that just happened, and his aura of invincibility enhanced.

The onslaught should have killed him, yet here he is still breathing, thinking 1st about his children, then about the lengths that Roberto Rossi would go through in order to see him dead. As Vincent waited for rescue, he considered how lucky he was to have the resources and foresight to be prepared for such an attack.

Upon finding Vincent alive and still breathing, one of his men yelled at the top of his lungs, "I found the boss, and we need to get a doctor immediately," as he struggled to help Vincent out of the full board compartment and onto his feet.

What seemed like an army of men came pouring down from the Capoli estate, some jumping in vehicles and others on foot patrol looking for any signs of the individuals who perpetrated this attack.

"The car looks like shit." Knuckles was busy observing the car.

The driver's limp figure was pulled out of the car while Knuckles growled at a group of men standing around, "You … scan the area, and if you find even a trace of their men in the area. You tell me!"

Just then, other men tried to open the back door. Vincent could hear them screaming into their microphones.

"WE FOUND HIM! GET THE DOCTOR NOW!"

"He was in the compartment! He is okay!" The other man called out. After placing the body of the dead driver on the ground, he peered his head into the car, and one of the men who was busy trying to open the completely mangled SUV finally had the door open.

The car had saved Vincent. The men carried him to the main house.

When Vincent stumbled into the house, Martin rushed downstairs. His face was a mix of worry and determination. "Call the family doctor immediately," he barked at the chief of staff, who nodded and quickly picked up the phone. Martin then turned his attention back to Vincent, guiding him to a comfortable chair in the living room.

"Sit here, Dad. Let's get you checked out," Martin said, his voice strained with concern.

Vincent was visibly shaken and waved off the fuss. "I'm fine, Martin. Really, I don't even have a scratch on me," he insisted, trying to reassure his son and the others who had gathered around, their faces lined with worry.

The doctor arrived quickly. He was a middle-aged man with a calm demeanor that suggested he had seen his share of emergencies. He approached Vincent in a professional yet gentle manner. "Let's take a look, Mr. Capoli," he said, starting to inspect him for any injuries. "Do you care about telling me what happened?"

Vincent raised a hand to stop him, pulling open his shirt to reveal a lightweight vest beneath. "This is why I'm okay," he explained. "I always wear this specialized Kevlar vest under my clothing. It's lightweight but strong enough to stop anything."

The doctor nodded, impressed. "That's smart, but we should still check for any bruising or internal injuries."

As the doctor continued his examination, Vincent held up the cloth that had been draped over him during the attack. "And this," he said, "is made out of experimental spider silk. It's almost indestructible. Nothing can penetrate it."

He paused, then elaborated, "I own a company that specializes in research and development for advanced materials. We've been working on creating clothing made from spider silk because it's incredibly strong—ten times stronger than steel—and twenty times lighter. This cloth is one of our prototypes. When the attack happened, I draped it over my body, knowing that bullets couldn't get through it."

The doctor inspected the cloth with interest, marveling at its potential. "Remarkable," he said, running his fingers over the smooth yet incredibly tough material. "This is a game-changer in personal protection."

Vincent nodded. "We've been testing it rigorously. I knew carrying it with me was a good precaution, and it proved invaluable tonight. If it weren't for this, the outcome might have been very different."

Even though Vincent's expression was solemn, he sighed as he said. "Being unprepared is a major problem in our line of work, Martin. This assault marked the start. Keep your wits about you and make the most of every opportunity."

Standing nearby, Johnny Viola interjected, saying, "Vincent, this spider silk material—if we can produce it on a larger scale, it could revolutionize our security measures. It would provide us a major advantage and make our guys safer."

After giving a little nod, Vincent continued. "All in due time, Johnny. It took three years and the silk of 1,000,000 spiders to create this blanket. We are working on a synthetic version that we can possibly mass-produce. The need to incorporate innovation into our defenses is evident, considering tonight's events. Staying one step ahead of our enemies is of the utmost importance."

Vincent continued, "We have other projects in the works that I am excited about. We're developing transparent surveillance film, no bigger than a credit card, that will stick to anything and is barely noticeable. These 'stickers' can provide audio and video within a 5-meter range and allow for GPS tracking." Vincent paused to gauge everyone's reactions. "We also have a biological weapon of last resort that could immobilize any group. I hope it never comes to that."

An air of refocused resolve pervaded the space. Thanks to Vincent's vision and their state-of-the-art technology, they escaped the attack today. With the doctor's inspection complete, the room was filled with a collective will to overcome the challenges that the Capoli family will face to reclaim their rightful place as the head of New York's criminal underworld.

Martin looked at the cloth, then back at his father. "You always have a plan, don't you?"

Vincent managed a weary smile. "It pays to be prepared, son. Especially in our line of work."

The tension in the room began to ease as everyone realized that Vincent was indeed unharmed. The doctor finished his inspection, confirming that there were no injuries. "You're in the clear, Mr. Capoli. Just try to take it easy for a while."

Vincent nodded appreciatively. "Thank you, doctor. I'll do my best."

Martin placed a hand on his father's shoulder. "We were really worried, Dad. I'm glad you're okay."

Vincent patted his son's hand. "I know, Martin. And I appreciate it. But we need to stay strong and focused. This attack won't be the last. We need to be ready for anything."

Despite the close call, Vincent's resilience and preparedness had seen him through once again. The incident only reinforced their commitment to each other and their cause.

The car seemed shattered from the outside, but because of the tinted windows, the assailants could not tell from the outside if their plan had worked or not. The black Escalade had done its due diligence.

This particular Escalade was far from ordinary. With advanced armor plating, it could withstand various types of assaults, including gunfire. This level of protection was vital for someone like Vincent Capoli, whose life was constantly shadowed by threats inherent to his position at the helm of a powerful criminal empire.

This fortress on wheels was not just a means of transport; it was a critical part of his survival strategy that enabled him to move with confidence in a world rife with danger.

Vincent sat in the living room and explained how he had saved himself. "When the attack started, I knew I had to act fast," he began, glancing at his family and the doctor. "The Escalade has a small panel on the floor that conceals an emergency exit. Glancing frantically around, I spotted it and knew what I had to do."

He continued, his voice steady but intense. "I reached down and yanked it open and peered into the darkness below. I remembered the safety compartment. It was big enough to fit me well." Vincent paused, recalling the moment vividly. "I slid down into the hidden compartment just in time. Through the cracked window, I caught a glimpse of the attackers. Their faces were masked, and their eyes were cold and ruthless. This was no random attack; it was a calculated, methodical strike against our family."

"I could feel the determination of those men. They were out to send a message."

Martin and the others listened intently, understanding the gravity of the situation. Vincent's quick thinking and the hidden features of the Escalade had saved his life. His recounting of the events painted a clear picture of the danger they were up against and the cunning of their enemies.

As Vincent finished, he looked around at his family. "We need to stay vigilant. This won't be the last time they try something. We must be prepared for anything."

Vincent took a deep breath and looked around the room, his eyes settling on each of his family members and close associates. "I appreciate your concern, but I need everyone to leave now," he said firmly. "Martin, Johnny, stay with me. We need to talk."

The room slowly emptied as everyone obeyed Vincent's command. Once it was just the three of them, Vincent motioned for Martin and Johnny to follow him to his study. The heavy door closed behind them with a decisive thud, sealing them off from the rest of the house.

Vincent sat behind his large mahogany desk and gestured for Martin and Johnny to take the seats opposite him. The study was filled with the scent of leather and the soft glow of the fireplace, casting flickering shadows on the walls lined with books and family photos.

"Tonight was more than just an attack," Vincent began, his voice low and steady. "The Rossi clan has openly declared war on us. They've crossed a line, and now it's our solemn duty to respond. We must eradicate them to ensure the Capoli family's survival."

Martin leaned forward. His face was etched with determination. "I've been expecting this, Dad. What's the plan?"

Vincent nodded, appreciating his son's readiness. "First, we need to fortify our defenses. Increase security around all our properties and ensure our key people are protected. We can't afford any more surprises."

"We also need to gather intelligence and find how they managed to get so close. We have to cut off their resources and allies." Johnny Viola, the first lieutenant, spoke up.

"Agreed," Vincent said, thoughtfully tapping his fingers on the desk. "We'll hit them where it hurts. Disrupt their operations, take out their key players, and show them that coming after us was a grave mistake."

Martin's eyes gleamed with a fierce light. "I'll take care of the security arrangements. Johnny, can you handle the intel?"

Johnny nodded. "I have contacts who can help. We'll find out everything we need to know."

"This won't be easy. We're going to need everyone on high alert. The Rossi's are ruthless, and they won't back down easily." Vincent leaned back in his chair, feeling the weight of his decisions.

Martin placed a reassuring hand on his father's arm. "We're ready for this, Dad. We've been preparing for a long time."

I know, Martin. And that's why we'll come out on top. But we need to be smart about this. No reckless moves. Every step we take must be calculated." Vincent met his son's gaze, a proud smile tugging at the corners of his mouth.

Johnny added, "We should also consider reaching out to our allies. Make sure they know what's happening and where we stand. We can't afford to be isolated in this fight."

"Good point, Johnny. I'll make some calls and set up meetings. We must rally our supporters and ensure they're with us." Vincent nodded in agreement.

The room fell silent for a moment as the gravity of the situation sank in. Vincent looked at the two men he trusted most, feeling a renewed sense of determination.

"This is our moment," he said quietly but firmly. "The Rossi's have pushed us to the brink, but we will not fall. Together, we will ensure our legacy continues."

As they left the study to begin their preparations, Vincent felt a fierce resolve building within him. The Rossi's had started this war, but the Capolis would finish it.

***

A fog of bewilderment and disorientation obscured Isabella's vision as her eyes flitted open. She could feel the thick, stagnant air pulsating through her body as the car's engine hummed rhythmically. Her limbs were wrapped securely with duct tape, and panic washed over her as she realized she was imprisoned.

As she struggled to catch her breath, she attempted to move, but the tape refused to budge, limiting her range of motion and making it extremely difficult to breathe deeply. She frantically combed the shadows for any clues that would lead her to her kidnappers, but the trunk held nothing save for the stifling stillness and the distant murmurs of their captors from the front seat.

"Boss, we got the bitch tied up in the trunk," one of the men said, his voice gruff and menacing. "We're keeping her at the storehouse for now."

Isabella's heart pounded in her chest, the sound of her own pulse thundering in her ears. She knew she had to stay calm, to focus on her breathing, but the agonizing tightness around her chest made it nearly impossible.

As the car sped through the night, Isabella's mind raced, trying to piece together what had happened. One minute, she had been at the restaurant, waiting for Jake, and the next... nothing. Her memory was a hazy blur, and the more she tried to grasp at the fragments, the more elusive they became.

Suddenly, a surge of panic gripped her. *Jake*. What had happened to him? Was he safe? The thought of him worrying, searching for her, sent a fresh wave of terror coursing through her.

The duct tape around her wrists and ankles cut into her skin as she frantically struggled against them, her heart pounding in her chest. She tried to cry out, to let him know she was still alive, but her voice was muffled, barely more than a strangled whisper. The car continued to speed down the dark, winding road, the voices in the front seat growing louder and more agitated.

"Dammit, she's awake," one of the men growled, his voice dripping with malice. "We will just have to knock her ass back out."

"She is so lucky that the boss wants her to come in in one piece, or else I would be having fun with her."

Isabella's heart sank as she fought to stay conscious. Her mind raced with a thousand horrific possibilities. She struggled against the fog clouding her thoughts. Her body was heavy and unresponsive as she overheard their conversation. "What did they have planned for her? And what did this mysterious "boss" of theirs want with her?" Every instinct screamed at her to stay awake, but something in her bloodstream kept trying to pull her back under, making it harder to resist with each passing second.

As the car careened around a sharp turn, she felt her body slam against the side of the trunk, the impact knocking the breath from her lungs. She squeezed her eyes shut, willing herself to stay conscious, to keep fighting.

The voices in the front seat grew more frantic, and she could hear the sound of a phone being dialed. "Boss, we got a problem. The bitch is awake."

There was a moment of silence, then a deep, menacing voice crackled over the speaker. "Take care of it. And make sure she doesn't make a sound."

Isabella's blood ran cold, and she felt another wave of panic wash over her. She had to get out of this and had to find a way to escape. But as she struggled against the unyielding tape, she could feel her strength fading, the fog of whatever drug they had used to subdue her threatening to pull her back under.

The car came to a sudden stop, jolting her body forward. She heard the doors open and the sound of footsteps approaching the trunk. She braced herself for what was to come, her heart pounding in her chest.

"Get her out of there," the deep voice commanded.

***

The twilight bled across the Manhattan skyline, painting the city in hues of rose and gold. Roberto Rossi, perched in his opulent high-rise apartment, took a long drag from his Cuban cigar, the smoke curling into languid rings that mirrored the cityscape sprawling beneath him. Tonight, however, the usual warmth of the liquor failed to reach him. A knot of unease tightened in his gut, a premonition that things weren't quite going according to plan.

With a curt nod, he gestured towards the two figures standing before him. His son, Marco, swaggered in, his face bursting with news. "Dad," he said as he waited for a dramatic pause, "We got the woman of one of their colleagues. Remember that goddamn 'Jake' character that you told us to keep our eye on, we tracked them down. My men are taking her to one of the east side storehouses. "We will break her dad."

"Don't worry. Everything is under control."

Roberto looked bewildered for a second, then said, "You mean Jake, the asshole who roughed up our guys at the Flamingo room?" Marco nodded, then Roberto's gaze flickered briefly to his top advisor, a man whose steely demeanor and calculating eyes earned him the silent moniker 'The Wolf.'

The Wolf, ever the strategist, entered with a sigh that spoke volumes. "There's… a complication, boss," he began, his voice a low rumble. "We almost had him, but Capoli had his car armored up. That thing was a small tank. We had many heavy guns, but they were not able to penetrate the vehicle. The driver did get hit, but I am not sure if we took him out."

The wolf was a tough, mean bastard, but sweat flickered down his forehead as he started to worry about what the boss would do to him.

A vein pulsed on Roberto's temple. "You should have nuked the goddamn thing. Let's see if my gun penetrated through that thick skull of yours." He took out a gun and pointed it to the Wolf's head. "I should kill you for this incompetence, but I don't feel like cleaning up the mess." He threw the gun down on the sofa.

He slammed his glass down on the mahogany table, the crystal clinking ominously. "You put a show of force, you say? Let's hope it was enough to rattle that self-righteous asshole Vincent Capoli. They should be rattled with the amount of firepower and the number of men that we have posted near their personal residence."

Marco, oblivious to the tension crackling in the air, puffed out his chest. "That's right, Dad! We left a real mess for his boys to clean up. They won't forget this anytime soon."

Roberto fixed his son with a withering stare. "This isn't some playground brawl, Marco. This is a war. And Vincent... well, Vincent never forgets, and he never forgives." He took another long drag from his cigar, the air thick with the scent of tobacco and unspoken threats.

"The brawl in the Flamingo Room at The Dirty Bird started because we asked that self-righteous prick to let us deal some drugs out of his casinos, but he refused. Then, the stunt we pulled at Francesca's party was set into motion to let Vincent Capoli know that he is not untouchable and not even his kids are safe from me. But now we have reached the point of no return, and we need to make the Capolis understand that we are the apex predators. Now, this assassination attempt means that we've drawn first blood," he conceded a hint of steel in his voice. "But the game has only just begun. Get me every operative we have. We need a plan, a counter-offensive. We need to hit them where it hurts and make damn sure they understand – New York belongs to the Rossis."

The Wolf, ever the pragmatist, chimed in. "Agreed, boss. A misstep now could be catastrophic."

Roberto nodded curtly. The city lights twinkled below, oblivious to the storm brewing in the opulent apartment high above. But for Roberto Rossi and his men, the die was cast. The battle lines were drawn. And as the last embers of the cigar glowed red in the ashtray, a vow hung heavy in the air – a vow of vengeance, a vow of power, a vow that promised to paint the glittering cityscape with the blood of their enemies.

Chapter 8: Whispers of Disappearance

"Please be okay," Jake mumbled, uttering a small prayer. He had rushed back to his car right after receiving a call from Agent Jackson. The agent had just called him back with an urgent update. On the phone, they had exchanged a few tense words. Jake was now racing against time, his foot pressing harder on the gas pedal as the empty roads blurred by. The dark sky loomed overhead, mirroring the storm inside him. Minutes passed in what felt like a never-ending race, his grip tightening on the wheel as he fought to keep control of both the car and his spiraling thoughts.

Finally, Jake arrived and sat at a table, his head down, trying to catch his breath. He had driven for hours to get home and is now meeting with Agent Jackson in person to discuss Isabella's disappearance. As he started composing himself, his phone buzzed in his pocket. In an instant, he whipped it out, his heart pounding. It was his cousin, Titiano.

He sighed and shut his eyes briefly before accepting the call and answering with a sober "Hello."

"Jake, where are you?" Titiano's voice was filled with concern.

"I can't stay put, man. I need to fucking do something." Jake answered in an exasperated tone. "She is in trouble, I know it!" He anxiously explained to Titiano.

"I know, man, but you can't rush the police now, can you? They have their ways of doing these things. What are you doing right now anyway? You are supposed to wait for the police to call you. Are you back at the police station?" Titiano was curious about what his cousin was up to at the ungodly hour of the night.

"Nah, I rushed back to the estate right after the meeting at the Police Department. There is this Agent I know that works for the FBI… The Jackson guy I told you about?" Jake held his throbbing head in his free hand.

"Yeah, the agents that keep bugging you?" His cousin wondered.

"Yep. I needed to make sure I had all the information before meeting him." He rubbed his eyes some more. Jake was entirely exhausted.

"How did you get there so quickly?" Titiano asked, surprised. Then he paused, realizing the time. "Oh, right, it's late into the night."

Jake sighed, trying to focus his emotions. "Yeah, the roads were empty, so I didn't care about speed. I just needed to get here as fast as I could."

"Man, you must be exhausted," Titiano said sympathetically. "You've been pushing yourself too hard. Don't do anything crass. Remember, you have to be smart when dealing with all the different characters involved in this scenario. Stay focused, and you will be the one who finds her. You just need to be level-headed."

Jake leaned back in his chair, feeling the weight of the day pressing down on him. "I just... I can't stop, Titiano. I need to find her."

"I know, Jake, I know," Titiano's voice softened. "But you need to take care of yourself too. You will be no good to Isabella if you cannot function."

He closed his eyes, the fatigue and worry mixing together. "I just feel so helpless. Every minute counts, and I can't afford to waste any time." Jake's voice broke towards the end.

"Listen," Titiano said firmly, "you're doing everything you can. You got here quickly, you're meeting with the agent, and you're not giving up. That's what matters."

Jake nodded, even though Titiano couldn't see him. "Thanks, Titiano. I just... I needed to hear that."

"Anytime, cousin. Keep your head up. We're all in this together. Keep me updated, and don't go driving on the road like a mad—"

Before Titiano could finish, Jake cut the call. His attention snapped to the arrival of the FBI. Agent Jackson and his partner Patrick Flanagan arrived in a sleek black sedan, its polished surface gleaming under the streetlights. Jake watched as the car door opened, the darkness spilling out with the two agents. Jackson stepped out first, his demeanor calm and authoritative, exuding a quiet confidence that put Jake slightly at ease.

From the passenger seat, Patrick Flanagan shot Jake a withering glare. His eyes were filled with irritation. Jake could almost feel the annoyance radiating off him. As Flanagan got out of the car, Jackson leaned in close and murmured something into his ear. Whatever it was, it caused Agent Patrick to wave him off dismissively, though the sharpness in his gaze didn't soften.

Behind them, Susan Collins emerged, her expression one of quiet observation. She glanced between Jackson and Flanagan, and their little chat made her eyes narrow in confusion. The other agent, Patrick, seemed to share her bewilderment, looking at the exchange with raised eyebrows.

Jackson, unfazed, straightened his jacket and approached Jake. "Jake," he began, his voice steady and reassuring, "we're here to help you. But you need to tell us everything."

Collins stood back and watched the interaction with a mix of curiosity and concern, their presence adding to the tense atmosphere.

"Jake," Jackson began, his voice steady, "we're here to help you, but you need to tell us everything. Every detail matters."

There was a glimmer of optimism in Jake's mind as he nodded. With her notepad in hand, Susan Collins remained silently positioned next to Jackson. She gave Jake a quick nod, and her eyes remained focused and attentive. In the meantime, Patrick Flanagan appeared annoyed and clinging to a coffee mug as if it were his only means of survival. While Jackson was looking at Jake, he said, "You look like a mess." as he rolled his eyes and sighed.

"Jake, this is Agent Collins and Agent Flanagan, whom you already know." Jackson introduced. "They'll be assisting with the investigation." Collins nodded again, her pen poised to take notes, while Flanagan barely concealed his annoyance.

"Alright, start from the beginning," Jackson prompted.

Jake took a deep breath while explaining the sequence of events that led to Isabella's disappearance. While speaking, he became aware of Flanagan's attention, which was fixed on him, as if Jake were the one responsible for destroying his evening.

"So, after I told them about her phone tracker, they just asked me to wait!" After telling them the entire story, Jake complained, "I rushed to meet with you because I know something is wrong. I can sense it. The police portrayed it to be a petty fight between a couple, but we were not at all fighting. If anything, we actually became exclusive." Jake raised his hands in frustration, and Agent Jackson patted his shoulder to calm him down.

"Did you see anyone suspicious around?" Jackson asked, his tone professional.

"No, she just vanished into thin air!" Jake continued, his voice wavering slightly.

Collins scribbled furiously, her eyes not letting go of her notepad. She did not speak, her presence appearing almost spectral as she took in every word that was being said. Following a little pause, she raised her head and addressed Jake, saying, "Jake, please try to calm down and let us do our work. You are aware that the police carry out procedures through set regulations, but we do not operate under the same restrictions?"

Flanagan gave a resounding nod and continued, "Yeah, pay attention to what she has to say." We can handle this."

On the other hand, all it took was one intense look from Agent Jackson to silence Patrick before he could speak. Flanagan's enthusiasm evaporated, and he took a step back, looking chastened. Collins took a quick peek at Jackson before returning her attention to her notepad and carrying on with her careful and quiet note-taking.

Jackson leaned in, his expression serious. "Jake, I need you to understand something. Both you and Isabella could be in imminent danger. We can't rule out that this is retaliation for the bust at Wonderland."

Jake's stomach began to churn whenever the word "Wonderland" was mentioned. It was then that thoughts of the FBI raid came flooding back to him, and he grimly nodded his head.

The unpleasant talk that took place between Johnny Viola and Knuckles during game night at the Capoli residence was brought to his mind. They had been talking about how the Rossi family had a trafficking operation based out of the Wonderland Gentlemen's Club. Knuckles had only mentioned it, but Jake passed that information on to the FBI. At the moment, it appeared that those remarks, along with Jake's previous actions, were returning to haunt him.

"We're committed to finding Isabella," Jackson assured, "and we'll provide all the resources we can. We will also get in touch with the NYPD. Do you have any idea who else might be into this or be after Isabella?"

Patrick took a long sip of his coffee, then muttered, "Yeah, great. Another sleepless night chasing shadows."

Jake shot him a look but didn't respond. He couldn't afford to care about Flanagan's attitude right now.

"We need recent photos of Isabella and any other information that could help," Jackson said, ignoring Patrick's comment.

Jake promptly handed over his phone to them and displayed the most recent photographs that he had taken of Isabella. Collins accepted the phone and proceeded to examine each photograph in great detail before nodding and returning it to Jake.

"Thank you," she said quietly, finally breaking her silence. Her voice was soft but firm, and her eyes met Jake's with a hint of empathy.

Jackson stood up, signaling the end of their conversation. "Jake, go home and try to get some rest. Let us handle it from here."

Jake hesitated but then nodded. "Alright. I'll let Aunt Mary and Rodney know what happened."

As Jake turned to leave, he felt a hand on his shoulder. He looked up to see Jackson's reassuring smile. "We'll find her, Jake."

As he walked away, Patrick grumbled about the fact that he had not gotten enough sleep and that his coffee was cold. Collins, who had not yet spoken, gave Jake one last nod before turning around and heading back to the vehicle. Jake walked to his own car, feeling a mix of exhaustion and hope. He drove home, replaying the conversation in his mind. He had to trust the professionals now.

"Well, the fucking FBI knows about it. I wish there was something else I can do." Jake mumbled to himself. The thought of this being mingled with the Capoli's rushed to mind often through the drive, but he brushed it off. "There could be no way that is linked to this."

Jake pulled into the driveway and took a deep breath, ready to face Aunt Mary and Rodney with whatever strength he had left. Walking in, he noticed that everyone had gone to bed, so he decided to wait until the morning.

Johnny Viola, along with two associates, were dressed in dark suits as they rode the elevator to the top floor of One Manhattan Square, one of the most luxurious apartments New York had to offer. The elevator's soft hum did nothing to ease the tension in the air. Johnny's face was a mask of determination, his sharp eyes flickering with the weight of their task.

While they stood silently next to him, the associates, who were carrying big black boxes that were full of equipment, had expressions that were just as dreadful. While the elevator was climbing, Johnny's thoughts were racing through the careful strategy that Vincent Capoli had devised. For this next stage, Vincent recruited his most capable men, and he placed his faith in Johnny to take charge of the small group.

The elevator doors opened with a gentle ding, exposing the luxurious corridor leading to the suite on the highest floor. It was a luxurious experience to walk on the velvety carpet, and the walls were covered with excellent artwork that exuded an air of luxury. Johnny reached into his pocket and took out a key, feeling the metal on his skin. They used it to enter an expansive suite that took up the entire top floor of the building.

He turned to his associates, his voice a low growl. "Let's make this fast. We install the equipment and then get the hell out of here."

They gave a firm nod, their faces grim like they were set in stone. Johnny put the key in the lock and turned it. The loud click resounded down the empty hallway. They walked into the room and were blown away by how luxurious the penthouse was. The view from the floor-to-ceiling windows of the city skyline was amazing, but no one took the time to look at it.

Johnny told his men to go to the corners of the room and start setting up the tools efficiently. As he watched them work, his mind spun with thoughts. This job wasn't like any other; it was the next step in Vincent Capoli's plan. It was more important than ever, and failing was not an option.

As they began to look around, they noticed a small statue in one corner of the room and a clock on the wall that looked extremely expensive. Each man reached into his respective bag and pulled out an exact replica of the clock and the statue. They replaced the original items with their replicas, carefully placing the originals in their bags. Then they both took out what looked like a pack of transparent stickers, about the size of a credit card, and attached a few to the walls and furnishings in the main room and the kitchen.

Johnny spoke into his earpiece, "Boss, the packages are in place. Please confirm the visual."

Martin Capoli, who was waiting in a Maybach parked at a busy restaurant on the street corner, flipped through a few apps on his iPhone. He glanced at the live feed from the cameras they had just installed and responded, "Visual confirmed. I can see and hear everything in there."

Johnny nodded, relieved. He turned to his associates. "Alright, we're done here. Let's get out."

As they finished installing the last piece of equipment, Johnny felt a cold sweat trickle down his spine. He knew that once they left, the game would change, and there would be no turning back.

One of the associates, a burly man with a shaved head, glanced up at Johnny. "We're almost done here."

"Good," Johnny replied, scanning the room one last time. "We don't have much time."

Just as they were about to leave, one of the guys noticed a picture on the wall of Roberto Rossi shaking hands with the mayor of New York City, Eric Adams. Panic flashed in his eyes. "Johnny, do you know whose fucking apartment we just broke into?"

Johnny's heart skipped a beat, but he kept his voice steady. "Don't worry about it. This is a job, just like any other. I'm going to double your fee for all the trouble."

The associate looked at Johnny, doubt still etched on his face, but he nodded. They slipped out of the suite as quietly as they had entered, the door closing with a soft click behind them. Back in the elevator, Johnny's heart pounded as they descended, each floor bringing them closer to the uncertain future that awaited them.

As they reached the lobby, Johnny turned to his men. "My Uber is going to be about 25 minutes out. Can you give me a ride to the restaurant down the street?"

The two men, still nervous, exchanged glances but knew this job was a big payday. They agreed to drop Johnny off.

The drive to the restaurant was nervously tense, the city's lights flashing by as they cruised through the streets. Johnny's mind raced with the implications of their actions, but being in the mob for so long, he knew how to stay calm in these situations. When they arrived at the restaurant, Johnny instructed them, "Go to the top of the parking garage. I'll go into the restaurant from a private entrance."

The men nodded, their faces taut with anxiety. They pulled into the parking garage, the car's tires squealing slightly on the concrete. "Good job tonight," he said, trying to ease their nerves. "We will be in touch about your bonus payment."

When the men got to the very top of the parking garage, it was dark. The city lights below barely reached this high, casting long, eerie shadows. Johnny instructed them to park in his assigned stall, a spot tucked away from the main traffic. As the car came to a stop, Johnny's mind raced, calculating every move he was about to make.

"Alright, guys," Johnny said, forcing a smile. "Thanks for the ride."

One of the men, the burly one with the shaved head, glanced at Johnny through the rearview mirror. "No problem, Johnny. Are we all good now?"

Johnny nodded, his expression blank, and replied, "Yeah, we're all good." As he got out, smoothing his suit and giving them a nod of reassurance.

He reached into the pocket of his jacket, feeling the cold metal of the Glock against his fingers, as his emotions went cold, and he turned his mind off. He moved quickly and shot both men in the head. Two bullets, each with pinpoint accuracy in the time it took for a normal person to sneeze. The noise resulted in a series of loud bangs, and then everything fell silent.

Johnny stood there for a moment, glancing around to make sure that the top floor of the parking garage was empty. The men slumped in their seats, their lifeless eyes staring blankly ahead. The death toll in this war could be massive, and sacrifices had to be made. Johnny took a deep breath and composed himself, as he had become accustomed to making these types of moves for the family over the years. There could be no loose ends. He walked over to their dead bodies and performed a quick inspection to make sure that their lights were out.

Johnny quickly popped open the trunk and pulled out a thick dark cover that he draped over the entire car. He then pulled out a cloth and applied a solution that he carried in his jacket pocket. He then used it to thoroughly clean his face, his hands, and jacket to remove any gunpowder residue or splatter. He didn't waste any time and walked straight toward the restaurant's private door. His mind was already racing with ideas for the next part of the plan. He tapped his earpiece as he got closer to the door and focused his demeanor with a sense of urgency.

"Martin," he said, his voice calm and steady despite the adrenaline coursing through his veins. "I just wrapped up all the loose ends. Meet me inside for cocktails, and let's get the cleanup crew to deal with the mess."

There was a brief pause, and then Martin's voice came through the earpiece, smooth and unbothered. "Understood, Johnny. I'll be there in a few minutes. Good work."

The only sound in the dimly lighted hallway was Johnny's footsteps echoing back to him. Pushing open the door, he entered the restaurant, the soothing music and bright light a welcome change from the dark, frigid garage he had just left. He sensed a tiny release of tension as he walked in, but he knew the evening was far from done.

He moved toward the bar, taking in the space with wide eyes. With a few late-night customers strewn about, the restaurant was rather deserted. As Johnny walked up, the bartender looked up and nodded to him.

"Evening, Mr. Viola. What can I get for you?"

"Whiskey, neat," Johnny replied, his voice steady. He needed something strong to turn off the killing machine and bring him back to reality.

As the bartender poured the drink, Johnny felt his phone vibrate in his pocket. He pulled it out and saw a message from Martin: "On my way up. Cleanup crew dispatched."

Johnny took a deep breath and felt at ease about the job being done on time. The bartender placed the glass of whiskey in front of him, and Johnny took it with a nod of thanks. He took a sip, the burn of the alcohol a welcome distraction from the thoughts swirling in his mind.

Martin entered the restaurant with a powerful and self-assured presence a few minutes after the door opened. He approached Johnny as soon as he caught his eye at the bar. "Johnny," Martin said, clapping him on the back. "Everything handled?"

Johnny nodded, taking another sip of his whiskey. "Yeah, it's done. No loose ends."

"Good," Martin replied, signaling to the bartender for a drink. "Now, let's get some drinks and talk about the next steps."

Johnny forced a smile, though his mind was still racing. The night was far from over, and the weight of it all was sending Johny into a state of ruthlessness and frenzy.

***

Isabella's Dream

Trapped in a deep state of unconsciousness, Isabella started to dream. She was at the restaurant with Jake and started feeling sick. Isabella staggered into a restroom, her head looming over the sink as she suddenly started feeling a sudden wave of nausea like she was about to pass out. Suddenly, a muscular woman arrived out of nowhere and seized Isabella with hands that felt like iron. Before Isabella could say anything, the woman stabbed her in the neck with a needle as the pain pierced all her senses, and then everything went dark.

"Jaa…" Before she could scream, the darkness had crept in.

Isabella could feel herself being transported through a heavy, murky atmosphere in the darkness. The air was thick, making every breath seem like icy smoke. She could hear muffled, warped echoes all around her, like she was being sent on a one-way trip to hell. Through the darkness, she could hear the echoes of evil men.

"Boss, we have the bitch tied up!" one shouted, his words reverberating through the void, each echo more menacing than the last.

A bone-chilling cold seeped into her very core, freezing her from the inside out. She looked around in horror as the River Hades materialized before her, its dark, swirling waters whispering of doom and despair. The river seemed to pull her towards it, promising a one-way trip to purgatory. Its currents were slow, relentless, dragging her deeper into the shadows.

The stillness was suffocating. She felt as if she were trapped in a never-ending void, where time stood still, and hope was a distant memory. The cold was unlike anything she had ever felt, a biting, all-encompassing frost that made her bones ache and her spirit waver. It was a cold that spoke of death, a chill that whispered finality into her soul.

Isabella knew she was dead or at least caught between life and death. Her mind screamed for escape, but her body felt heavy and unresponsive. Every second in this icy limbo stretched into an eternity, the darkness pressing down on her, squeezing the life from her lungs.

Even though it was very quiet, something moved. There was a weak pulse, a flicker of warmth, that fought back against the cold. At first, it was weak and hard to notice, but over time, it got louder and more insistent. It seemed like her very being was fighting against the darkness to get back for the light.

The cold got stronger and wrapped around her like a vice as if it could feel her struggle and wanted to put it out. The whispers got louder and more evil as the darkness got darker. The cold clawed at her, trying to pull her back into the abyss, and her body shook uncontrollably.

As she fought her way back, her eyes opened slowly. She had awakened, soaked in sweat, and her breathing was all over the place. Every time she took a breath, it felt like a fight. Her chest heaved as she tried to stay steady. Even though the room was dark and strange, she was no longer in that heavy void. She was still scared from the dream, but she was back in real life and desperately trying to hold on to the thin threads of truth.

Her hand reached up, trembling, to find an iron collar locked around her neck. A heavy chain attached to the collar led to the wall, anchoring her in place. Panic set in as she tried to stand, realizing with horror that she was completely naked.

The room around her was pitch black. She couldn't see her hands even when she held them directly in front of her face. The air was cold and damp; the only sound was the faint, haunting whisper of someone crying in the distance. She strained her ears, trying to make sense of her surroundings, but the darkness was impenetrable.

Isabella's breath came in short, ragged gasps. She was shaking from the inside out, tears streaming down her face. She covered her mouth with her hand, trying desperately not to make a sound. Her mind raced with fear and confusion. Where was she? Why was this happening?

"Jake," she whispered, her voice trembling. "Jake, where are you? Please, find me."

She closed her eyes, trying to summon his face in her mind. The thought of him brought a fresh wave of tears, and she missed him so much it hurt. He had always been her rock, the one person she could rely on no matter what. She thought about when they were together at the restaurant, his reassuring smile, the warmth of his embrace. She clung to those thoughts, using them to keep the fear at bay.

The whispers in the distance grew louder, and she could make out more voices now, muffled and indistinct. She strained to hear, hoping for some clue about where she was or what was happening. But the darkness was absolute, and the whispers only added to her fear.

"Please, God," she prayed, her voice barely a whisper. " Please help me get out of here."

She tried to move again, testing the strength of the chain. It held fast and unyielding as she felt around the floor, hoping to find something, anything, that could help her. But there was nothing, just cold, hard stone.

The crying in the distance continued, a haunting reminder of her own helplessness. She wondered who else was here and what horrors they were enduring. The thought made her stomach churn with fear and disgust.

She hugged her knees to her chest, trying to make herself as small as possible. The darkness pressed in around her, suffocating and relentless. She felt utterly alone, trapped in a nightmare with no end in sight. The cold stone floor bit into her skin, and the iron collar around her neck felt heavier with each passing second. She closed her eyes, focusing on Jake's face, his warm smile, and the way he made her feel safe. She clung to those thoughts, using them as a lifeline in the overwhelming darkness.

Her thoughts drifted back to the muscular woman who had attacked her. Who was she? Why had she done this? The questions swirled in Isabella's mind, adding to her confusion and terror. She tried to piece together what had happened, but it all felt so unreal, like a twisted dream.

She forced herself to take deep breaths, trying to calm her racing heart. She couldn't afford to lose hope, not now. She had to believe that Jake would come for her, that he would find a way to rescue her from this nightmare. As she tried to stand, a wave of cold reality hit her—she was completely naked. The room around her was pitch dark, the kind of darkness that swallowed everything.

She stretched out her hands, attempting to get her bearings, but she couldn't even see them in front of her face. Panic clawed at her chest as she realized she was alone in what felt like a damp, musty cellar. The air was thick and oppressive, filled with the scent of mold and decay.

In the silence, she could hear faint whispers and the sound of someone crying in the distance. The cries were soft, almost ghostly, and they sent chills down her spine. She strained her ears, trying to make out any other sounds, but the darkness seemed to swallow everything else.

Her body began to shake uncontrollably, the terror and cold seeping into her bones. Tears started to flow, hot and fast, burning trails down her cheeks. She clamped her hand over her mouth, desperate to stifle her sobs. The last thing she wanted was to draw attention to herself.

Isabella's mind raced with the images of her capture and the dream she had just awoken from playing on a loop. The muscular woman, the needle, the darkness—it all felt too real. She prayed silently, her thoughts a jumbled mess of fear and hope.

"Please, Jake," she whispered into the void, her voice barely audible. "Please find me." The whispers in the distance continued, a haunting backdrop to her silent prayers. Isabella knew she had to stay strong, for herself and for Jake. She couldn't let the darkness win. She had to hold on to the hope that Jake was looking for her somewhere out there and he wouldn't stop until he found her.

Jake was sprawled across the floor. His body was wracked with intense pain shooting up his torso from doing 300 sit-ups in the immaculate gym on his aunt's estate. Sweat poured off him, soaking the mat beneath as he gasped for breath. His mind, seeking refuge from the present agony, drifted back to a point ten years earlier.

He was in the dojo with his sensei, Randy, being forced to sit on the floor in seiza for hours while holding two glasses of water in each hand. The memory was vivid. Every time his arms tired and the water began to drop, Randy would whack him on the head with a shinai. The sound of the bamboo stick cracking against his skull echoed in his mind, mingling with Randy's relentless voice yelling, "Focus!" The pain in his arms and shoulders had been unbearable, but his mind and willpower refused to let him drop the glasses. That lesson in endurance and focus had never left him.

Now, Jake was channeling that same intensity, working out like a madman in order to push his limits. He pushed heavy weights, his muscles screaming in protest. His eyes kept flicking to the clock, counting down until he could officially report Isabella missing. He had to wait 24 hours, a cruel eternity in his mind where he felt every second.

Horrible scenarios ran through his head, each one worse than the last. He saw Isabella trapped, hurt, calling out for him. He saw her in the hands of people who would do unspeakable things. Each vision fueled his workout, pushing him to lift more, to push harder. He needed the physical pain to drown out the mental torment.

Minutes passed like hours as he desperately planned how he could get Isabella back. His mind raced, crafting and discarding plans, searching for any clue, any hint of where she might be. The ache in his heart was far worse than the pain in his muscles. He grabbed his phone and texted Agent Jackson.

"Can I be actively involved in the search for Isabella?" He typed, his fingers moving fast as he stared at the screen, willing a reply to come.

Time crawled as seconds felt like hours, and Jake's mind refused to be still, with each heartbeat a reminder of Isabella's absence. He dropped to the floor and started another set of sit-ups, pushing his body to the brink. The pain was a distraction but a necessary escape.

As he finished up, a special alert from Channel 6 News flashed on the television. Jake's inner psyche commanded his attention because there was something familiar about this newscast. He grabbed the remote and turned up the volume, his eyes glued to the screen.

The reporter was outlining two strange and disturbing occurrences that had taken place recently.

"In Kansas City," she began, "a patient was dropped off at a hospital in critical condition. Portions of his arms had been surgically removed at the elbows, and portions of his legs had been surgically removed at the knees. Medical staff are baffled by the precision of the amputations."

Jake felt a slight shiver run down his spine as his brain comprehended the gruesome details that unfolded.

"Police have also made a horrifying connection," the reporter continued, "in Atlanta, Georgia, another individual was mysteriously delivered to an emergency room. Portions of his spine had been surgically removed, rendering him unable to stand or sit up. In both cases, their tongues had also been surgically removed, leaving them unable to communicate."

The reporter's voice maintained its professional tone, but the underlying horror was palpable. "Authorities are investigating these cases as potential acts of torture due to the surgical precision involved and the specific nature of the injuries."

As she spoke, the segment transitioned to show pictures of the two men. Jake felt a wave of anxiety for a second as he forgot how to breathe. He recognized them instantly. These were the same two amateur thugs that he had encountered at Francesca's birthday party who had come there specifically to grope and harass her.

Thoughts of that night came rushing back and how he ended up in a fight with these thugs while defending Francesca's honor. The last he heard was that these guys went to jail and then were bailed out. Jake's mind raced, piecing together the clues, and then, all at once, he came to a strange realization. This had to be the result of these guys challenging the Capoli family, and the brutal, calculated nature of these mutilations seemed to be unmistakable mob-style retribution. Instead of fear, Jake felt a strange thought forming in his mind—maybe the Capolis were the ones who could help him get Isabella back.

The thought was unsettling, but Jake couldn't shake it. The Capolis had resources, connections, and a ruthless efficiency that could be precisely what he needed. His mind whirled with the possibilities, and a cold determination began to settle in his chest.

He needed to find out more. If the Capolis were involved, he had to figure out how to use that to his advantage. The news segment ended, but Jake's mind was far from calm. His pulse raced with a mix of fear and hope, his thoughts a tangled web of plans and uncertainties.

As he stood there, staring at the now-muted television, the gravity of the situation pressed down on him. He needed to act, and he needed to act fast. The Capolis were dangerous, but they might also be his best chance at finding Isabella.

***

FBI Bureau Chief Sean Brady was on a call with Agent Jackson, Patrick Flanagan, and Susan Collins. The mood in the room was tense, the weight of their recent meeting with Jake pressing heavily on everyone. "Alright, let's go over this again," Brady's voice crackled through the speaker. "Jake's friend from college has disappeared, and all our Intel points to the Rossi clan. What's our next move?"

Agent Jackson leaned back in his chair, his eyes narrowing. "We met with Jake, and he's desperate. His friend Isabella is from California, and her disappearance is making waves. Jake's aunt is powerful, and we can't afford a PR disaster."

Susan Collins, who had been taking meticulous notes, looked up. "Chief, why is Patrick so off-tempered with Jake? It's not helping the situation."

Before Patrick could respond, Agent Jackson chuckled. "Oh, they got off on the wrong foot. Some miscommunication over the delivery of a glazed donut." He chuckled, but she just raised an eyebrow and returned to the topic unamused.

Patrick grunted, clearly not appreciating the joke. "Let's focus on the task at hand."

"Agreed," Brady said, his tone sharp. "We need to tread carefully. The Rossi clan is dangerous, but we have an opportunity here. Use the Wonderland bust as the reason for the raids. We need to hit their known criminal businesses hard. While we're at it, let's see if we can dig up any information about Isabella."

Jackson nodded, his mind already working through the logistics. "We know their operations are spread out. Roberto Rossi has fingers in many pies. We can start with his clubs and warehouses."

"I want coordinated raids. No room for mistakes. Collins, you're on Intel. Flanagan, you'll lead the tactical team. Jackson coordinated the efforts on the ground. We need to find out what happened to Isabella, but we also need to make sure we're not blowing our cover." Brady's voice was firm.

"Chief, we have a few leads on their operations. I've been following their money trail. Rossi's got several businesses that are fronts for illegal activities. If we hit them simultaneously, we might catch them off guard." Collins spoke up with a steady voice.

"Good work, Collins," Brady said, his tone approving. "We need to move fast. The longer Isabella is missing, the colder the trail gets. And we can't afford to have Jake or his aunt making too much noise about this."

Patrick leaned forward, his expression serious. "We have to be prepared for resistance. Rossi's men are heavily armed and won't go down without a fight."

Jackson agreed and nodded. "Things have been worse. But we need to be smart about this. We can't have any deaths on our end."

"I know it's hard, but Isabella needs to come back." It's the right thing to do, not just for Jake. Let us show these crooks they can't get away with this," Brady answered in a softer tone.

There was a moment of silence as everyone absorbed the weight of the mission ahead. The tension was palpable, but so was the resolve.

"Let's get to work," Brady said finally. "I want updates every hour. And remember, this isn't just about taking down the Rossi clan. It's about finding Isabella and bringing her home safe."

When the call finished, the agents looked at each other with determination. Collins went back to work. She quickly typed on the keyboard to look up maps and bank records. Patrick took a look at his gear and started gathering tactical equipment for the upcoming battle. Jackson started to call people to plan the raids' details. The trio began to get ready, and the weight of their task became clear, which was to find Isabella and bring her home No matter what.

***

In the opulent office that Vincent Capoli had occupied, the lights had been dimmed to the point that they gave the space an air of solemnity. He was participating in a conference call, and his tone was composed and authoritative. His ever-loyal enforcer, Knuckles McGee, a huge figure of muscle and terror, sat across from him. He maintained his loyalty. A palpable sense of expectation pervaded the atmosphere.

"Tim, phase one of our counter-offensive is complete," Vincent said, his voice smooth and composed. "We now have full surveillance capabilities on Roberto Rossi's main residence."

Tim Scott's voice crackled through the speakerphone, confident and resolute. "Good to hear, Vincent. I'm in the process of getting the rest of the puzzle pieces together. We'll be ready to bring the fight to Roberto soon."

Vincent leaned back in his chair. Remember how we first connected, Tim? "How did our lives intersect, and how did that alter everything?"

From the other end, Tim let out a chuckle. "Difficult to forget!" I was a prominent attorney who worked for one of your companies during that time. Following that, I was suddenly accused of the suspected murder of my fiancee. This came out of nowhere. The circumstances surrounding her disappearance were shrouded in mystery."

Knuckles shifted slightly, his attention focused on the conversation. Johnny Viola, leaning casually against the wall, was also interested in hearing this story. The fight against Rossi was at last starting, and he couldn't wait to get his hands dirty again and be in the middle of the conflict.

"You were in a tight spot," Vincent continued, his eyes narrowing slightly as he recalled the past. "Because you were my employee, I couldn't let that scandal bring unwanted attention to our operations."

Tim's voice softened, the gratitude evident. "You found her, Vincent. My fiancée had run away with someone else, trying to set me up to collect on her own death insurance policy. You made her confess. You saved my life and my career."

Vincent nodded. "It was the right thing to do. And now, your loyalty to me is something I value deeply."

In the years since then, Tim has dedicated his profession and time to ensuring that Vincent's businesses and operations were insulated from any attacks from law enforcement or other mob interests. Vincent gave a quick nod to Johnny and Knuckles, who were listening intently and then returned his focus to the call being made. "Tim, I have faith that you will organize things on time. It is optimal that we dismantle Rossi's operations as quickly as possible."

Tim's tone was consistent. And without a doubt, Vincent. I owe that to you completely. We are going to take him down, one piece at a time.

Johnny observed Vincent with a mixture of admiration and reverence because, at this point, he was utilizing the tactical skills of a four-star general. Vincent Capoli was in complete command of the situation. In addition to his rigorous planning, his self-assurance was immovable. Despite the fact that Knuckles is often a stoic figure, he glanced at Vincent with an expression that exuded respect.

Vincent's thoughts were racing as he considered the many methods and tactics that they would employ. This was just the beginning of the surveillance that was conducted on Rossi's apartment. Every action was precisely planned, and every move was calculated. Considering that there was no room for error, he would make certain that none of them occurred.

Following the continuation of the call, Tim went into depth about the actions he was taking in order to acquire the remaining intelligence that was required. Vincent paid close attention, his thoughts already two steps ahead of the conversation. He was well aware that bringing Rossi down would eliminate a potentially deadly competitor and send a strong message to anyone who had the audacity to compete in the future.

As the call came to an end, Vincent responded to Tim by saying, "Keep me updated." We may be quickly approaching the end game, and a calculated strike might just end this conflict.

The room was completely silent as soon as he concluded the conversation. In anticipation of Vincent's subsequent directive, Johnny and Knuckles both kept a close eye on him. Vincent rose to his feet, and his aura made him appear as if he were 10 feet tall. The metropolis he ruled with an iron grip was in his sights as he made his way to the window and looked over it. A familiar quote that he had read as a child filled Vincent's mind for a second: "Strength and courage are my virtues as I carry the weight of life."

Johnny, who was Vincent's left hand, was always characterized as being an unpredictable loudmouth and hot head, but just as these qualities displayed passion, he was extremely loyal and ready to further the Capoli agenda no matter the cost. Knuckles was seen as Vincent's right hand, a strong tactical thinker whose massive build and strategic muscle represented the strength of the family.

It was obvious to everyone in the room that Vincent Capoli was in command of the situation. All of the rules had been established, the game was ready to be played, and Vincent was prepared to guide them to victory.

***

Extremely cold, to the point of bone-chilling. Isabella experienced the sensation of being confined within a horrible refrigerator. She was curled up into a tight ball and shivering violently. Her tears mixed with the dirt that was on her face, which was badly bruised. Her body was covered in a multitude of scratches and bruises, each one serving as a terrible reminder of the trauma that she was unable to recall in its entirety. Every time she moved, the tight metal collar that was around her neck and binding her like some kind of animal made her feel as if she was being choked.

She struggled to piece together how she had ended up in this nightmare, but her memories were a foggy, jumbled mess. One thing was clear, though: unless a miracle happened, someone was certainly coming to get her. And they were going to violate her in the worst way possible if they hadn't already. The thought made her stomach churn, and fresh waves of tears streamed down her cheeks.

The faces of Isabella's parents flashed in her mind, their worried expressions haunting her. In all the confusion, she did not know how many days had elapsed since she had been captured. By now, they had to know that she was missing. Isabella could not bear the thought of them not knowing what had happened to her.

Then, her thoughts shifted to Jake. "Oh God, Jake," she sobbed, her heart aching. "Please be safe. Please, don't let anything have happened to him."

The idea that Jake might be suffering the same fate, or worse, was unbearable. Was he also in chains, in some dark, cold place? Or had he been killed? The questions gnawed at her, each one more terrifying than the last.

"Jake," she cried out softly, her voice breaking. "Please, if you're out there, come find me. I need you."

Her mind drifted to the stories she had heard about people who disappeared into darkness. Did any of them ever come back unscathed? Or were they all lost forever, broken and destroyed? The thought made her shudder. "Is this what happens to people who disappear?" she murmured to herself. "Do they ever come back? Or am I doomed to stay here, alone and scared?"

As she moved, the cold metal of her collar cut into her neck, a continual reminder of her shackle. To no avail, she embraced herself even more firmly in an effort to stave off the chill and the terror. In addition to the physical agony, the shame of her predicament was a terrible aching. Her humanity and dignity were snatched away as she was ensnared and rendered powerless, like an animal.

Anger and despair tore at her soul. Her hands quivered as she strained to free the collar. As she desperately tried to free herself, her nails dug into her own flesh, and her fingers clawed at the metal. However, the collar remained steadfast, its hold firm and unbreakable. As she tugged on it, the biting depth increased, causing her neck to ache in excruciating anguish.

"Please, let me go," she pleaded, her voice quivering. "Please, let me go."

No matter how much she clawed at the collar, it would not budge. The metal was excessively robust and stable. As her fingers lost grip on the slippery surface, her feelings of helplessness and embarrassment intensified. Even this most fundamental constraint became too much for her to overcome.

Her eyes welled up with hot, bitter tears. As she drained her vitality from each one, it was as if her hope were dwindling. The shame of her incarceration was like a stifling oppressor; it made her feel helpless and diminutive. She was defenseless, exposed, and held captive by her assailants.

The icy, black walls reverberated with Isabella's low sobs. She was so distraught that she shook from head to toe as she buried her face in her knees. Defeated and crushed, she had never felt worse. Beyond its practical function as a restriction, the collar around her neck served as a powerful emblem of her captivity and an ever-present reminder of her powerlessness.

She screamed, "Why is this happening to me?" but her voice hardly carried. "What the hell did I do to deserve this?"

"Please, God," she whispered, her voice barely audible. "Help me. Get me out of here. I don't want to die like this."

She tried to think positively, to hold on to the hope that someone would find her. Maybe Jake was already looking for her, refusing to give up until he brought her home. The thought gave her a small glimmer of hope, but the harsh reality of her situation quickly overshadowed it.

The darkness around her seemed to close in, pressing down on her with a suffocating weight. She could hear the faint sound of someone crying in the distance, a haunting echo that made her feel even more isolated.

"Who else is here?" She wondered aloud, her voice shaking. "Are they suffering like me?"

She wished she could reach out to them to offer some kind of comfort. But she was trapped, just as they were, and there was nothing she could do. The helplessness was overwhelming.

As she lay there, curled up on the cold, hard floor, Isabella tried to cling to the memories of happier times. She thought about the times she and Jake had spent together, laughing and loving each other. Those memories were her only solace in this dark, terrifying place.

But the fear was relentless, and the cold seeped into her very bones. She felt like she was slipping away, her hope dwindling with each passing moment. She needed to stay strong for herself and for Jake. But it was getting harder with every second.

"Please," she prayed, her voice a desperate plea. "Don't let this be the end. I want to see Jake again. I want to go home."

The tears continued to flow, her sobs echoing in the darkness. She didn't know how long she could hold on, but she knew she had to try. For Jake, for her parents, for herself. She had to keep fighting, even if it felt like she was fighting a losing battle.

***

Roberto Rossi was having dinner with an attractive young woman on his private yacht off the coast of New England. The evening was calm, the gentle sway of the ocean creating a soothing backdrop for their intimate meal.

The woman, with her long, flowing hair and sparkling eyes, leaned in close, a playful smile on her lips. "Roberto, you have to try this," she purred, holding a forkful of pasta up to his mouth. "It's simply divine."

While she fed him, Roberto smiled and shrugged. With his eyes never taking off of hers, he enjoyed the smooth taste. Without raising his voice, he said, "Delicious." "But not as captivating as you."

Her cheeks turned a little red as she laughed. "Oh, you flatter me, Roberto." Along the back of his hand, she ran her finger. "What else can I do to make your evening more enjoyable?"

Roberto looked at her with laughter in his eyes. " Darling, just be yourself. That is more than enough."

The chief stewardess arrived at that precise moment, her posture conveying a courteous attitude. "Sir, you have an urgent phone call," she whispered as she gently came in closer to him.

When Roberto made his way to a private room, his dazzling smile began to fade as he excused himself from the situation. The expression on his face became sterner when he picked up the phone. He questioned, "What exactly is it?"

"Boss, the FBI is at it again," the voice on the other end said, tense and hurried. "They just came in with a search warrant and tore up the place."

Roberto's jaw tightened. "I knew sooner or later those fools would come looking into my locations ever since that fiasco at Wonderland. But they will find nothing. I've been working overtime to move my operations around and clear out anything the FBI would think to look for."

The man on the other end hesitated. "Boss, one of the agents had a picture of a girl they asked one of our guys about. Beautiful, long dark hair, Mexican, looks like she's around 23. One of the guys overheard the FBI agents refer to her as Isabella."

Immediately, Roberto felt a shiver run down his spine. It turned out that his gut feelings were correct when he suspected that the Jake figure had anything to do with the Wonderland security breach. The only reason the FBI would start looking for Isabella is if they discovered that she had some sort of connection to Jake.

"Damn it," Roberto muttered under his breath. "Jake."

Roberto's mind raced. He knew the implications of the FBI's interest in Isabella. She was leverage, a way to get to Jake. He couldn't allow their search for Isabella to put him under more scrutiny, but he also needed to find out what Isabella knew. He needed to act fast.

"I want her alive," Roberto said, his voice cold and calculated. "I need to handle this personally. Make sure no one touches her."

"Understood, boss," the voice replied. "We'll keep her untouched."

Roberto hung up and immediately dialed another number. His expression was one of ruthless determination as he waited for the call to connect. When it did, his voice was direct. "I want Isabella kept alive. No one touches her. I'll deal with her myself."

The man on the other end hesitated, sensing the urgency in Roberto's tone. "Yes, boss. We'll make sure she's unharmed."

Roberto ended the call, his mind already strategizing his next move. He couldn't afford any mistakes. Isabella was the key to getting back at Jake and the FBI. He needed to extract every bit of information she had, and he wanted to be the one to break her.

As he returned to the dinner table, his charming facade slipped back into place. The young woman looked up at him, her smile curious. "Is everything alright, Roberto?"

"Just some business," he said smoothly, taking his seat. "Nothing that can't wait."

But in his mind, the wheels were already turning. He would get to the bottom of this, and he would make sure that Jake and the FBI paid dearly for crossing him. His instincts had been right, and now it was time to act on them.

He poured himself a glass of wine, lifting it to his lips with a calm, controlled motion. The battle had begun, and Roberto Rossi was ready to fight. The evening's serenity was a stark contrast to the storm brewing inside him. He was determined, ruthless, and ready to do whatever it took to maintain his empire and exact his revenge.

Chapter 9: Blood Bonds

A few days went by, though Isabella couldn't tell exactly how long because, in the pitch darkness, time seemed to stand still. The cold was relentless, and the hope that someone would save her was dwindling. Sometimes, she would lose the feeling in her hands and feet, and the numbness would spread and consume her like an unwelcome guest.

The swollen eyes ached from crying nonstop, while hunger carried out constant pangs in her stomach in the form of protest. She hadn't eaten for what felt like an eternity, and her body had become weak and trembled from deficiency. Each minute dragged on and blended into nothingness.

Thinking about how many days had passed, she rubbed her hands in a cold corner when three men stormed into the room. The sudden onslaught of blinding lights made Isabella wince and squeeze her eyes shut. The harsh light burned through her eyelids, leaving her temporarily blinded. She could hear the men moving around her, their footsteps heavy and their voices loud and cruel.

"Get up, you dog!" one of them yelled, his voice shrill and grating. "But not just any dog. We have ourselves a bitch here, folks!" One of the gruff men with the huge flashlight let out a throaty laugh and deliberately shined the light in her eyes.

Isabella flinched at the insult, her heart racing. She could barely see anything through the intense brightness; her world was reduced to a haze of light and shadows. Cold water suddenly drenched her, the shock of it making her gasp and shiver violently. The icy water soaked her naked body and chilled her to the bone.

Another voice chimed in, this one rough and gravelly. "What kind of dog do you think she is? I say she's a Chihuahua, weak and pathetic."

"No way," the shrill-voiced man argued. "She's more like a German Shepherd, acting tough but still just a bitch."

The third man, who smelled strongly of weed and wore a brown leather jacket, laughed. "It doesn't matter what kind of dog she is. She's nothing."

She struggled to catch her breath, the cold water making her teeth chatter uncontrollably. She could barely make out their figures through the blinding light, but she could feel their presence, looming and oppressive.

The man with the goatee and high voice knelt down beside her, his face close to hers. "You hear that, bitch? You're nothing!"

The most muscular of the three seemed to hold some authority over the others. He stepped forward with a heavy bag in his hand. "Enough talk," he growled, his voice deep and commanding. "Feed her."

The others fell silent as he produced a packet of dog food, the crinkling sound of the bag echoing in the stark room. He poured the contents into a bowl, the dry kibble rattling as it fell. Isabella's stomach churned with a mix of hunger and disgust.

The man in the brown leather jacket shoved the bowl toward her, spilling some kibble onto the floor. "Eat up, bitch. It's all you're getting."

Isabella stared at the bowl, her vision slowly adjusting to the light. Seeing the dog food made her stomach twist in revulsion, but hunger gnawed at her insides. Her hands trembled as she reached for the bowl, her fingers brushing against the cold metal.

"Look at her," the man with the goatee sneered. "Pathetic."

Isabella's body was shaking with fear and shame, and her tears mixed with the cold water running out of her hair. Instead of giving up in the face of shame, she became like a fire. With a sneer, she grabbed a piece of the food and threw it at the man in the brown leather jacket.

"This is not fit for human consumption," she defiantly spoke out, her voice strong despite her trembling body. "I am a person, not an animal."

The big, mean man stared at her with dark, merciless eyes. "Eat," he commanded, his tone leaving no room for argument. "You want to survive, don't you?"

Isabella's stomach growled, but she refused to give in. "I will do no such thing," she retorted. "I have money. My family is rich. Let me go, and you will be well compensated."

The men exchanged glances, surprised by her defiance. The man in the leather jacket leaned down, his breath hot and smelling of weed. "You think we care about your money?" he taunted. "You're nothing here."

Isabella's resolve only hardened. "To hell with you," she hissed. "You're so fucking dumb not to take the money because now, I'm going to see you in hell after I kill you."

The men laughed, and Isabella could hear their mean enjoyment. But she didn't back down. "Boys, I think we need to teach her a lesson." The man sitting on the stool had clearly had enough of the confidence and bravery Isabella was demonstrating.

As soon as he finished his sentence, the other two men slowly walked towards Isabella. The weak soul was too numb to know what was being conspired in front of her.

The man with the beard stepped forward, becoming angry as he did so. He growled and took off his belt, saying, "You need to learn your place." The man in the leather jacket raised his leg and gave a light kick to her shoulder. "Eat up bitch. No one's fetching you out." Before she could react, a hard punch landed on her cheek when she turned around to say something to him. She skipped across the wet floor and hit the wall with her body because the blow was so strong. She felt pain in her cheek that went all the way through her head. She could taste blood, and it had a coppery tang.

"Shut up, bitch," he spat, his eyes gleaming with malice. "You're not a person. You're a dog."

He swung the belt at her, and the buckle hit her skin with a loud, painful bang. She really wanted to cry, but instead, Isabella bit her lip. The pain was completely unbearable. Suddenly, it was a good thing that her body was numb from the intense cold. Isabella was determined not to let them see her break down.

"Still think you're tough?" the man with the goatee sneered, delivering another blow.

Isabella's vision blurred with tears, but she lifted her head and met his gaze. "Yes," she said through gritted, blood-stained teeth. "You can beat me, but you won't break me."

The man's eyes narrowed in frustration. "We'll see about that," he muttered, swinging the belt again.

Each strike sent waves of agony through her body, but Isabella's spirit intensified with every lash. In the back of her mind, she forced her psyche to enjoy the heat that each lash brought against the freezing cold because she would survive this.

Screaming her defiance with every hit, her voice echoed off the cold, dark walls.

"Go to hell!" she shouted. "You hit like a girl!"

The beating continued, and she could feel the blood pooling under her skin, the bruises forming, but she remained defiant and would not give in.

Finally, the man with the goatee stepped back, panting with exertion. "You're not worth the effort," he spat, turning away.

"Eat," The man in the leather jacket shoved the bowl of dog food closer to her. He demanded again, his voice laced with irritation.

Isabella pushed the bowl away with a shaking hand. "Shove this up your ass," she said, her voice hoarse but determined. "I'd rather die today with dignity, rather than give you the satisfaction of seeing me eat that."

The men exchanged frustrated glances, unsure of how to break her spirit. The big man's eyes darkened with fury. "You're going to regret this," he warned, but Isabella's eyes burned with defiance.

"I regret nothing," she replied. "And when I will get the hell out of here. I will make sure you all pay for this."

The largest one of them all had resided in the back and perched himself on a stool. He looked at her with a menacing gaze and waited for the other two to stop snickering. "So, this bitch *really* still thinks she can buy us. Do you even know who we are?" He looked at her and waited for an answer.

Isabella looked up slowly and replied, "Yes, you are a scumbag loser who likes to beat on defenseless women with two fucking retarded idiots as friends."

She lay there and held her face as if trying to gauge the throbbing pain that had elicited in her jaw. She winced as soon as she touched it. The intensity augmented to an extreme, and it made her gag as her body recoiled from its effect, and she dragged herself to the corner. The pain was off the severest degree that her body could not decipher what else to do.

"I think you broke my jaw assshole. Thanks a lot!!" She choked out the words as she tried to regain her balance and somehow managed to fight back. But all that she could manage was a few wobbles here and there.

The man in the Goatee was yet to leave. He stayed in the shadows near the exit, observing her trying to get up from the slippery floor. Before locking the doors, he delivered one final verbal blow, "Remember, the only reason we're not fucking you right now is because you're being saved for the boss." The man adjusted his brown leather jacket and said, his voice dripping with contempt. "You're nothing but a toy for him to play with."

It was hard to see, and the iron taste filled her mouth. She kept hearing the sound of their feet stomping around in her head. The room fell silent; the only sound was that of her ragged breathing. She tried to curl up, her body shaking uncontrollably. The cold metal of the collar bit into her neck, reminding her that she was still a captive. She closed her eyes, trying to block out the pain and humiliation, but the memories of their brutality were seared into her mind.

With a trembling hand, she reached up and touched her swollen cheek, wincing at the sharp pain. The blood trickled down her face; the buckle had cut deep into the flesh and had managed to create cuts all over her body. Suddenly, the rage and frustration within her boiled over, and she let out a guttural scream, punching the wall with whatever leftover energy she had.

***

The coffee machine's silent buzz was the only sound that chimed in the entire meeting room. Agent Jackson was seemingly the most content man in the room with his brew, while the rest sat there with grim faces, waiting for the Zoom call to connect. Agents Flanagan and Collins were also in attendance, waiting for the wifi network to connect and start the meeting with Bureau Chief Sean Brady.

"You would expect the FBI to have a better connection," Agent Jackson chuckled. "Sir, there is a network lag from the other side, mainly because of the weather." His assistant was quick to deliver an answer.

"That is even worse!" His hearty laugh made Agent Collins giggle as well, but he quickly silenced due to Flanagan's death stare. After mere minutes, four faces appeared on the screen, all reflecting stoic and serious demeanors. The recent raids on Roberto Rossi's businesses yielded some significant findings, but they did not provide the information they were desperately seeking.

"Chief, we've hit several of Rossi's key locations," Agent Jackson began, his voice steady but tinged with frustration. "So far, we haven't found anything directly related to Isabella's whereabouts."

Brady's expression hardened. "What have you found, Jackson?"

Jackson took a deep breath. "At one of Roberto's distribution centers near Howland Hook, we confiscated a container full of cocaine, heroin, and fentanyl. It's a significant haul and a major blow to Rossi's operations. But... it's not what we were hoping for."

Agent Flanagan chimed in, his face etched with worry. "We're getting closer to the point where we could actually charge Roberto with something substantial. The drugs alone are enough to lock him away for years."

"But," Agent Collins interrupted, her voice soft yet firm, "we're still no closer to finding Isabella. We need to start setting realistic expectations with Jake. It's been a few days..."

Jackson nodded, his jaw clenched. "I know. And I think it's time someone spoke to Jake about the possibility that we might never find her."

Brady's eyes narrowed. "And you're volunteering for this, Jackson?"

"Yes, Chief. I know him the best. I think I can handle it."

Brady sighed heavily. "Alright, Jackson. But be careful. This is a delicate situation. We can't afford to lose his trust."

Jackson nodded, the weight of the task settling heavily on his shoulders. "Understood, Chief. I'll handle it."

Jackson leaned back in his chair and rubbed his temples when the call stopped. He dreaded talking to Jake because he knew what a difficult conversation this could be, but it had to be done. His mind was racing as he picked up the phone and called Jake.

"Jackson," Jake's voice came through the line, hopeful and desperate. "Do you have any news? Did you find anything?"

"Hey, Jake," Jackson greeted him gently. "We need to talk. Are you free?"

Jake's voice was tense. "Did you find any new leads?"

"What about Isabella? I would have hoped that we would be gaining traction by now. What is happening with her search? I provided the GPS link and expected that police would have found her by now," Jake's anxiety was clear through the phone.

"Jake," Jackson said, trying to keep his voice steady, "we need to talk about this in person. Can you meet me at the Mamane Cafe?"

"Alright, I'll be there as soon as I can." Jake hesitated, fear and hope mingling in his voice.

Later, at the Mamane Cafe, Jackson arrived to find Jake already seated, his face drawn with worry and exhaustion. Jackson joined him at the table, his expression somber.

"Jake, I need to be honest with you," Jackson began, his tone serious. "We're doing everything we can to find her, but it's been a few days at this point. We need to start preparing for the possibility that we might not find her."

"No! You can't say that! You can't give up on her!" Jake's eyes widened in horror.

"We're not giving up," Jackson said firmly, leaning in closer. "We're still looking, but we need to be realistic. The more time passes, the harder it becomes to find her. I know it's not what you want to hear, but we have to prepare for every possibility."

Jake's eyes became defiant, and he shook his head vehemently. "She's out there, Jackson. I know she is. I can't give up on her. won't."

"I know, Jake. I know. And we won't stop looking. But we need to be ready for whatever we find. We have to be strong, for Isabella's sake," Jackson's own voice broke for a few seconds.

Those words from Jackson hit them both hard, and they sat there in silence for a moment. As they faced the harsh truth of their position, the cafe around them seemed to fade away. Jackson knew they had a long way to go, but he also knew they had to go through it together, no matter how difficult it was.

***

Jake had barely slept. His nights were filled with restless tossing, and his days were consumed by physical exhaustion. He spent most of his time running, lifting weights, and practicing Uechi Kata. The rigorous discipline was his only escape, his way of coping with the gnawing fear and helplessness he felt over Isabella's disappearance. He pushed himself to the brink, performing Seichin 100 times perfectly, his muscles screaming in protest. He repeatedly punched the makiwara, toughening his hands until they were raw and bruised.

The relentless training wasn't enough to distract him from the worry. Jake's mind kept drifting back to Isabella. Every hour that passed without news was another hour of torment. He knew he couldn't keep this up forever. He needed help, and he needed to talk to someone.

The next evening, after another grueling session, Jake realized he could no longer shoulder this burden alone. It had been a few days since Isabella's disappearance, and initially, Jake had hoped she would be found quickly, especially with potential mob ties involved; he wanted to keep it as quiet as possible. However, the reality of the situation was setting in, and he needed his family's support now more than ever. Aunt Mary had just returned from a business trip, and this was the first chance Jake had to gather everyone together. He approached Rodney, determination firming his voice.

"Rodney," he began, visibly worn but resolute, "we need to sit down with Aunt Mary tonight. It's important. There's a lot you both need to know."

Rodney looked at him. Concern etched on his face. "Of course, Jake. What's going on?"

"It's about Isabella," Jake replied.

They all sat down for tea in the living room, and Aunt Mary waited for him to speak up about his concerns. The tone with which Jake had asked them to listen made them highly concerned.

"What is it, Jake? What's wrong?" Aunt Mary came down and sat right next to him. She patted his shoulder in a tender way, "You know I am like your mother. Whatever is wrong, we will deal with it!"

Jake hesitated for a moment, then began to explain. "Isabella has disappeared. It's been days, and I haven't heard anything. I've been calling off sick at work because I can't focus on anything else."

Aunt Mary gasped, her hand flying to her mouth. "Oh, Jake, that's terrible! What happened?"

"I don't know. We were having dinner, and she went to the washroom and never returned. I looked and looked. It just... it is like she vanished in thin air. So, one thing led to another, and now I have been working with the FBI, but we haven't found any leads so far. I may be in over my head, Aunt Mary. I don't know what to do," he answered in a low tone.

Jake took a pause to let that information sink in. He waited for Aunt Mary to regain her composure after the initial shock wore off. He kept his gaze down and stayed ever so calm, then he continued, "I've been pushing myself so hard, trying to stay strong, but it's getting harder every day. I *need* to find her. I can't rest till then."

Aunt Mary leaned forward, her eyes filled with empathy. "Jake, you don't have to go through this alone. We're here for you, whatever you need."

Jake nodded, his throat tight. "I just don't know how to keep going. Every time I close my eyes, I see her. I can't sleep, I can't eat. I'm afraid that something terrible has happened to her."

"We'll find her, Jake. We won't stop until we do," Rodney squeezed his shoulder gently.

"I also need to tell you about the Rossi family. It's not just about Isabella's disappearance. It's more complicated than that." He wiped his face and leaned forward, bracing himself to tell her in detail.

"Tell us everything, Jake." Aunt Mary's tone was more serious.

"It all started a few months ago. I was at a bar, and there was a fight breaking out. I stepped in to break it up, and that's when I first encountered some of Rossi's men. They weren't happy with me getting involved. Later, at Francesca's birthday party, things escalated. Rodney and I had to step in to save her from a dangerous situation. Ever since then, I've been spending time with them, trying to keep an eye on things. But now, with Isabella disappearing, I don't know if it's just a random event or if it's connected to everything else that's been happening." Jake nodded, swallowing hard.

Rodney's expression hardened. "You think the Rossis are behind this?"

"I don't know. It's possible. They're dangerous, and they don't forget grudges easily. I'm worried that Isabella might be caught up in something because of me." Jake shrugged, his eyes filled with worry.

"What can we do? How can we save Isabella!?" Jake called out his worries in the room. He had no clue what to do.

"First," Aunt Mary said firmly, "we need to take care of you. You're exhausted and stressed. I'll have my physician give you a diagnosis so you can take FMLA leave from work. You need to focus on finding Isabella without worrying about your job."

Jake nodded, relief washing over him. "Thank you, Aunt Mary. That would help a lot."

"Go take a shower and try to rest," she said softly. "We'll handle things from here. The position I am in today, I didn't come here by being passive. I know how to deal with such people. I will use my resources to resolve this situation. Please, do not worry because you have me on your side."

Jake stood up, feeling a bit lighter. "Thanks, Aunt Mary. Thanks, Rodney."

As he left the room to head to his shower, Aunt Mary turned to Rodney, her expression serious. "Rodney, we may need to use your other skills."

Rodney frowned, knowing exactly what she meant. "You mean my military training?"

"Yes," Aunt Mary replied. "Jake is in over his head with these people. If the Rossis are involved, we need someone who knows how to handle dangerous situations. I trust you to protect him and help us find Isabella."

Rodney nodded with determination in his eyes. "I'll do whatever it takes, Maam. We'll get her back."

Aunt Mary sat down on the sofa, deep in thought. She then whipped out her phone and started her plans to help Jake.

***

In his sophisticated and fortified space, Vincent sat with ease and an air of calmness. Something which he had manifested for a long time. His well-thought-out plan had been going smoothly.

Sitting in front of a wall of high-definition monitors, he observed the display of various angles of live surveillance footage from Roberto Rossi's lavish apartment. The underground Capoli lair was the perfect place for planning battles in the underworld.

The polished mahogany glowed from the lighting of the monitors. Placing the heavy whiskey glass with a loud thud, Capoli patiently waited. The game was afoot, and he sat there as the mastermind behind it all.

The dominos were about to be set off, and everyone was in position, waiting for Vincent to give the green light. He sipped the amber whiskey in silence, wearing an earpiece. He watched Roberto Rossi sleeping peacefully on one of the monitors.

In a low, smooth voice, Vincent spoke, "Let's begin." His words were calm but carried an air of authority that brooked no argument. In a swift movement, the man beside him, Knuckles McGee, silently acknowledged it, brought his earpiece closer, and spoke into it. His voice was gruff yet composed and well-rehearsed. "Blue team, go. Red team, stay in the hall and manage surveillance."

The command set a flurry of activity into motion. Vincent looked at the screens and saw the blue team move with purpose and accuracy. They were dressed in sleek black combat gear. They walked through the hallways of Roberto's apartment building in sync with each other and without making a sound. Each person knew what their job was because they had spent countless hours getting ready.

As the blue team got closer to Roberto's apartment door, Vincent leaned forward and widened his eyes in excitement. "Remember," he said into the talk mic, "every step should be calculated. Make certain he knows who's in charge."

As Knuckles watched the action, his fingers flew over the keyboard to ensure the red team kept a safe boundary and continued watching without interruption.

All at once, someone from the blue team placed an explosive on the door. The explosion shattered the silence, blasting a hole in the wall. Whilst the booming noise resonated in the hallway, the next trail of events unfolded in a smooth motion. Vincent's men stormed into Roberto Rossi's apartment, masks covering their faces and smoke-filled grenades in hand. The grenades hissed as they hit the floor, filling the room with thick, choking smoke.

The commotion from the blast had caught everyone in a frenzy, and Roberto's men were completely off guard. While they could recover from their confused states, Vincent's man shot out multiple rounds of bullets. Roberto's guards fell to the ground, struck down by precise headshots. The blue team moved with military precision, and their training was evident in every movement.

"Where is Roberto?" One of Vincent's men shouted, his voice muffled by his mask. He grabbed a terrified guard by the collar, shaking him roughly. "Where is he?"

"I don't know!" the guard stammered, his eyes wide with fear. "He's in the bedroom, I think!"

Another of Roberto's men tried to make a run for it, but a member of the blue team caught him with a swift, brutal blow to the head. He crumpled to the floor, unconscious.

"Secure the perimeter!" the team leader barked. "Find Roberto. Now!"

The team spread out, methodically clearing each room. They moved quickly, their guns ready, eyes scanning through the smoke for any threats. One by one, they rounded up Roberto's men, binding their hands and forcing them to the ground.

In the middle of the chaos, the team leader discreetly took out a pack of transparent stickers and started attaching them to walls and to some of the clothing that he saw lying around. He then took out a thick bottle and sprayed a thick grayish residue around the apartment that seemed to disappear on contact.

Hearing the commotion, Roberto jumped to his feet and bolted to his master bedroom. His heart pounded in his chest as he darted into his main closet, a space the size of an average apartment. He pressed a hidden button on the wall, and all the doors around him snapped shut. A computerized voice intoned, "Lockdown secured."

Roberto had managed to make it to his safe room, a fortress with steel walls impenetrable to any attack. He leaned against the cold metal, trying to catch his breath, listening to the chaos unfolding outside.

"Where is he?" one of Vincent's men shouted, gripping a guard by the collar. The guard whimpered, blood trickling from his mouth.

"I don't know! He disappeared!" the guard cried out, his voice cracking with fear.

Another of Roberto's men, already bloodied and bruised, groaned from the floor, "He must be in the safe room. It's the only place he could go."

Frustration simmered among Vincent's team. Just then, one of the men received an urgent message from Knuckles McGee. "Hurry up and get the hell out of there. The police might be on their way."

The leader of Vincent's blue team glanced at his watch and barked, "Wrap it up! We need to be gone in 60 seconds."

Before leaving, they made a brutal statement. Two more of Roberto's men were shot in the head, their bodies crumpling lifelessly to the ground. The leader of the blue team turned to the remaining guards; his voice was cold and menacing.

"Tell Roberto," he said, his eyes hard, "that Vincent Capoli is coming for him. There's nowhere he can hide."

With that, Vincent's men disappeared into the night, leaving behind a scene of chaos and a clear message: the hunt for Roberto Rossi was far from over.

As he watched the events on TV, Vincent felt a sick sense of relief at getting even for the attempt on his life. He smiled coldly as he watched Roberto's men being killed one by one. But there was a little bit of sadness that they hadn't been able to kill Roberto.

Vince sighed as he left the monitoring room and went into a different room, where Tim Scott was already on a video call waiting for him. Tim's face showed up on the big screen, and he looked serious but calm.

"Tim," Vincent greeted, taking a seat. "The raid on Roberto's home went as planned. We didn't get him, but his men were dealt with."

Tim nodded. "Good to hear, Vincent. I've got some news on my end as well. Remember those thugs who dared to touch Francesca at her birthday party?"

Vincent's eyes darkened at the memory. "What about them?"

"They've been taken care of," Tim replied, his voice cold and measured. "One was dropped off at a hospital in Kansas City, and the other in Atlanta, Georgia. They're not dead, but they probably wish they were. I made sure they paid a heavy price for trying to assault one of the Capoli children."

Vincent's expression softened slightly, a hint of gratitude in his eyes. "Thank you, Tim. Francesca means the world to me. They needed to understand that no one touches a Capoli and gets away with it."

Tim leaned in closer to the camera, and his voice dropped to a whisper as he talked about the plot. "The message was sent very clearly. They are not going to touch anyone in the Capoli family again. Those hospitals will have to deal with the effects for a long time."

Vincent nodded, and his eyes showed that he was happy. "All right. Wonderful. We are making our message clear to all of our enemies."

Tim smiled for the first time in a long time. "Thank you for always making sure our family is safe, Vincent. Please let me know if you need anything else."

"I will," Vincent told him. "Thank you once more, Tim. Tonight, we both did a good job."

Because the call was over, Vincent leaned back in his chair and felt calm. The night's events sent shockwaves through the underworld, and the Capoli name was once again linked to fear and honor. When Vincent took a big breath, he was already thinking about what he would do next in his fight with Roberto Rossi.

***

It had been a few hours since Isabella stayed in a fetal position on the cold floor. She had passed out from starvation and had laid in the same spot where she was beaten brutally. After a while, she whipped her eyes open and realized where she was. Reality struck when she recalled the most recent events.

Isabella lay on the cold, hard floor, tears streaming down her face as she desperately tried to stay warm. Her body was completely numb from the relentless beating and the bitter cold that seemed to seep into her very bones. There was no protection for her now frail naked body against the freezing air, and every breath she took felt like inhaling shards of ice.

Over the past few days, she had started to lose hope of ever being rescued, knowing that statistically, very few people make it out of her situation alive. The darkness around her seemed to close in, amplifying her sense of isolation and despair.

"Please, someone help me," she whispered through chattering teeth, her voice barely audible. The hunger pains were excruciating, causing severe disorientation. She could no longer remember the last time she had eaten, and her stomach felt like it was being twisted in knots.

She curled up into a tighter ball, trying to conserve what little warmth she had left. Her mind wandered to thoughts of Jake, her parents, and a life that seemed so distant now. The memories of happier times only made the present agony more unbearable.

"Jake, where are you?" she sobbed, her voice cracking. "Please find me. I need you."

Isabella started having more persistent thoughts of ending it all. The idea of slipping into eternal sleep seemed like a merciful release compared to the torture she was enduring.

"I can't do this anymore," she whispered to herself, her voice filled with despair. "I can't take this pain."

Thoughts of dying right now seemed blissful, and there was hardly a thought where she could come to another conclusion. She thought about giving up, but a small, stubborn part of her wouldn't let go. She thought of Jake's face and how his eyes showed love and power. He didn't want to give up on her, and she couldn't either. The resolve in her voice was faint, but it was there. She clung to the hope that somehow, against all odds, she would be rescued. The darkness around her was suffocating, but she focused on that tiny glimmer of hope, using it to keep her going. If she died now, the agony would end, and maybe, just maybe, she would be warm again. She only needed to figure out the quickest way to do it.

As Isabella lay there pondering how to take her life, she heard a lot of footsteps coming through the cold, dark room. Fear and despair were dancing together in her chest like a crazy tune. It scared her when she heard a heavy door open and then slam shut. After a while, a rough, scary voice from an old man broke through the quiet like a knife.

"We're coming back to get you again tomorrow, bitch," he yelled. "So you better be ready."

"Please, no more," she whispered to herself, tears streaming down her face. But surprisingly, they were not after her at this time.

When the quiet broke for a moment, she heard something that made her blood run cold. Someone was sobbing very loudly, and their voice was filled with terrible pain. The cries were raw and full of pain, just like hers. Isabella felt terrible for whoever was going through the same thing she was.

She listened to the sobs and felt a strange link to someone she couldn't see. She saw a reflection of her pain in their cries. The thought of another person going through this hell gave her a little strength. The cries continued, and Isabella felt a strange sense of solidarity. She wasn't ready to give up yet. Not while there was someone else fighting to survive.

"We'll make it," she whispered, almost as if trying to send a message to the unseen sufferer. "We have to hold on."

Isabella waited a while, listening to the sobs that echoed in the darkness. Summoning her courage, she whispered, "Hey, are you okay? What did they do to you?"

A faint voice replied, filled with despair. "I'm gonna kill myself. It's the only way to get out of this hell."

The girl's words struck Isabella like a blow. "No, please don't say that," she whispered back, her voice trembling. "What's your name?"

"Stephanie," the girl replied, her voice barely above a whisper.

"Hi Stephanie, my name is Isabella, and I wish that we could have met under different circumstances," Isabella replied.

Stephanie continued, "Almost two weeks ago, I went to Walmart to pick up a few things. While I was shopping, I noticed a straggly-looking guy following me at different points, but I didn't think anything of it."

Isabella listened intently, her heart aching for Stephanie. "What happened next?"

"When I went to put the groceries into my car, two men drove up in separate vans and blocked me in on either side," Stephanie continued, her voice shaking with the memory. "They grabbed me and shoved me into one of the vans. The other men took my keys and jumped into my car. They drove away with everything."

"That's horrible," she whispered. "Did you see their faces?" Isabella felt a surge of anger and sorrow. "Did you see their faces?"

"They wore masks," Stephanie replied, her voice filled with frustration. "It all happened so fast. They brought me here, and after torturing me for a while, they now take me upstairs every day. I have to get dressed and entertain whatever man comes there. If I resist, they beat me unconscious."

Stephanie's voice broke with emotion. "I can't do it anymore, Isabella. Every day is a nightmare."

Tears filled Isabella's eyes as she imagined Stephanie's ordeal. "I'm so sorry," she said softly. "I can't even imagine what you've been through."

Isabella took a deep breath, her resolve hardening. "Stephanie, listen to me. You have to stay strong. No matter what, I will find a way to get us out of here. These men will pay for what they're doing." Her sobs quieted a bit, and she whispered, "Do you really think we can get out of here?"

"Yes, I do. We just have to hold on a little longer. I know it's hard, but we can't give up." Isabella nodded, even though Stephanie couldn't see her.

"Good," Isabella said softly. "We'll get through this together. We have to believe that help is coming. I'm not giving up, and neither should you. I am going to make them fucking pay."

***

The conference room was filled with heated arguments, voices overlapping in frustration. The tension was palpable; even the closest assistants were asked to step out. Agent Jackson, his face a mask of determination and frustration, turned to his colleagues, Susan Collins and Patrick Flanagan.

"We're not getting anywhere with the usual methods," Jackson said, his voice low but intense. "We need to think outside the box. We brought Jake into this mess, and I feel responsible."

Collins and Flanagan exchanged glances, their expressions mirroring Jackson's concern. "What are you suggesting, Jackson?" Collins asked.

"I'm suggesting we break the rules," Jackson replied, his eyes narrowing. "We need to find Isabella, and we need to do it fast. Are you with me?"

Collins nodded. "Count me in."

Flanagan agreed as well. "Let's do it."

Jackson picked up his phone and dialed Jake's number. "Jake, it's Jackson. Can you meet us at the Mamane Cafe? There's something important we need to discuss."

"I'll be there as soon as I can." Jake didn't hesitate.

As Jackson, Collins, and Flanagan walked to the cafe, thoughts of what they were about to do ran through their minds. When they got there, Jake was already sitting down, and his face was tense and worried. Jackson joined him at the table, and Collins and Flanagan sat in a booth nearby.

"Jake, I need you to sit quietly and let me explain what's happening," Jackson began, his tone serious.

Jake nodded, his eyes fixed on Jackson. "Go ahead."

He took a deep breath. People have been interested in you, Jake, ever since you came into town and stopped that fight at the bar. The FBI knew you would be interesting to the Rossi and Capoli families. Then you stopped the fight at Francesca's party and gave us the information that led to the Wonderland bust, news all over the country. Isabella, just going missing for no reason seems like too much of a coincidence.

Jake's eyes widened. "Are you saying the Rossi crime family is involved?"

"That's *exactly* what I'm saying," Jackson confirmed. "We've been conducting various raids on Roberto's businesses, trying to get any information we can about Isabella. So far, we've found almost nothing."

Jake's fists clenched in frustration. "So what do we do now?"

Jackson leaned in closer. "We're going to break the rules. We need to hit them harder and get information by any means necessary. We can't afford to play by the book anymore."

Jake looked at Jackson, a mix of hope and fear in his eyes. "I'm in. Whatever it takes to find Isabella."

"Good," Jackson said, his voice firm. "We'll need to move quickly and be careful. This is dangerous, but it's our best shot at finding her."

Collins and Flanagan rejoined them, their faces set with determination. "We're ready," Collins said.

Jackson nodded. "Alright. Let's get to work."

Agent Jackson looked Jake square in the eyes, his expression earnest and filled with regret. "Jake, I'm deeply sorry for my part in trying to make you an informant. I would do anything to find Isabella, even if it costs me my job or my life. But you must be ready for the possibility that she may already be dead."

Jake just listened, his mind churning. Jackson's words hurt extremely, but they also made him very determined. Shortly, he closed his eyes and thought about the determination he had built up over many hours of training. They were loaded with a warrior's determination when he opened them.

"Thank you, Agent Jackson," Jake said quietly. "Thank you for all the information. Please keep me updated, and if there's any way I can join the investigation, I'd be truly grateful. Isabella is very important to me."

Jackson nodded, a mixture of admiration and sorrow in his gaze. "I will, Jake. We'll find her, one way or another."

After the meeting ended, Agent Jackson, Susan Collins, and Patrick Flanagan huddled together to formulate a plan. They knew they had to go off-grid and take extreme measures. Their strategy was simple: go after any high-ranking official in the Rossi family until they discovered the location of the Rossi family's human trafficking operations. It was their best shot at finding and freeing Isabella.

Meanwhile, Roberto Rossi sat in his safe room, still reeling from a massive hangover from the night before. He watched on his monitors as Vincent's men stormed his apartment, which encompassed the entire top floor of One Manhattan Square. They used an explosive to blow a hole in the wall, trying to dismantle as many cameras as they could while making their way into Roberto's lavish estate. He could see them shooting his men in the head and demanding to know his whereabouts. Luckily, he had made it to the safe room in time, and the reinforced walls kept him secure.

Roberto immediately called his son, Marco. "Send reinforcements ASAP," he barked, his voice a mix of anger and desperation.

As he waited, he began pulling out guns and ammunition from hidden compartments within the safe room. He knew Vincent Capoli would respond to the previous attack, but a direct assault on his personal residence was risky, even for Vincent.

"This means war," Roberto muttered, his eyes narrowing with fury. He knew the two men had passed the point of no return. "I will not rest until I personally kill Vincent and every member of his family." He couldn't get rid of another thought: Jake. The FBI had been raiding his businesses to look for this Isabella, and now he was certain that Jake's involvement had somehow started this whole chain of events. He became even angrier as he thought about Jake and the cruel and painful payback he was planning.

"I'll make him pay," Roberto growled, gripping his gun tightly. "And as for Isabella..."

He paused, a cruel smile spreading across his face. "I won't kill her. No, that would be too easy. I'll make her live the rest of her life in service to me. She'll experience a thousand lifetimes of hell on earth."

As he sat there, surrounded by his arsenal, Roberto's mind raced with plans for retribution. He imagined Jake's look when he realized Isabella was alive, suffering endlessly at Roberto's hands. It would be the perfect revenge.

Meanwhile, Vincent's men had retreated but continued their search throughout the building. Roberto remained hidden, his mind a storm of vengeful thoughts. He vowed to turn the tables and strike back with a fury that would make Vincent Capoli regret ever coming for him. The lines had been drawn, and Roberto was ready to take things up a notch.

Roberto could still hear the faint sound of gunshots inside his fortified room as he plotted his next steps. He would expand his empire at any cost and make damn sure that those who dared to challenge him would pay dearly.

Jake had a crushing sense of resolve and clarity as he stepped out of the meeting with Agent Jackson. Since the FBI confirmed Rossi's probable involvement, Jake decided that Vincent Capoli, already at war with Rossi, could supply him with the required aid and resources to get Isabella back. He requested a meeting with Vincent by calling the Capoli estate's main house and leaving a message. Despite the seriousness of the situation, his voice remained calm.

Vincent was surprised by Jake's unannounced arrival at the Capoli estate. He graciously consented to meet with Jake privately. They met in Vincent's study, where the air was heavy with the aroma of cigars and plush mahogany furnishings. Jake exchanged a few pleasantries, drew a big breath, and then explained.

"Mr. Capoli," Jake started, his voice steady but filled with urgency, "I need to tell you everything. I want you to know who I am, how I came to break up that fight at the Flamingo Room, and why I'm here now. I respect the Capoli family deeply, even though I know you're involved in organized crime."

Vincent raised an eyebrow but remained silent, listening intently.

Jake explained about moving to New York after his college graduation and the events that led up to the present. Jake continued, "The FBI tried to recruit me. I didn't want any part of it, but I did tell them about what I overheard regarding Wonderland. At this point, I desperately need your help and resources to rescue Isabella. She means everything to me."

As Vincent pondered Jake's remarks, he reclined in his chair and narrowed his eyes slightly. "Jake, requests of that magnitude are never granted without a price," he added, maintaining a composed but resolute tone.

Jake nodded, understanding the gravity of what he was asking. "I know, Mr. Capoli. I'm willing to do whatever it takes."

Vincent's expression softened slightly. "You've saved both of my children on separate occasions, Jake. For that, I am in your debt. I'm quite fond of you because you're a hard-working young man with good values."

Jake looked down, humbled by Vincent's words.

Vincent continued, "Honor and loyalty mean everything to me. If I move forward to help you, we will be formally united. I will consider you a member of the family, and we will take care of each other for the rest of our lives. But know this, Jake: there can be no more betrayals."

"I understand," Jake replied, his voice resolute.

Vincent nodded. "I will never ask you to be directly involved in any illegal activities. But if I ever need you, the price you will pay for my help now is that you can never refuse my request."

Jake took a moment to absorb Vincent's words. The implications were heavy, but his resolve was unwavering. "I agree," he said firmly. "I am grateful for your request."

Vincent stood up and extended his hand. Jake took it, and they shook hands firmly. Then, in a gesture that took Jake by surprise, Vincent pulled him into a fatherly hug.

"You've got a good heart, Jake," Vincent said quietly. "We'll get Isabella back."

Jake felt a sense of relief wash over him. For the first time in days, he felt a glimmer of hope. He pulled back and looked Vincent in the eye. "Thank you, Mr. Capoli. I won't let you down."

Vincent smiled a rare, genuine smile. "Call me Vincent. We're family now."

Jake nodded, his heart swelling with a mix of gratitude and determination. "Alright, Vincent. What's our next move?"

Vincent's expression turned serious again. "We need to find out where the Rossi family is holding Isabella. My men will start gathering information immediately. We'll use every resource at our disposal."

Jake listened intently, feeling a newfound sense of purpose. He knew the road ahead would be dangerous, but with Vincent's help, he felt more confident than ever that they would succeed. The bond they had just formed was strong, forged in mutual respect and a shared goal.

Before leaving, Jake turned to Vincent, his expression earnest. "I have one request. If the family finds Isabella, I want to be directly involved in any rescue."

Vincent nodded, understanding the depth of Jake's need to be part of the mission. "I agree, Jake. You'll be right there with us."

Jake felt a surge of gratitude and determination. "Thank you, Vincent. I won't let you down."

After Jake left, Vincent sat back in his chair, his mind replaying the events of their meeting. He felt a rare twinge of guilt, recalling how he had initially set Jake up to inadvertently expose Rossi's human trafficking operation to the FBI. This move had made Jake a target, putting him in grave danger. Vincent sighed deeply, vowing to do whatever it took and use all his resources to help Jake get Isabella back.

A seemingly unrelated recollection from his youth slipped into Vincent's mind. He remembered reading a book called "Teste di Moro," and a smile slowly spread across his face. The book was about two young lovers who were head over heels for each other. They faced insurmountable odds, but through faith and determination, they ended up together. The comparison made

Vincent laugh out loud. Although he considered himself a patron of the arts, he found himself involved in a real-life romance rekindling.

"Funny how life imitates art," he murmured, a touch of irony in his voice.

Vincent's thoughts turned back to the pressing issue at hand. He couldn't shake the image of Jake's determined face and the genuine love he had for Isabella. It was rare to see such pure dedication, and it struck a chord within Vincent. He strongly wanted to protect and support Jake in this dire situation.

Leaning forward, he picked up his phone and dialed a secure number. "Johny, it's Vincent. We need to ramp up our efforts. I want all eyes on Rossi's operations. Pull every resource we have. We need to find Isabella, and we need to do it fast."

Johny Viola's voice crackled through the speaker. "Understood, boss. We're on it."

After hanging up, Vincent sat back and continued to think. The dangers of crossing Rossi were not lost on him, nor were the strengths, resources, and tenacity of the Capoli family. No one else could have made it through this perilous ordeal unscathed.

As he bore the brunt of the blame, the room fell silent. Yet, after a long period of feeling aimless, Vincent experienced a revitalization of his sense of purpose. Assisting someone who had displayed tremendous bravery and honesty was just as important as any consideration of power or profit. He had an obligation to finish what he had started, to go after Roberto, and to help Jake.

Chapter 10: Shadows Can Shift

The living room of the lavish mansion echoed with worries of tomorrow. Aunt Mary had been left in shock after her conversation with Jake. She had not moved an inch from the sofa. As meticulous as she was, she had started planning the next move in how to help Jake and give him an advantage in this crazy situation while securing his future with Isabella. She was such a sweet girl, and Isabella was someone worth saving. She focused her efforts and started planning how she could utilize her resources to make the biggest impact on the outcome of this situation.

"Maam, are you okay? You seem lost in thought." Rodney was passing by and noticed her in the same place as before.

"Yes, Rodney, I am just thinking about what possible implications my next actions will have." She rubbed her eyes and tried to refocus. "It's just that I consider Jake to be my own and want him out of this mess as soon as possible. His parents aren't even here, and they don't even know what their son is going through. So, I will use my assets to make sure he does not get himself in trouble. Until we have everything planned, let us keep our further plans to ourselves."

Rodney nodded. "Let me fix you a good cup of tea to soothe those nerves."

After a while, when he returned, they both looked at each other. A silent acknowledgment that their meddling had to happen. "No way in hell am I leaving that child alone in this. Isabella, the poor girl, got caught up in the middle of all of this. I can't even fathom what treatment she must be receiving. I do hope that she stays safe and returns to Jake. He looked too happy with her," she said, looking at her jasmine tea.

Sitting in the armchairs with their tea in hand, Aunt Mary and Rodney talked about the urgent issues at hand. Rodney gave Aunt Mary a bulky packet containing several documents. "I've compiled all the research I've done on the matter," Rodney said, his voice steady but serious. "This includes everything I could find on the Rossi family, their operations, and potential leads on Isabella's whereabouts."

Aunt Mary took the folder, her expression calculated as she began to leaf through the pages. She added this to the pile of other paperwork. Her work seemed to grow as the hours passed by, but she sat near it, remaining unfazed. "Thank you, Rodney. This is thorough work. We need to ensure Jake has all the support he needs." She signed another document and threw it in the piel she had rummaged through already.

"Ma'am, I'm sure Jake can care for himself, but the underworld is dangerous. I want to stay close to him during this process. The people we're dealing with cannot be trusted," Rodney nodded, his eyes earnest.

Aunt Mary looked up from the documents, her eyes meeting Rodney's with a mix of surety for her nephew. "I want you to be careful, Rodney. You have become an important family member, and this is a dangerous mission. Though I am sure Jake and you are both clever enough to know how much people are to be dealt with."

Rodney smiled softly. "I'm happy to help, Maam. Jake is like a brother to me, and I'll do whatever it takes to keep him safe."

They continued their discussion as the evening light faded, and Aunt Mary managed her paperwork with an unfazed vigor. Aunt Mary set the documents aside and took a sip of her tea. "I've rearranged my weekly meetings to be home when Jake is here. Let us make sure he has everything he needs when all hell breaks loose."

With a creak as the front door opened, Jake entered Aunt Mary's dimly lit hallway. His eyes displayed exhaustion from his meeting with Vincent. The aroma of a delectable dinner, one that contained all of Jake's favorite dishes, awaited him in all of its glory. The expensive spread was quite a wholesome diversion that he faced from the chaos he was experiencing mentally. Aunt Mary noticed him as she glanced up from the living room, a bright smile lighting up her face.

"Jake, come in," she called, her voice filled with affection and concern.

He walked into the cozy living room, the soft glow of the evening light casting a serene ambiance. Aunt Mary stood up from her chair, holding a sleek, modern watch in her hand. "Some food will be good for you, you know." She gently urged him to sit.

"I have something for you," she said, extending the watch toward him. "I want you to always wear this. It has a GPS tracker, so I can always stay in touch with you and know where you are."

Jake took the watch, his fingers brushing against the cool metal. He looked at her gratitude and exhaustion in his eyes. "Thank you, Aunt Mary. I'll wear it all the time. I'm sorry for causing all this trouble."

Aunt Mary stepped closer, placing a gentle hand on his shoulder. "You're not causing any trouble, Jake. We're family, and families stick together, no matter what. I can't give you many details right now, but I promise you, we're doing everything we can to look into Isabella's disappearance."

He smiled emphatically, but his eyes reflected how tired he was. "I… I don't know what to say."

She walked up and gave him a big hug. "We're going to find her, Jake. No matter what it takes, we'll bring Isabella back."

***

The place was similar to the freezer, and with no clothes on their bare skin, they had no choice but to warm themselves with what little breath they had left in them. Isabella sat in her cell, her hands rubbing together to generate some warmth in the frigid air. She eyed the bowl of dog food on the floor, her stomach gurgling loudly. Her lip was swollen, and she smelled of piss and blood, the scent making her stomach churn even more. She felt utterly dehumanized, but a spark of defiance still burned inside her.

"Isabella?" came a frail voice from the next cell. It was Stephanie, sounding more fragile than the day before.

"Yeah, Stephanie, I'm here," Isabella replied, her voice hoarse but strong.

"Are you okay?" Stephanie asked, her voice trembling. "I'm scared they'll kill me."

"They didn't kill you yet, did they?" she replied firmly. "Don't worry. We'll get out of this, and I'll take my revenge on these bastards." Isabella spat out a mouthful of congealed blood, the coppery taste lingering.

Stephanie's voice wavered. "I don't know how much more I can take, Isabella. They... they're monsters."

Isabella glanced around her cell, the cold, hard walls closing in on her. "Listen, Stephanie, we need to look out for each other. Memorize everything about these men – their faces, their voices, their routines. It's the only way we'll find a weakness."

"Okay. I'll try," Stephanie sniffled, but there was a note of resolve in her voice.

Trying to ignore the stinging agony in her injured lip, Isabella inhaled deeply. She recalled the men who had assaulted her. She'd committed their manners and demeanors to memory. One person's commands appeared to be the most important. His distaste for getting his hands filthy was evident from the way he backed off during the beatings. "There's one guy," Isabella said quietly, "the one who gives the orders. He doesn't like getting his hands dirty. That's something we can use against him."

Stephanie's voice was barely a whisper. "What do we do?"

"We stay strong," Isabella replied. "We watch, we wait, and when the time is right, we fight back. We'll get out of here, and we'll make them pay."

Stephanie's silence spoke volumes, but Isabella knew she was listening, drawing strength from her words. Isabella rubbed her bruised hands together again, ignoring the pain. She remembered how she refused to let them see her break.

"We're going to get through this, Stephanie," Isabella said, her voice a low, determined growl. "I promise you that." Isabella felt her tummy churn more loudly than usual. Her hunger competed with her defiance as she looked at the dog food bowl. She refused to let them enjoy watching her eat food like a beast. She would be able to survive somehow. Isabella's eyes burned with determination as she leaned back against the cold, damp wall. As the minutes ticked by, something within her began to shift. She turned to the wall, knowing Stephanie could hear her.

"Stephanie," she called out, her voice steady and fierce.

"Yeah?" Stephanie replied, her voice shaky.

"If I'm going to die in this hellhole, I'm not going alone," Isabella said, her tone hardening. "I'm taking at least one or two of these motherfuckers with me."

Stephanie was silent for a moment, then responded, "Isabella, what are you saying?"

Isabella's eyes burned with a new intensity. "I'm done being their victim. The next time they come for us, I'm fighting back. I don't care if it's the last thing I do. They're going to pay for what they've done."

Stephanie took a deep breath, the strength in Isabella's words igniting a spark of hope within her. "Okay," she whispered. "We'll do it together."

Isabella nodded, even though Stephanie couldn't see her. "Together," she affirmed. "We'll make them pay."

The image of the man who issued the orders remained vivid in her thoughts. She'd figure out how to utilize it and turn the tables on their captors. The individuals who had abused and insulted her would face severe consequences. She closed her eyes and focused on the sounds surrounding her, memorizing every footstep and creak of the floorboards above. Isabella could hear Stephanie's breathing steady as she drew power from her words. They weren't broken yet. And as long as they had each other, they would continue to fight, hope, and live.

***

Vincent was in his war room, a safe place to plan and keep an eye on things. A dim glow from the monitors cast a cold, eerie light over his sharp features, drawing attention to the lines of determination that were already there. A live feed from Roberto Rossi's estate was shown on the walls, which were covered with a grid of screens that caught every angle and shadow. Vincent's fingers tapped a steady, thoughtful beat on the shiny mahogany table. It was a physical representation of the endless calculations going on in his head. His sharp, unwavering eyes looked at every monitor with surgical accuracy, not missing a thing.

The room was like an extension of his mind, a command center where every piece of knowledge was a weapon, and every second was important. The room had an exciting feel to it as if something big was about to happen. Vincent leaned forward and narrowed his eyes as he looked for patterns and weak spots. He was ready to make his next move in the deadly dance of revenge and power.

Vincent sat across from Tim Scott. Vincent's face was a mask of calm, but his eyes shone with pride as Tim spoke. "The substance my men sprayed all over Roberto's apartment is a timed-delayed radioactive decay weapon," Tim explained, his voice smooth and confident. "For the first two hours, it's perfectly harmless. After that, it transforms into a specialized radioactive agent that attacks the nervous system and brain of anyone in contact with it."

Vincent leaned back in his plush leather armchair, and the man was satisfied. His fingers drummed lightly on the ornate mahogany desk, a gesture that betrayed his barely contained satisfaction. He had built his empire through a lifetime of cunning, strategic maneuvering, and an unwavering resolve to maintain his dominance in their shadowy realm.

Now, as the pieces fell into place, he allowed himself a moment of self-assurance, secure in the knowledge that his enemies would soon feel the full weight of his power. Tim, who he trusted, was sitting across from him with a cigar in his hand. As he took a slow, thoughtful drag, the spark gave off a soft glow, and he acknowledged with a respectful nod how brilliant their plan was.

As the head of the Capoli family, these two knew how important the situation was and were happy that their carefully laid plans were finally paying off. While they talked, Vincent's lieutenants would come in and out of the room, whispering in his ear about operations and other management chores. Vincent paid close attention and either nodded or gave short directions before turning his attention back to Tim.

Tim continued, "The beauty of this weapon is in its delayed activation. Roberto and his men will think they're safe, but after two hours, the substance becomes lethal. It takes about ten days for the symptoms to fully manifest, causing a slow, painful death. During the initial period, they won't even know they've been exposed."

Vincent's smile widened as he took a sip of his wine. "Brilliant," he murmured. "And after twenty-four hours, the substance reverts to its harmless state, leaving no trace. That's why we kept some of Roberto's men alive. Like insect spray, they'll spread the poison to the whole colony."

Tim nodded his head in agreement, and his eyes sparkled with a mix of seriousness and intensity. "Yes, that. Roberto's men will bring the toxic material back to him, even though they don't know it. It will happen soon enough."

Vincent silently raised his glass and then put it down. Then he put up his hands and pointed to the monitors that showed the different live feeds from Roberto's house. "Tim, the big picture is to make sure that Roberto and his men are killed one by one." It's like we turned their safe place into a death trap. Tim, taking a deep breath in, slowly let out his smoke, which curled around his head. "And the stickers placed on the furniture and clothing?" he asked, already knowing the answer but wanting to hear it from Vincent.

Vincent leaned forward with an even more serious look. "The stickers are very high-tech transmitters." They send out any sound within five meters and give you a video as well as exact GPS coordinates. Some of these stickers were put on Roberto's men's clothes during the first and second attacks on his apartment. Most people don't notice them because they look like transparent tape.

"So, not only have we poisoned them, but we're also tracking their every move." Tim nodded, tapping ash into a crystal ashtray.

"Precisely," Vincent said, his voice low and smooth. "Breaking into Roberto's apartment wasn't just about trying to kill him directly. We've set in motion a plan that ensures his downfall through both biological warfare and constant surveillance."

A lieutenant entered the room, whispering something urgent into Vincent's ear. Vincent nodded, acknowledging the update, and turned back to Tim. "We're closely monitoring the whereabouts of Roberto's men. This will lead us to Roberto himself. But there's another important matter at hand." Tim looked puzzled for a second. "What is it?"

"I promised Jake we'd find Isabella. This isn't just about taking down Roberto anymore. We have to rescue her." Vincent's expression grew serious. Tim nodded and proceeded to take on drags of his cigar and reveled in how beautifully the plan had carried itself out. "We'll find her, Vincent. And we'll make sure Roberto doesn't get a chance to regroup. We need to hit him hard and fast."

The determination in Vincent's jaw was evident as he nodded his head. "Agreed. We go on the offensive, giving him no breathing room until he's destroyed."

Vincent's lieutenants continued to bring in updates, each one painting a clearer picture of their progress. The live feeds showed Roberto's men moving about, unaware of the deadly game unfolding around them. He leaned back in his chair, casually checked his phone, and then started reading a random article while periodically looking at the monitors to see how far they had come.

Following his gaze, he saw how, despite an entire team keeping an eye on Vincent, he didn't seem to keep his attention off the screens. "Oh, you need to have a little more trust in them, old man. Our men are trained to be discreet. They know the stakes." He smiled when Vincent looked at him at that comment and raised an eyebrow.

"Tim, the only reason I sit here and not actively manage is because I have planned this and overlooked its execution very carefully. I *know* for a fact that it will depend on the cards we play. It's just that this entire ordeal reminded me of my brother just now. "I think he would have enjoyed this If he were alive, that is." A sudden thought crossed Vincent's mind, and he smiled. "This reminds me of a story I once read, where the hero systematically dismantles his enemy's defenses from within. We're doing the same, only in real life."

Tim chuckled, taking another puff of his cigar. "And with much higher stakes."

"We will win this conflict, Vincent, and to make sure those who wronged us pay dearly." Tim raised his glass in agreement. The game was on, and Vincent knew victory was close at this point. He just needed to make sure they were successful in the end.

***

Roberto Rossi stood under the shower on his yacht, the water cascading over his muscular frame. His mind was a whirlwind of anger and introspection as he recounted the events of the raid on his luxury apartment. The rising steam formed A hazy barrier on the glass, mirroring the fog he was experiencing in his thoughts. In an effort to gain some perspective amidst the commotion, he rubbed his forehead against the smooth, cool surface.

"Damn Capoli bastards," he muttered, his voice low and filled with venom. "They think they can walk into my home, my sanctuary, and get away with it?"

The cold water pounded against his skin, but it did nothing to quell the fire raging within him. His fury was a living thing, growing with each passing second. He clenched his fists, feeling the tension coil through his muscles.

"I need better security," he growled, the words echoing off the tile walls. "No more of these incompetent fools. I need professionals, people who know how to keep threats out." The water continued to flow, mingling with the steam that now enveloped the entire shower. Roberto's mind raced, piling up the tasks he needed to accomplish. He couldn't afford any more lapses. The Capoli family had struck a nerve, and he would ensure they paid for it dearly.

"I'll find them," he promised himself, his voice a harsh whisper. "Every single one of them. And I'll make them suffer."

He slammed his fist against the wall, the impact resonating through the small space. The pain was a welcome distraction, grounding him momentarily in the physical world. But it was fleeting, and his thoughts soon returned to the attack. "How did they manage it?" he wondered aloud, his eyes narrowing as he tried to piece together the breach. "I'll rip apart every inch of that apartment until I find the leak."

The steam grew thicker, almost suffocating, as his anger boiled over. He knew he couldn't stay in the shower forever. There were plans to make, people to interrogate, and a security team to overhaul.

"Capoli," he spoke, the name like it was a curse word. "You will regret your decision to come after me." Roberto Rossi stepped out of the shower, the steam still clinging to his skin as he wrapped himself in a luxurious bathrobe. The soft fabric did little to soothe the rage simmering within him. He left the bathroom and made his way to the private meeting room atop his yacht, a space meticulously decorated with fine art and sleek, modern furniture. The large windows offered a stunning view of the ocean, but Roberto's eyes were fixed on the task at hand.

Waiting for him was his son, Marco, and his lieutenant, a gruesome-looking man known as the Wolf. Marco's face lit up with relief when he saw his father, but Roberto was all business. There was no time for pleasantries. "Dad, I'm glad you're okay," Marco began, but Roberto cut him off with a wave of his hand.

"We don't have time for that now," Roberto said sharply, his voice sharpened. "We need to call in all available reinforcements. The FBI raids have left us vulnerable, and we can't afford any more breaches."

Standing in silence by Marco's side, the Wolf finally spoke, "I've already started mobilizing our men, boss. We've got teams securing our key locations, but we need more manpower to ensure everything is covered."

Anger flashed in Roberto's eyes as he glanced up at the wolf. Almost nothing had gone according to plan, and it was always at Roberto's expense. He looked outside the window to calm his rage and thought how shouting at them wouldn't improve things. An action plan was needed right now, and he had to change his position in the game as soon as possible. Roberto paced the room, his mind racing. He had to be a little more hands-on with the plan to bring down Vincent. "Good. We need to fortify our defenses and prepare for a counter-offensive against the Capoli family. Do they seriously think they can strike at us and get away with it? They need to understand why smart people fear the Rossi organization.

"What's the plan, Dad?" Marco leaned forward, his expression serious.

When Roberto turned back to his son and the Wolf, he briefly glanced at the crashing waves on the shore. We must assault them in their vulnerable areas and simultaneously attack all of their enterprises. I am going to tear their kingdom to shreds.

I've got a list of their key locations. We can start planning our moves tonight." The Wolf cracked his knuckles, a dangerous gleam in his eye.

"Do it," Roberto commanded. "And make sure we have eyes on every member of the Capoli family. I want to know their every move."

Marco understood his father's desire to quickly get done with the matter of the Capolis and then added, "We should also find out who their allies are. Cut off their support and isolate them."

Roberto nodded. "Exactly. This is a war, and we need to treat it as such. The Capolis won't know what hit them."

"Marco, I need you to oversee the security of our main operations. Make sure every man knows what our expectations are and what the price is for failure. Wolf, I want you to handle the intel and planning for our counter-offensive. We strike hard, and we strike fast."

Both men nodded, understanding the gravity of their mission. Roberto walked over to the large windows, staring out at the endless expanse of the ocean. The calm waters belied the storm brewing within him.

"We got too comfortable never having an enemy of this size with the balls to challenge us," Roberto said quietly, almost to himself. "Now, we're taking the fight to them. The Capolis will regret the day they ever thought they could challenge us."

Marco and the Wolf exchanged a glance, both feeling the weight of Roberto's words. This was more than just a retaliation; it was a declaration of war. The powerful and violent energy emanating from him was clearly in stark contrast to the beautiful bathrobe he wore, which looked out of place. Roberto began to talk, his voice low and filled with hate. Marco and the Wolf, his most trusted subordinate, observed as Roberto began to reveal his thoughts.

"We need to come out of the corner swinging," Roberto declared, his eyes burning with rage. "We're going to hire specialists, the best in the business. Mercenaries, hackers, anyone who can give us an edge. We need to bring in as much muscle as possible to overwhelm the Capoli clan and the FBI."

He paced back and forth, his hands clenched into fists. "I don't care how much it costs. I have very deep pockets, and I will make sure we see the Capoli family go down. I want to urinate on their graves," he spat, his face contorted with hatred.

Marco nodded, his face serious. "I'll reach out to our contacts and get the best people on this."

The Wolf added, "I know a few teams that specialize in this kind of operation. They won't come cheap, but they're worth every penny."

"Do it," Roberto commanded, his voice shaking with intensity. "I want to hit them so hard they never see it coming." Roberto maintained an angry yet coldly calculated demeanor as he detailed his plans. As he told them what they needed to do, he flew into fists of rage like a man hell-bent on winning at all costs.

While everything was going on, Vincent Capoli was sitting in his own war room, listening in on the talk. Roberto was utterly unaware of this. One of the clear stickers his men put on one of Roberto's goons stuck to their coat. This was the one they didn't hurt during the raid.

After the attack, this goon took Roberto to his boat, and his coat was now near Roberto's meeting room. Vincent leaned forward, straining to catch every word. The signal was faint, but he could still hear enough to piece together Roberto's plans. He listened as Roberto ranted and raved, his own face a mask of grim determination.

"We have a location on Roberto," Vincent said, turning to Tim Scott, who stood beside him. "Let's get our men in position. It's time to finish this." Tim nodded. There was a fierce light in his eyes. "I'll get everything ready. We'll hit them hard."

On the yacht, Roberto's anger glowed bright red and reached a fever pitch. Both Marco and the Wolf looked at each other and knew how angry and determined Roberto was. They knew what was at stake and what their jobs were. The price for failure could be death or worse. Roberto looked at his son and lieutenant, his expression softening slightly, but the fire in his eyes remained. "We're going to show them who they're dealing with. The Rossi family should be feared."

"Don't worry, Dad, we are on it." Marco nodded and went into another room to start executing these plans as Roberto's men scurried around.

Little did Marco know, and as far as he and the Wolf were concerned, every effort was already too late. Vincent was already a few moves ahead and in the process of changing the game's parameters before Rossi could move anything forward.

Vincent and Tim were already getting their own troops ready as they moved to carry out their plans. Both teams knew that their next few moves would be very important for the game.

It was the calm and commanding voice that Vincent proclaimed. "This is over now."

"We are going to catch Roberto for good and bring Isabella back home." Tim gave a firm nod and looked very determined.

"Let's get this done."

***

The rancid smell of chemicals was not the only foul odor at the warehouse. It was dark inside the building, and the smell of sweat and desperation was strong and unsettling. Agent Jackson and Patrick Flanagan carefully made their way through the maze of boxes and machines, keeping their guns drawn and looking at every shadow. There was a lot of anxiety in the air, and beads of sweat ran down their foreheads, shining in the dim light from the dirty windows high up. Jackson's heart pounded in his chest as he strained to listen for any sound that might betray the presence of the perpetrators. He glanced at Flanagan, who was just as tense, his face set in a grim mask of determination. They had been tracing the buyers of the heroin, cocaine, and fentanyl that had been confiscated from Roberto Rossi's distribution center, and now they were closing in on their targets.

Flanagan knew it was time to move in when Jackson gave him a nod. Jackson broke through the door and yelled FBI, holding up a badge. Flanagan then changed from a well-trained spy to a wilder, more dangerous person. The guy who seemed to be in charge of the drug operation at Rossi's location was standing next to a table full of plastic bags full of white powder. He moved with a wild ease, and his eyes were fixed on that man.

Flanagan, seemingly out of nowhere, hit the guy who appeared to be in charge against the wall, charging at him without saying a word. The collision caused a lot of confusion. The way Flanagan took out the target made Jackson even more shocked. "What the hell do you think you're doing here, buddy?" Flanagan snarled, his voice a low, menacing growl.

The man tried to stammer out a response, but Flanagan cut him off, driving his fist into the man's gut with brutal force. The man doubled over, gasping for air, but Flanagan gave him no respite. Flanagan grabbed a chair that was nearby and swung it hard. The metal frame of the chair made a horrific impact on the man's side.

Despite the fact that the man yelled in agony and fell to the ground, Flanagan was just getting started. The chair was used repeatedly to knock the shit out of the guy in charge, with each whack sounding like crushed bone.

Looking at it made Jackson sick to his stomach. On other occasions, he had witnessed Flanagan displaying anger; nevertheless, this was something entirely different and frightening. "Patrick, Go Easy!" There was a shout from Jackson, but Flanagan was unable to hear it. The individual who was lying on the ground sobbed as he attempted to protect himself from the unrelenting punches by curling his body into a protective ball around himself.

With a final, savage swing, Flanagan threw the chair aside and grabbed the man by his bloodied shirt, lifting him off the ground. "Who's your supplier?" Flanagan demanded, his face inches from the man's. The man's eyes were wide with terror, his breath coming in ragged, desperate gasps.

"I-I don't know!" the man cried, blood and saliva mingling on his lips. "I swear, I don't know!"

Flanagan shook him violently. "Bullshit!" he roared. "You're going to tell me everything, or I swear to God, I'll break every bone in your body."

"That's enough, Patrick," Jackson said firmly, his voice cutting through the haze of violence. "We need him to talk."

With a touch on Flanagan's shoulder, Jackson moved forward. Flanagan paused, hold becoming firmer before he finally let go and let the man fall to the floor. The man attempted to crawl away while mumbling words of pure pain as his body seized up in agony.

Jackson knelt beside the man, his tone softer but no less insistent. "Give us the information we need, and we can end this here. Who provides for you?"

The man sobbed, his body shaking. "It's… for the Wolf. I do not know who he is or who he works for. That is all I know. I just got employed here, and I swear there isn't much I know." Jackson placed a hand on Flanagan's shoulder. They had confirmed their suspicions about the place, and now they had key suspects who also linked them to Roberto.

Agent Jackson whispered into his headset, his voice calm yet forceful. "Collins, turn off your microphone," he ordered. Susan Collins, who was waiting in the car, complied right away, knowing that the situation inside had gotten out of control. Inside the warehouse, the mood was tense and filled with a distinct sense of danger. Flanagan used brute muscle to lift the drug gang leader over his head and place him in a chokehold.

As he hurled the man to the ground with a fast and forceful move, the victim's neck landed with a painful thud on the concrete. The gang leader lay motionless. Without missing a beat, Flanagan switched his focus to another member of the group, his eyes icy and ruthless as he did so. He seized the man and hauled him up with almost animalistic force. Meanwhile, Jackson surveyed the room, spotting another individual attempting to flee. Jackson fired with experienced precision, striking the fleeing man in the shoulder. The man shouted and clutched at his wound.

"You're all going to jail," Jackson declared, his voice ringing out across the room. "But if you don't want to end up underground, you'll tell us what we want to know. We want the location of Rossi's trafficking operation – the one he still has active."

The men in the room looked at each other, fear etched on their faces. One of them, shaking and pale, stammered, "Rossi will kill us all."

Just as he finished speaking, Flanagan lunged forward, grabbing the man in a chokehold. Jackson moved in beside him, his expression one of grim determination. He pressed his gun to the man's ear, the cold metal making the man flinch. Without warning, Jackson fired, blowing off the man's entire earlobe. The man howled in pain as blood spattered about him. "What makes you think we won't kill you?" Jackson shouted into the man's other ear, his voice a harsh, intimidating growl. The man's screams echoed through the warehouse, the sound mingling with the groans and cries of the others who had been subdued.

"You heard the man," Flanagan tightened his grip, his biceps bulging with the effort. "Talk, or you won't get another chance," he growled.

The man in Flanagan's chokehold gasped for breath, his eyes wide with terror. "Okay, okay!" he choked out. "I'll tell you. Just… please, don't kill me."

Jackson eased back slightly, giving the man room to speak but keeping the gun trained on him. "Start talking."

"The operation," the man gasped, blood trickling down his neck from where his earlobe had been, "it's… it's at the old shipping yard, down by the docks. They move the girls through there, keep them in containers until they're ready to be shipped out." Flanagan and Jackson had a knowing look as they exchanged looks. Their lead was in hand.

"Good," Jackson said, his voice hard. "Now, if any of you think about warning Rossi, remember what we did here tonight.

We will find you, and it will be much worse." When Flanagan let go of the man, he collapsed on the floor, wailing and grabbing his ear. After the agents' rigorous questioning, the remaining gang members' swagger crumbled. They appeared obviously terrified.

With a step back, Jackson stowed his weapon. In response to his command, "Secure them," Flanagan wasted no time binding the hands of the surviving gang members who were still conscious.

"Collins, we've got the location. Get the team ready. We're moving out." They prepared to leave; Jackson spoke into his earpiece again.

"Copy that. I'll alert the others." Collins's voice crackled back.

Just as they were about to leave the warehouse, another man emerged from the shadows, frantic for the entrance. Jackson reacted immediately, raising his rifle and firing. The shot boomed out, and the man slumped, screaming and grasping his leg. The expression on Flanagan's face was icy and threatening as he walked over. He pressed his boot firmly against the man's injured leg, prompting another yell of pain. "If you don't want to lose this leg, you better tell us something useful," Flannagan said.

The man whimpered, his hands scrabbling at the floor in a futile attempt to escape the agony. He was too scared to speak, but another man, cowering in the corner, stepped forward, his eyes wide with fear. "Wait, wait!" he pleaded. "I heard something. There's a new hotel by the airport – the Euphoria. Rossi brings in high-end clients there. They're looking for... for girls."

Jackson's eyes narrowed as he processed this information. He pulled out his phone and called the FBI to report the lead. "We've got a new location," he said, his voice crisp and authoritative.

"The Euphoria Hotel by the airport. Rossi might be operating out of there. Send backup."

After securing the remaining men in a locked room, Jackson, Flanagan, and Collins hurried to their car, the urgency of the situation propelling them forward. As Jackson drove, his mind raced with possibilities while his gut told him that he was going in the right direction. They had to move quickly if they were going to catch Rossi and rescue Isabella.

Jackson dialed Jake's number, feeling a mix of hope and apprehension. "Jake, we've got our first solid lead on Isabella," he said as soon as Jake answered. "Sit tight. We're checking out a hotel by the airport."

"What's the name of the hotel?" Jake pressed, his voice taut with anxiety.

"I can't give you that information right now, Jake. It's too dangerous." Jackson hesitated, knowing the risks of involving Jake directly.

Jake's voice hardened. "Jackson, I gave the FBI information when it counted. You owe me at least one favor in return." There was a long pause. Jackson knew Jake was right. He had earned the right to know. "Alright," Jackson relented. "It's the Euphoria Hotel, by the airport. But stay out of it, Jake. Let us handle this."

"I understand," Jake said, though his tone suggested otherwise.

As he got ready for action, Jake slipped into a dark gray athletic tracksuit, which hugged his powerful physique. His motions were deliberate, smooth, and well-rehearsed. With the familiar feel of their weight, he reached for a set of brass knuckles and tucked them into his pockets. After that, he delicately inserted a short, thick, and heavy lead pipe inside a little duffel bag after feeling its chilly, solid heft. At long last, he completed the set with a miniature sledgehammer, fierce and stocky in build. Everything seemed to be following a script he had practiced over and over again.

"Madam, Jake just received the call. It's time for me to go operational." Rodney called Aunt Mary as soon as Jake left the estate, a sense of duty reflected in his calm voice.

Aunt Mary's response was also calm but laden with concern. "Godspeed, Rodney. You two come back home to me safe."

Jake drove with single-minded focus, the engine of his car humming as it sped down the road. His mind replayed the words of his sensei from years ago. Randy's voice was clear and stern in his memory: "When you get ready to go into battle, you have to focus your mind. In some ways, you need to turn it off to feel your instincts. In war, you have to be merciless. Never let your enemy get back up, or they will have another chance to hurt you."

Jake let those comments reverberate in his mind, shaping his decisions and behavior. His tensed fingers gripped the steering wheel even more tightly. While he drove, the city lights sped by in a haze, and the continuous thump of the tires on the road filled his ears like a drum.

In an effort to quiet the tempest of feelings raging inside him, he inhaled deeply. His thoughts were aided to drift away by the chilly night air that blew in through the crack in the window. Maintaining concentration was crucial; he needed to control his wrath and transform it into power and accuracy. All of Jake's senses were on high alert, and he remembered every detail of his environment.

As he deftly made his way across the metropolis, he could see the impending encounter ahead of him in the lengthy shadows created by the lamps. His sensei's lessons had grounded him in the present, so his mind was clear even though his heart was pounding.

He pulled over and waited for a moment to settle himself as he neared the spot. To make sure everything was in his duffel bag, he gave it one more check. Everything needed for the task at hand was on hand, including the miniature sledgehammer, lead pipe, and brass knuckles.

After securing the bag, he threw it over his shoulder and stepped out of the vehicle. The building loomed ahead, its dark silhouette stark against the night sky. On the inside, Jake's mentality was a stronghold of tenacity. The adrenaline pumping through his veins was visible, and he could feel his body getting ready for action. The sentiments expressed by Randy struck a chord deep within him, "Be merciless. Never allow them to get back up again."

Jake took one more long breath before beginning his approach, his footfall soft but deliberate as he moved closer. Hesitation was no longer an option at this point. In order to get Isabella back, he was prepared to do whatever he needed. Both his thoughts and his body were in perfect alignment for the fight that lay ahead of him. His determination was unrelenting.

Isabella and Stephanie had rehearsed this moment countless times. The sound of footsteps echoed down the corridor, and they immediately fell silent. The tension in the air was palpable. The door to Isabella's cell burst open, and three men stormed in, turning on the blinding white lights that seared her eyes. Isabella squinted against the harsh glare, her heart pounding in her chest.

But tonight was different. Instead of the usual taunts and beatings, one of the men carried a giant water hose. Without warning, he turned it on her, the force of the water slamming into her with brutal intensity. Isabella felt like her skin was being peeled off her body. She gritted her teeth, refusing to give them the satisfaction of hearing her scream.

"Fuck you!" she spat, her voice barely audible over the roar of the water. "You think this will break me?"

The man with the hose sneered, increasing the pressure. Isabella's body was pushed against the wall, the water battering her mercilessly. She struggled to stay upright, her muscles straining with the effort.

"You need to get cleaned up because the boss wants to see you tonight," one of the men said, his tone mocking. He threw a towel at her feet, the coarse fabric landing in a soggy heap. Another man stepped forward and removed the collar from her neck. The metal felt cold and unforgiving against her skin.

"I'm not going anywhere with you, bastards," she hissed, her voice steady despite the terror gnawing at her insides. Isabella glared at them, defiance burning in her eyes.

The man who had spoken grabbed her roughly, his fingers digging into her arms as he threw her over his shoulder. Isabella kicked and struggled, her body writhing in a desperate attempt to break free.

"Let me go, you piece of shit!" she shouted, her fists pounding against his back. But her captor was unfazed, his grip ironclad.

As they left the cell, Isabella heard Stephanie's faint whisper, "Stay strong and be safe."

Chapter 11 Fortiudo Venatus

Jake was the first to arrive at the Euphoria Hotel. He jumped out of his car, donning a pair of large sunglasses, and began patrolling the lobby with an air of nervous energy. The opulent surroundings did little to calm his racing heart. The grand chandeliers and plush carpets seemed out of place for the grim task at hand.

Ten minutes later, Agent Jackson and his team arrived. They spotted Jake almost immediately. His amateurish attempt at blending in, complete with the sunglasses at night, made him stick out like a sore thumb. The car erupted in laughter. Agent Flannagan yelled, "What the hell does this guy think he is doing?" trying to catch his breath from laughing. The sight brought a welcome relief from the tension leading up to that moment. The FBI team decided that if they make it out alive, then they would teach Jake how to maintain his cover without looking so ridiculous and suspicious. Jackson eventually recovered enough to call Jake over and meet them in their van, parked discreetly in the lot.

"Alright, Jake, listen up. You'll need to stick close to Flanagan and follow his lead." Inside the van, tension was high yet focused. Agent Jackson outlined the idea in a dominating manner.

"This hotel is 100% owned by Roberto Rossi. It's invitation-only, which fits the profile of a human trafficking operation. We believe we've got the right place." Leaning forward, Agent Collins clarified.

Jackson nodded. "Collins and I will go in posing as a couple looking to dine at the restaurant and book a room. Flanagan and Jake, you two will put on janitorial uniforms. This will allow you to move through the hotel without drawing attention." There was a certain ease and relief in this plan. Jake felt sure and certain. Maybe the involvement of the uniform would help him conceal the lead pipe and brass knuckles he had stashed in his duffel bag. "Got it," he said, his voice steady. "We'll keep an eye out and report anything suspicious through the headsets."

With the plan in place, they moved quickly. Jackson and Collins adjusted their appearances, transforming into a seemingly ordinary couple, while Flanagan and Jake changed into janitorial uniforms. Jake felt a mix of nerves and determination as he put on the outfit, tucking his weapons securely away. They entered the hotel through a service entrance, and Jake tried to calm his nerves. The uniform helped him blend in, and he focused on the task at hand. They moved methodically, Flanagan taking the lead and Jake following closely behind, pushing a cart laden with cleaning supplies.

As all of this was going on, Jackson and Collins strolled into the foyer, perfectly in character. They strolled up to the front desk, grinning and chit-chatting like any other couple out on the town for the evening.

After Jackson had reserved a room, they headed to the bar and looked around for anything strange. The decor of the hotel was opulent, with soothing music playing in the background and dark lighting. The bar area was full of smartly dressed customers, but Jackson and Collins were on guard, their eyes darting everywhere. An hour went by with nothing happening. Jake and Flanagan had searched every floor but found nothing. Tension started to build. Jake couldn't get the thought out of his head that they might not be where they should be.

"Anything?" Jackson's voice crackled in Jake's earpiece.

"Negative," Flanagan responded. "We've checked all the obvious spots. Nothing so far."

"Keep looking," Jackson replied. "We can't afford to miss anything."

As they continued their search, Jake's thoughts drifted to Isabella. He had to find her. He couldn't let her down. The stakes were too high. His focus sharpened, and he redoubled his efforts, checking every nook and cranny. Jake believed the cleaning suit was brilliant because it allowed him to conceal his pipe and brass knuckles discretely. As they walked through the hotel's service hallways, he could feel the weight of his hidden weapons, which reminded him of his goal. Even though he was tense, the musty smell of cleaning supplies and the hum of machines filled the room. He opened his eyes wide, looking for signs of something strange.

Back at the bar, Collins leaned in closer to Jackson, pretending to whisper sweet nothings. "I'm starting to think this might be a bust," she murmured.

"Stay sharp," Jackson replied, his eyes scanning the room. "We're not done yet."

***

There were tears running down Stephanie's face as she recalled the discussions she had with Isabella when she was now incarcerated. They had vowed to do everything they could to make it out alive, and if they couldn't, they would at least take a few of their captors down with them. The thought gave her a small, flickering hope amidst the overwhelming despair. Suddenly, the sound of approaching footsteps echoed down the corridor. Two men appeared at her cell door, with faces painted with deception and twisted with the lust of cruelty. "Get up, bitch," one of them snarled as he unlocked the cell and grabbed her roughly by the arm. "It's time for you to go to work again."

Stephanie exerted great effort to resist their hold, but the men were unrelenting. As she stomped down the poorly lighted corridor, her feet barely making contact with the floor, she was forcibly removed from the cell. A further source of agony for her was the fact that the cold, hard floor scraped against her bare feet. They halted at a side elevator and pushed her into it without any hesitation. The mechanical walls of the lift made her feel as though she was being suffocated, and the only thing that broke the silence was the sound of her own frantic breathing. A dinging sound marked the opening of the doors, which revealed a sterile and clinical-looking changing area. A small sink with a toothbrush and a few toiletries sat on a shelf, and hanging on a hook was a striking red dress.

One of the men pointed to the dress. "Put it on," he ordered. "And you better make this client happy, or it could be your last night on this earth."

The scarlet outfit sent shivers down Stephanie's spine when she observed it. It clung to every contour like a cheap satin lingerie, leaving little room for creativity. Even though it gave her the willies, she knew she had to wear it nevertheless. With quivering hands, she took up the dress as she stared at the men, who had emotionless, icy eyes.

As Stephanie changed into the red dress, one of the men leaned against the wall, watching her with a sneer. "This one's easier to handle than the new bitch," he remarked to his companion.

"Yeah, that new bitch, she's a handful. Just got dragged away for a meeting with the boss," the other man chuckled darkly. "I'd like to see how long she lasts. Bet she won't be so tough after a few rounds with the boss. I hear that he is a mean, sadistic character." Hearing those words, Stephanie's heart sank, thinking about Isabella, but it also reignited a spark of defiance within her. She thought to herself, He's right. This might be my last time on this earth, so I'm going to fucking make it count. She settled herself, determined to face whatever came next with courage. The water from the shower washed away the dirt and grime, but it did little to alleviate her terror. Her attention was fixed on the impending confrontation as she brushed her teeth.

Even though she was aware she had to remain strong, the circumstance was weighing her down. This was her chance to stand up and prove she wasn't going down without a fight. She thought about Isabella and their pact. The idiot henchman came back within half an hour. With one hand on hers, they began to drag her back towards the elevator. Stephanie's body tensed and prepared, her face expressionless as her thoughts raced. She could feel the chill of the metal bracelets digging into her wrists as they ascended to the eleventh floor of the elevator. The men were virtually carrying her down the corridor into a magnificent suite as another set of elevator doors opened as they passed. Her surroundings' stark contrast and lavishness appeared to be mocking her predicament.

Suddenly, they noticed a clean-cut guy in a janitorial outfit walking toward them. It was Jake. He cast a quick glance in Stephanie's direction, his eyes focusing on hers with a questioning expression. "Is everything okay here, miss?" he inquired, his voice steady yet betraying his concern. A tear streamed down Stephanie's cheek as she made an apparent yet quiet cry for assistance by simply saying no. Then suddenly, Jake was shoved hard by one of the men with her. His tone was one of reprimand

and exclusion. I don't understand why you're even on this floor. You are not allowed in this area.

"Just doing my job," he said, his voice calm despite the tension. "Didn't mean to intrude." Jake stumbled back a step, his hands raised in a placating gesture. The men hissed at him, distracted. Stephanie took advantage, her head racing. She realized she had to act immediately. "Please," she muttered, shaking but determined. "Don't let them take me."

Jake's gaze grew determined. She looked desperate, and he knew he couldn't let this continue. "I think you need to let her go," he added, approaching closer and standing firm. Before the man could finish his sentence, Jake pulled out his brass knuckles and landed a left hook square on the guy's temple. The man collapsed, pulling Stephanie down with him. The second man, reacting quickly, pulled out a knife and swung at Jake. However, he had already anticipated the move. He dodged the attack and immediately pulled out his lead pipe. With a swift motion, he struck the man's hand, causing the knife to clatter to the ground. Stephanie instantly jumped for the dropped knife. She did a front roll, like a gymnast, and stabbed the man Jake had hit before. Her motions were precise, driven by repressed fury. Her screams echoed through the hallway as she stabbed him in the throat, mouth, and finally, the eye.

With each stab of the knife, she let out her focused rage, "You're coming with me, motherfucker!"

Jake was too late to respond to Stephanie's tantrum. He opened up when the second attacker lunged at him. Jake assumed a solid Uechi-dachi stance, body ready to strike. With an effortless grace, Jake gave him a straight kick to the jaw as the assailant attempted to move.

After tumbling to the ground and trying to raise himself, the man discovered that the pipe strike had shattered his hand. Before Jake could take another breath, Stephanie fixed her gaze on the fallen attacker. With a grim determination, she shoved the knife she had in her hand straight up his ass. The man's scream pierced the air like a choir boy hitting a high note, and in that instant, Jake took out his pipe and cracked the man hard on the back of the head hard. The attacker went down and out like a light, blood gushing from the base of his skull.

Jake quickly helped Stephanie to her feet. "Hey, let's get you out of here," he said, his voice urgent but gentle. They raced towards the elevator, Jake talking loudly into his headset. "Agent Jackson, Flanagan, we've got a situation! We're coming down from the 11th floor. Be ready!"

As they reached the elevator, Jake glanced back at the chaos they had left behind. He felt a mix of relief and adrenaline, knowing they had only moments before more trouble arrived. The elevator doors slid open, and they stepped inside, the small space suddenly feeling like a sanctuary. Stephanie leaned against the wall, her breath coming in ragged gasps. "Thank you," she whispered, her eyes wide with a mixture of fear and gratitude.

Jake nodded, his focus still sharp. "We're not out of this yet. Just hold on."

Three men were playing a furious game of poker at a table in a small hotel security room. The only source of light in the room was a bank of monitors showing different camera feeds from around the hotel. A burly man with a full beard among the men looked up at the monitors and gave them a second look.

"Holy shit!" he yelled, his eyes widening as he saw the fight unfolding on the screen. The other two men immediately jumped up from their seats, the poker game forgotten. They rushed to the control panel, frantically hitting a series of buttons. Alarms blared throughout the hotel, and the man grabbed the intercom, his voice panicked. "We need all available security personnel to be ready! This is an omega-level event!"

Meanwhile, Jake and Stephanie were descending rapidly in the elevator. Jake pulled out a key card from his pocket and handed it to Stephanie. "When we reach the parking lot, find a white Tesla. Get in and lock yourself inside. Don't open the doors for anyone except me or the FBI."

Stephanie took the card with trembling hands, her eyes wide with fear. Jake then pulled out his phone, showing her a picture of Isabella. "Have you seen her? She nodded and answered in a shaky voice, "Yes, I've been locked away in a dark basement with no lights. The only time I saw any light was when they forced me to go to one of the rooms in the hotel. I talked to someone named Isabella through the walls. They took her to someone they called the Boss maybe two hours ago."

The elevator doors opened, and Jake hurriedly escorted Stephanie through the lobby and out a side door. "Go!" he urged her. She took off, sprinting toward the parking lot.

Jake quickly slipped on his brass knuckles, the cool metal fitting snugly against his fingers. His eyes caught sight of a small sledgehammer propped up beside the door. He grabbed it, feeling the weight and balance, and headed back inside, his mind focused on finding Isabella.

Through his earpiece, Jake shouted, "Agents Jackson, Collins, Flanagan, I think there's a sub-basement under the restaurant where they're holding all the girls. But they just took Isabella somewhere else. We need to move fast!"

In response to his words, the hotel's security systems sprung into action. With a loud click, all the doors that led into the hotel were closed, preventing them from leaving the space. Numerous men, some of whom were armed with firearms, began to pour into the lobby, their expressions displaying a grim determination. Even though the tension in the air was apparent, Jake knew that a fight was about to occur.

Once a vision of elegance and tranquility, the foyer had become a battleground. Jake positioned himself in close proximity to the restaurant's door, paying close attention to his surroundings. He could pick up on the sound of footfall in the distance and the quiet hum of the alarms. He tightened his hold on the sledgehammer, getting himself ready for the storm that was approaching.

He glanced around, spotting Agent Jackson and Collins making their way toward him, their expressions serious. Flanagan was close behind, his eyes scanning the room for threats. The team was ready for action, and their movements were coordinated and efficient.

"Jake, we need to get to that sub-basement," Jackson said, his voice urgent but controlled. "Lead the way."

Jake nodded, his jaw set with determination. "Follow me," he said, starting to move towards a discreet door near the back of the lobby. The sound of gunfire erupted behind them, and Jake turned just in time to see one of the armed men aiming his weapon.

"Get down!" Jake shouted, swinging the sledgehammer with force. The man went down with a grunt, the weapon clattering to the floor. Chaos erupted as more security personnel entered the fray, their guns trained on the FBI agents and Jake.

"It's going to take longer for us to request backup because this one is off the books!" Colin shouted. Agent Collins and Jackson raced towards the lobby, their guns drawn and eyes scanning for threats.

They burst into the lobby and immediately spotted a group of Rossi henchmen dressed as security personnel, all in black jackets. One of the men from the surveillance team pointed at Jake and yelled, "Yeah, that's him!" Another henchman sneered, "Let's teach him a lesson."

Jake saw them closing in and knew he had to act fast. Without hesitation, he charged at the nearest henchman, landing a brutal punch to the face with his brass knuckles. The man staggered, blood spurting from his nose, and Jake followed up with a swift kick to the gut, sending him crumpling to the floor.

Seeing another henchman reaching for his revolver, Agent Jackson reacted quickly, firing a shot that hit the man square in the chest. He fell back, his body hitting the ground with a heavy thud. Collins shouted, "It'll be about 25 minutes before backup arrives!"

Most of the henchmen pulled out their guns, and the lobby erupted into a chaotic firefight. Bullets whizzed through the air, shattering glass and splintering wood. Jake dropped to the ground, crawling on his knees towards safety. He moved quickly, his mind focused on survival and finding Isabella.

Out of the corner of his eye, Jake saw Patrick Flanagan grabbing one of the men in a headlock. Flanagan's face was a mask of fury as he wrestled the man to the ground, pressing a pistol to his head. "You picked the wrong fight!" Flanagan growled before firing a shot that silenced the man permanently.

Jake could hear Flanagan shouting to Collins and Jackson over the ding of gunfire, "Is everything okay?"

"We're holding up, but we need to push through!" Jackson yelled back, his voice barely audible over the chaos. He fired off a few more shots, hitting another henchman who had been trying to flank them.

As Jake crawled toward the hallway, Isabella consumed his thoughts. He knew she was somewhere alive in this hellhole, and he couldn't let anything stop him from finding her. The sound of gunfire and shouts faded into the background as he focused solely on his mission.

He reached the relative safety of a hallway, pausing for a moment to catch his breath. The adrenaline coursing through his veins made his heart pound in his ears, but he forced himself to stay calm. He had to be smart and think like Randy had taught him: stay focused, stay alive, and never let the enemy get the upper hand. Jake pressed himself against the wall, peering around the corner. The hallway was clear for now, but he knew it wouldn't stay that way for long. He had to move fast, find the entrance to the sub-basement, and locate Isabella before it was too late. With a few minor bruises, Jake managed to get to the elevator. He pressed the button for the sub-basement, shouting into his microphone, "I'm going to get the girls!"

Agent Collins' voice crackled back urgently, "Wait for backup, Jake!"

Ignoring her, Jake remembered Stephanie's words about the service elevator being the pathway to the sub-basement. In little time at all, he located it and started descending. With the basement's lift doors slamming open, Jake's senses were heightened. He could hardly see anything in the pitch-blackness that engulfed him. In the distance, a barely audible sound of approaching footfall grew increasingly audible.

Without thinking, Jake tensed up and prepared to defend himself. Out of the gloom came a figure that swung at him. As a reflex, Jake locked up with the assailant and captured him in a judo-style headlock. This guy was strong and able to break free with very little effort. Jake stepped back into the darkness and grabbed his mini sledgehammer. As the attacker pursued, Jake motioned like he was about to execute a kick, which made the assailant go into a semi-defensive posture. Jake immediately switched gears, took the mini sledgehammer, and hit the attacker squarely in the head and then in the leg hard. Jake did not know if the guy was dead or not, but he was certain that this gentleman was not getting back up.

Within his thoughts, Randy's words resounded, "It's time to turn your mind off now." Jake cautiously made his way down the hall, following the wall as he looked for the girls. Moving further, he felt the cold, wet concrete beneath his fingertips. Someone suddenly snatched him from behind. One of the attackers grabbed his side, and then a third leaped on top of him, all before he could land a decent punch. Kicking and stomping, they wrestled him to the ground, attempting to beat him down.

Jake ducked his head in defense and dragged one of his assailants down by the leg. He then began violently elbowing the man in the face as the other two persisted in their unrelenting punching and kicking attacks. Jake went into defense looking for an opening. Suddenly, Jake heard a loud thump. Out of nowhere, two of his assailants passed out, and the guy Jake was fighting on the ground was being dragged away. A mysterious stranger lifted the man Jake had been hitting the ground and proceeded to repeatedly punch him in the face. Dazed, Jake got to his feet and exclaimed, "Whoa, easy! I am the good guy!"

"I know you're a good guy, but I am the Batman." A familiar voice responded.

Jake recognized the voice instantly. "Rodney?"

"How did you find me?" Jake asked, still catching his breath.

Rodney smiled, "That immaculate watch your aunt gave you? It's not just for decoration. I've been tracking you."

Relief washed over Jake as Rodney handed him a headlamp. The powerful beam cut through the darkness, revealing the grim reality of their surroundings. They moved swiftly, searching the basement. Jake continued to announce, "Don't worry, everything will be okay!" as he desperately tried to open the doors of each cage. It's okay now! Still holding out hope that Isabella would be among them, he shined his headlamp into each stall. There was no indication of Isabella in the faint light, but terrified, desperate faces were revealed. Refusing to give up, he continued pressing forward.

Susan Collins and Agent Flanagan were still deeply involved in a gun battle in the lobby. The sound of gunshots reverberated off the walls as bullets flew through the air. In order to avoid detection, Agent Jackson dove behind an uncovered table and strained his ears for a signal of reinforcements. At long last, he could make out the increasingly deafening beat of helicopter blades. To the rescue! "The FBI has arrived!" he exclaimed to his group.

As soon as word got out, multiple squads of FBI agents stormed the hotel, weapons drawn, in an effort to capture Rossi's men. As the agents systematically eliminated the remaining goons, the mayhem in the lobby became even more intense. Rodney and his associates retrieved little bomb devices from their duffel bags in the basement. Rodney cautioned the females, "Stand back," as he fastened the gadgets to the jail doors. The prisoners were set free as a succession of deafening explosions detached the doors from their hinges.

"Move, move, move!" Rodney shouted, herding the girls towards Jake.

"Jake," Rodney said urgently, "the FBI is on the premises. My team and I have to vanish, but we'll stay ready. If you need us again, just call."

"Thank you, Rodney," Jake replied, his voice filled with gratitude. "I won't forget this."

Gathering the girls, Jake led them to the service elevator. "Stay close and keep moving!" he urged. They crowded into the elevator, and as it ascended, Jake's thoughts remained fixated on Isabella.

As the elevator doors opened to the lobby, Agent Collins and Agent Jackson rushed to them. "Get them out of here!" Collins ordered, her gun still drawn.

"Follow us!" Jackson added, leading the group towards the exit while the rest of the FBI continued battling Rossi's henchmen.

Outside, the night was alive with flashing lights and the hum of helicopters. The girls were quickly ushered to safety by other agents. Just as Jake was about to step outside, his phone rang. It was Vincent.

"Jake," Vincent's voice was calm but urgent. "We have intel that Isabella was just taken to Rossi's yacht. Sit tight; my men and I are going to do everything we can to bring her back to you."

Jake felt a surge of relief mixed with dread. "Thank you so much, Vincent. There's a lot I need to tell you. I'm on my way."

Vincent's voice softened slightly. "Stay safe, Jake. We'll get her back."

Once outside, Jake pulled Agent Jackson to the side. "Listen, Jackson," he began urgently, "I'm also working with Vincent Capoli to get Isabella back. We've tracked her to Rossi's yacht. I'm going to confront Rossi and kill him if I can for everything he's done to her."

"My team and I are coming with you." Agent Jackson's eyes widened in surprise but quickly steeled with determination.

"No. Stay here and try to get a search warrant. I'll signal you when it's time to strike. I can't have you throwing away your career over this. Just promise me one thing – you will leave the Capolis out of this." Jake shook his head firmly. Agent Jackson nodded, his expression tense but resolute. Jake turned and sprinted away, yelling into his watch, "Rodney, I need you and your team to pick me up now!"

As he dashed through the chaotic scene, Jake glanced back at Jackson. "Make sure you get Stephanie out of my white Tesla and take her statement!" he shouted, his voice edged with urgency.

Jackson called back, "You're walking, talking, and acting like an FBI agent super spy, young man!"

Jake barely registered the words as he continued running, his heart pounding with fear and determination. The night air was thick with tension, every second feeling like an eternity. He could hear the distant sounds of sirens and the chaos of the ongoing raid behind him, but his mind was laser-focused on the mission ahead.

Suddenly, a sleek black SUV screeched to a halt beside him. The door swung open, and Jake didn't hesitate for a second. He leaped into the vehicle, breathless but resolute. "We've got a location on Rossi's yacht," he said, his voice steady despite the adrenaline coursing through his veins. "Let's move."

Chapter 12: Navis Bellica

Roberto's luxurious white yacht gleamed under the moonlight, and it stood anchored by the pier. Its sleek design contrasted sharply with the dark, chaotic underworld it was about to witness. The vessel's opulent exterior, adorned with intricate details and lavish furnishings, betrayed no hint of the violence and turmoil that was soon to erupt within its confines.

A short distance away, parked discreetly in the shadows of a nearby street, Vincent sat in his black Escalade. The SUV was equipped with state-of-the-art surveillance equipment, and Vincent's sharp eyes scanned the live feeds from multiple cameras strategically placed around Roberto Rossi's lavish yacht. Despite the chill inside the car, the tension was palpable, causing Vincent's men to break a sweat as they monitored the screens.

The yacht itself was a floating palace, meticulously maintained with no expense spared. It gleamed under the moonlight, its sleek lines and luxurious fittings making it a small fortress at sea. His attention to detail is evident in every inch of the vessel, from the polished teak decks to the opulent interiors decorated with rare artwork and plush furnishings. This was no mere pleasure craft; it was a symbol of power and wealth, a mobile stronghold for the Rossi empire.

"Getting out of that vessel alive and alone is not possible. I know my men will follow through on my expectations." Vincent was always two steps ahead. In his discussions with his lieutenants and his son Martin, he had meticulously planned every move. They knew that the yacht was more than just a floating mansion—

it was Roberto's command center, a place where he felt untouchable. But Vincent was determined to shatter that illusion.

"Remember, we're not just watching. We're controlling the narrative. Every move they make, every conversation they have, we need to know." The subtle growl in Vincent's was the definitive roar—a battle cry.

The entire plan was set out. Martin, who was in contact with the other security, exclaimed. "Our men are in position, and we have eyes on every angle. What about the FBI?" He asked.

Vincent allowed himself a small, confident smile. "I don't have my contacts for nothing." Just then he was cut off by the crackle of voice on the radio. "We're ready when you are, Vincent. Just give the word."

"It's time," Vincent said. "Let's show Roberto what happens when he tries to play us."

Then there was the matter of Jake. If he didn't arrive soon, they would risk losing the element of surprise, and more importantly, Isabella might not make it. Had Isabella not been on the ship, Vincent may not have been so careful and blew the entire thing up. But the FBI was too far deep into the matter, and he could not afford them coming after him, not when people like Roberto existed.

Beside him, his most trusted personal guard sat alert, his gaze fixed on the screens. "Sir, we can't wait much longer," he said, his tone respectful but firm. "If we delay, we might lose our chance, and the girl… she might not make it."

Vincent's jaw clenched. He had promised Jake he would wait, but the situation was becoming increasingly dire. "I know. I am just waiting for someone, trying to keep my side of the bargain,"

Vincent replied, his voice a low growl. "But we need to give Jake every possible moment to get here. He deserves that chance."

He nodded, understanding his boss's dilemma but knowing the risks all too well. He glanced back at the yacht, its pristine surface mocking the dark secrets it harbored. "Prepare the teams," he ordered, his decision made. "We'll give Jake five more minutes. If he's not here by then, we go in."

As if his guard had the next steps already mapped out in his mind, he swiftly pulled out his tablet, displaying the exquisite blueprints of the yacht. These blueprints, detailed and intricate, highlighted the luxurious and sophisticated design, reflecting the opulence of its owner. The guard relayed precise orders through his earpiece, his voice calm but authoritative. Around the yacht, the Capoli men, strategically positioned, tensed in readiness, their faces set with determination.

Vincent glanced at the clock, each tick amplifying the sense of urgency. This wasn't just any yacht; it was a floating palace owned by Roberto Rossi. His empire spanned continents, his influence reaching into the darkest corners of power. This yacht, with its lavish interiors and state-of-the-art security systems, was a testament to his vast fortune and meticulous nature.

Just as Vincent was about to give the final command, his phone buzzed with a message. It was from Jake: "You guys go ahead, I will join you." Just then, a few lights flickered on the yacht, showing some activity. It seemed as if Roberto's men were readying themselves to go offshore.

"Sir, there is activity on the yacht. The men stationed outside are not on site. This way, we will lose the girl. I request for immedia…"

"We will move in now. Jake will catch up." Looking straight ahead, Vincent muttered. "I am not letting him get away this time."

His guard nodded, relaying the updated orders. "Teams, advance and board the yacht. Execute the plan."

The Capoli men moved with military precision, their dark clothing blending seamlessly into the night as they closed in on the yacht from all sides. The first team boarded silently; their footsteps were absorbed by the sleek deck beneath them. The air was thick with tension, each man hyper-aware of his surroundings, scanning for any sign of movement.

They spread out swiftly, securing key positions with practiced efficiency. Vincent, from his vantage point in the SUV, could almost feel the weight of their anticipation. His pulse quickened, mirroring the urgency of the operation. The men's hushed communications crackled in his earpiece, each coded phrase a testament to their discipline and focus.

The yacht's luxurious exterior, glistening under the moonlight, belied the danger that now permeated its every corner. Vincent's eyes darted between the screens, tracking their progress, heart pounding in sync with each silent step taken by his team. The night was theirs, and every second counted.

"First team in position," came the whispered report through the earpiece.

"Second team advancing," another voice followed.

Vincent watched the screens intently. This had to go perfectly. Any mistake could cost them dearly.

"Third team, let me know your status. You seem to have the most activity on your end." Vincent's man has a copy of the people who were supposed to be on the yacht.

"The yacht is pretty big, and Roberto is a careful guy. He must have 3 to 4 people stationed at the back end from where you are supposed to surround.

"Yes, Alpha, we have sight of two of their guards. It seems like they are aware of the dangers and have learned about the action at the hotel. Let us isolate these two, and then we will give the signal for the other teams to move in. Bravo out."

The leader of the second team, just then, broke through the radio and communicated in an urgent manner. "There is activity on the side of the deck. Our team got rid of one of theirs and sent him overboard. We are ready to advance. We need your go-ahead. Knuckles McGee out."

"Proceed," Vincent ordered, his eyes never leaving the surveillance screens. He watched as Knuckles McGee's team moved in from the port side, their movements a blur of coordinated efficiency. They encountered another guard, and within seconds, he too was dispatched, his body disappearing into the dark waters below.

Bravo team, having cleared their initial targets, signaled to the other teams. "All teams, proceed to secondary positions. Engage at will. Bravo out." The yacht, now fully surrounded, became a hive of activity. Capoli's men moved through the shadows, systematically eliminating the outer defenses. Gunfire erupted, sharp and loud in the night, marking the start of the full assault. The serene vessel was now a warzone, its opulent interior shattered by the sounds of battle.

"Sir, we're encountering heavy resistance on the upper deck," one of the team leaders reported. "We need reinforcements."

Vincent clenched his fist, frustration gnawing at him. "Stay focused. Push through. Jake will be there any moment."

Alpha team broke into the upper deck, moving quietly so that the luxurious lounge, which used to be a sign of wealth, wouldn't let the people inside know what was going on. No one moved the furniture or damaged the walls, which kept the appearance of peace. But when they started fighting close up with Rossi's men, the room quickly turned into a battlefield, with broken furniture and the sharp crack of gunfire that was being held back. The Bravo team moved quickly and deadly as they moved up from the lower deck.

Every step was carefully thought out to block out any sound that might have let them know they were there. They cleared room after room, and what they did was a dangerous dance of efficiency. Rossi's guards were defeated by the team using silenced weapons and hand-to-hand fighting.

The members of Knuckles McGee's team went discreetly through the crew rooms, and their footsteps were scarcely audible on the port side of the yacht. Every step ahead proved to be a potential death trap due to the tiny hallways that turned into chokepoints. They encountered significant opposition, but they were aware of their objective, which was to remain as silent as possible in order to avoid being discovered.

In order to eliminate potential dangers, the men communicated with one another through hand signals and silent takedowns. With unwavering determination and skillful application, they were able to gain each step. In the darkness, the remainder of the staff on board the yacht continued to be blissfully unconscious of the violent conflict that was taking place.

Suddenly, Knuckles McGee found himself in a surprise attack. An enemy lunged at him from a hidden alcove, landing a powerful punch that knocked Knuckles McGee to the ground. The force of the blow made his vision blur, but he quickly rolled to avoid another strike.

"McGee!" one of his men whispered urgently, rushing to his aid. The team sprang into action, and in a blur of movement, they managed to fend off the immediate attackers. But something snapped inside Knuckles McGee. As he got back on his feet, it was as if an inner demon had been unleashed. His eyes darkened, and his usually controlled demeanor gave way to a brutal, primal rage. "You think you can take me down that easily?" he growled, his voice low and menacing.

Knuckles McGee moved with a terrifying efficiency, his fists and feet a blur of violent activity. He grabbed one of the attackers, slamming him against the wall with bone-crushing force. Another assailant tried to sneak up behind him, but Knuckles McGee spun around, delivering a savage kick to the man's ribs that sent him sprawling.

The brutality of Knuckles McGee's attacks was shocking. He didn't just subdue his enemies—he made sure they wouldn't get up again. He pounded his fists into another man's face with such fury that his knuckles bled, but he didn't stop until the man was unconscious.

One of his team members, watching the scene, muttered, "Damn, McGee, remind me never to get on your bad side."

Knuckles McGee, breathing heavily, looked at his team with a fierce intensity. "We don't leave any threats standing. Not tonight."

The team, galvanized by Knuckles McGee's ferocity, continued their mission with renewed determination. They moved through the yacht like shadows, eliminating any resistance with swift, silent precision. Knuckles McGee led the way, his inner demon now a driving force, ensuring that anyone who dared to cross them regretted it deeply.

In the end, the violent struggle went unnoticed by the rest of the yacht's occupants. Knuckles McGee's team had accomplished their mission, but not without a brutal reminder of the lengths they were willing to go to protect their own. As they regrouped, Knuckles McGee's bloodied knuckles and fierce gaze served as a testament to the ruthlessness required in their world.

"Let's finish this," Knuckles McGee said, his voice steady but filled with an underlying menace. "No one messes with the Capoli family and gets away with it."

Even though Rossi's men were well-trained, they couldn't handle the planned attack. Alpha, Bravo, and McGee's teams carried out their missions with surgical precision, keeping people guessing and giving the impression that everything was normal to those who couldn't see the storm that was happening just out of sight. Vincent's raid on Rossi's yacht began with an intensity that mirrored the stormy night. The luxury yacht, which once epitomized opulence and tranquility, quickly transformed into a chaotic warzone. As the teams boarded the vessel under the cover of darkness, the initial silence was shattered by the sharp cracks of gunfire and the grunts of hand-to-hand combat.

From his command post in a nearby location, Vincent monitored the situation closely. His Escalade was equipped with the latest surveillance technology, allowing him to coordinate the attack in real-time. He watched as Alpha, Bravo, and Knuckles McGee teams moved with precision, each team member carrying out their roles with military-like efficiency.

"Alpha, Bravo, McGee—proceed as planned. We need to find Isabella and take out Rossi," Vincent's voice was calm but commanding through their earpieces.

Just then, the sound of the chopper pierced through the air, and it made Vincent tear his gaze from the many surveillance screens spread out infront of him.

"Sir, is that…Jake?"

The helicopter carrying Jake sliced through the night sky with an ear-piercing scream as it roared towards the scene. The chopper dipped low towards the yacht, and a beam of light pierced the darkness, revealing chaos below. Jake prepared to touch down right on top of the yacht, with Rodney and his elite squad trailing closely behind.

"Fuck. Where did he get that?" Vincent was amazed.

As the helicopter hovered above the yacht, Jake's heart pounded with a mix of anticipation and dread. The rotors whipped the air into a frenzy, drowning out all other sounds. With a deep breath, Jake pulled out his phone and quickly typed a message to Vincent.

"Vincent, this is Jake. We're jumping onto the yacht now. Be ready for us."

He hit send and then secured his phone, giving a quick nod to Rodney and his team. They were ready. The helicopter lowered, and the deck of the yacht loomed closer. Jake could see Vincent's men engaged in intense combat, pushing forward with determination. As the helicopter lowered further, he noticed a man waiting for him, clearly one of Roberto's goons. Jake had anticipated this, planning his move even as he fell through the sky.

"Here goes nothing," Jake muttered to himself, steeling his nerves.

He leaped from the chopper, his body cutting through the air with precision. Before his feet touched the deck, he executed his plan flawlessly. With the grace of a trained fighter, Jake's elbow drove into the shoulder blade of the waiting man. The blow was powerful and precise, causing the man to stumble forward in pain.

Without missing a beat, Jake grabbed the man by his lower torso, using his legs to lift and rotate him. In one fluid motion, he swung the man around and then brought him crashing to the ground. Jake landed softly, using the man's limp body to cushion his fall. The man groaned, barely conscious. The rush of adrenaline washed over Jake, and he got to his feet. He tightened his grasp and pressured his weight; the blow from the impact had brought the goon near to his death.

Rodney and his squad landed moments later, quickly fanning out to secure the area. "Nice move, Jake," Rodney called out, a hint of admiration in his voice. The goon lay on the ground, gurgling out blood and the remnants of his guts.

"Thanks, but we're just getting started," Jake replied, his eyes scanning for more threats.

As they moved through the yacht, Jake and his team encountered more of Roberto's men. The yacht, a lavish fortress, was filled with intricately decorated rooms and opulent hallways. Despite its beauty, it was now a battleground.

Jake led the way, his training and instincts guiding him through each encounter. He dispatched enemies with a combination of martial arts and tactical maneuvers, each move calculated and efficient. Rodney and his team followed suit, their elite training evident in their coordinated actions.

They cleared room after room, ensuring no one was left to ambush them. The tension was palpable, but Jake remained focused. Every step they took brought them closer to their goal: ending Roberto's reign of terror.

As the teams penetrated deeper into the yacht, the resistance grew fiercer. Rossi's men regrouped, mounting a determined defense. The Capoli teams encountered surprise attacks, fortified positions, and a relentless barrage of gunfire. The once serene yacht was now a cacophony of explosions, gunshots, and the cries of combatants.

In one particularly intense moment, Jake found himself face-to-face with a heavily armed guard. The man raised his weapon, but Jake was faster. He lunged forward, knocking the gun out of the man's hands and delivering a swift punch to his jaw. The guard crumpled to the floor, unconscious.

"Keep moving!" Jake shouted to his team. "We're almost there!"

As they approached the heart of the yacht, the sounds of battle began to fade. Jake knew they were nearing the end of their mission. He took a deep breath, preparing for whatever lay ahead.

Vincent's voice came over the earpiece again. "Stay focused, push through. We can't afford any mistakes."

In the yacht's main salon, the Alpha team found themselves surrounded. The ornate room, filled with priceless art and elegant furnishings, had transformed into a deadly trap. Rossi's guards poured in from all sides, their sheer numbers threatening to overwhelm Alpha. The team fought fiercely, using the environment to their advantage. Tables became barricades, and statues were wielded as improvised weapons.

Pretty paintings soon splattered with blood, and the once-elegant tables adorned with fine china became a chaotic mess. Men fell to the ground, and heavy boots crushed the delicate china, the sound of shattering porcelain mixing with the grunts and cries of battle.

"Hold the line!" shouted Rodney, his voice barely audible over the chaos. He swung a statue at an advancing guard, the heavy bronze piece connecting with a sickening thud.

Jake was in the thick of it, his fists flying as he tore off multiple attackers. Suddenly, he felt a sharp pain in the back of his head. One of Rossi's men had hit him with a chair. Staggering forward, Jake shook off the daze, his vision blurring for a moment. But then something snapped inside him. It was as if he was possessed.

"You're gonna regret that," Jake growled, his voice dripping with fury.

With angry eyes, he turned to face the person who had hit him. He promptly and severely hit the attacker on the head, knocking him out and leaving him lying on the ground.

Alpha was in a fight with two guards nearby. A broken piece of china became his homemade weapon, which he used to cut one guard's arm and kick the other in the chest. He yelled, "We have to push through!" to get the team going. The fighting intensified, and the beautiful salon was now a war zone. Blood smeared the walls, and the air was thick with the scent of sweat and fear. Jake continued to fight with relentless fury, every punch and kick driven by the need to protect his family and bring down the Rossi clan.

Another guard lunged at Jake with a knife, but he sidestepped and twisted the man's arm, disarming him and delivering a powerful elbow to his face. The guard crumpled to the ground, out cold. Rodney, seeing an opening, barked out orders. "Alpha team, regroup! We're taking this fight to the heart of the yacht!"

Jake nodded, adrenaline pumping through his veins. "Let's move!"

In the midst of the chaos, Jake took center stage. He moved with a fluid grace, every motion honed by years of combat training. He disarmed an attacker with a swift twist, using the man's own momentum against him. A spinning kick sent another guard crashing into an antique mirror, shards flying everywhere.

Jake didn't pause. He grabbed a heavy lead pipe protruding from his pants leg, swinging it with precision to fend off two more assailants. One guard lunged at him, but Jake ducked, countering with an elbow to the ribs followed by a Uechi Uppercut that left the man sprawled on the floor.

"Vincent, we need backup in the main salon!" the Alpha team leader shouted into his earpiece, his voice strained with effort.

Jake heard the call but kept his focus, knowing they had to hold their ground until reinforcements arrived. He caught a glimpse of a guard aiming a gun at his teammate and, without hesitation, launched himself at the attacker. They grappled, but Jake's superior skill prevailed. He twisted the gun from the guard's hand and delivered a knockout punch.

Even with all the chaos, Jake's presence inspired his group. Driven by his unwavering enthusiasm and strategic acumen, they engaged in combat with revitalized vibrancy. Once a haven of opulence, the main salon was transformed into a battlefield, with every angle bearing witness to the intense conflict taking on inside.

"Good, McGee. Now, I want you to divert to Alpha's position," Vincent ordered, his eyes scanning the monitors. "Reinforce their location and continue the search for Isabella." The Bravo and McGee teams rapidly changed their trajectory to assist Alpha. The combined power of their arrival shifted the tide, forcing Rossi's soldiers to retreat. The once beautiful salon lay in ruins, strewn with lifeless bodies and broken glass.

Vincent felt a mixture of contentment and unease as he viewed the screens. The search for Isabella was growing more desperate, but they were making progress. The further they dug, the more obstacles they met. Rossi obviously sensed an onslaught was coming and had beefed up his defenses.

"Move forward," Vincent encouraged. "We're running out of time."

Once the lower decks were clear, the Bravo team went to the ship's engine room. The fighting got worse because of the limited area. They had to get through a maze of tools and machines, and each turn brought a new danger. Rossi's men set up ambushes from maintenance shafts and secret alcoves because they knew they had an edge in these small spaces. Every sound, movement, and hit was amplified by the small area, making a symphony of battle.

Bravo moved forward, they ran into strong resistance. One of Rossi's guards charged Bravo's point man from behind a big turbine, starting a bad punch fight in the metal cage. But just as the point man was about to give up, Jake charged forward and became the center of the fight.

Jake's movements were precise and deadly. He blocked a punch aimed at his face, countering with a quick jab to the guard's solar plexus. The guard staggered, and Jake seized the opportunity, delivering a spinning Uechi kick that sent the man crashing into a toolbox. Another guard appeared from a maintenance shaft, but Jake was ready. He ducked under a swinging pipe, then launched himself at the attacker, using the confined space to his advantage. He delivered a series of rapid punches, each one connecting with brutal accuracy.

The sounds of fists hitting flesh and grunts of pain echoed through the engine room. Jake's relentless assault left little room for Rossi's men to counter. He grabbed a wrench from a nearby tool rack and swung it with force, knocking another guard unconscious. The Bravo team, inspired by Jake's prowess, pushed forward with renewed vigor.

One of Rossi's guards tried to ambush Jake from behind, but Jake sensed the movement. He spun around, using the wrench to block a knife attack, then disarmed the guard with a swift kick to the wrist. A powerful elbow strike to the temple rendered the attacker unconscious.

Despite the fierce resistance, Jake and Bravo's squad steadily advanced. The confined quarters of the engine room became a battleground where Jake's skill and determination shone. Every move was deliberate, every strike calculated.

With the immediate threat neutralized, Jake led the Bravo team deeper into the engine room. They navigated the maze of machinery and tools, aware that time was running out. Each step brought them closer to their goal, and Jake remained at the forefront, his focus unyielding.

Vincent's voice crackled through the earpiece. "Good work, Bravo. Keep pushing. We're almost there."

Knuckles McGee's crew was assigned to guard the crew quarters and the surrounding storage spaces in the meantime. They moved with lethal accuracy, quickly, brutally removing the danger. Every contact was a violent, orchestrated dance. Knuckles McGee himself was ambushed by one guard, but the assailant gasped for air as a fast sidestep followed by a kick to the gut. Knuckles McGee did not hesitate; he sent the guard smashing into a bulkhead with a strong roundhouse kick.

"Any sign of Isabella?" Vincent's voice crackled through their earpieces, a constant presence driving them forward.

"Negative, still searching," Knuckles McGee responded, his voice steady despite the chaos around him.

As Knuckles McGee's team continued their sweep, they secured prisoners for interrogation. Each captured guard provided valuable information, their fear of Capoli's men outweighing their loyalty to Rossi. One guard, trembling and bruised, spilled details about the yacht's layout, bringing them closer to their goal.

However, the cost was high. In the confined corridors, four of Vincent's men fell. The first was caught in a brutal crossfire as they rounded a corner, bullets tearing through the narrow space. Another was ambushed by two of Rossi's men and dragged into a storage room, where he fought valiantly but was overwhelmed by sheer numbers. A third was taken out by a hidden blade, a silent strike in the chaos. The fourth, bravely trying to save a teammate, was shot down as he provided cover.

Vincent's frustration grew with each report of a fallen man. "Stay focused," he urged over the comms, his voice tense with suppressed rage. "We can't let their sacrifice be in vain." The gunfire was deafening, ricocheting off metal surfaces. Bravo's leader signaled for a flanking maneuver. Two soldiers crept along the narrow pathways, using the shadows to their advantage. They emerged behind the barricade, catching Rossi's men off guard. In the ensuing melee, fists and elbows flew, the confined space turning every encounter into a desperate struggle for survival. Knuckles McGee's team, having cleared the crew quarters, moved towards the storage areas. Here, the fighting was equally brutal.

One of Knuckles McGee's men engaged in a fierce hand-to-hand fight with a guard, their bodies slamming into shelves and crates. Knuckles McGee himself took on a particularly large opponent, dodging a heavy punch before landing a swift kick to the man's knee, followed by a series of rapid punches to his face and torso. The guard collapsed, blood streaming from his nose.

"We're getting closer," Knuckles McGee panted into his earpiece, wiping sweat and blood from his brow.

The Bravo team regrouped and was ready to go to the next phase after they neutralized the defenders in the engine room. As they continued to explore the vessel, the stench of blood and gunpowder became more pungent. The grim remnants of the violent conflict between two powerful factions were visible on the once-pristine deck. Even though there was still a long way to go, Vincent's troops were unyielding.

As for Jake, he went to join Rodney'team, who was waiting for him.

"Go, go, go!" Rodney shouted over the roar of the helicopter blades.

They quickly joined Vincent's men, their presence adding a powerful boost to the assault. Without a moment's loss, Knuckles McGee's team met with his unit and informed him of their proceeding to the lower deck where the VIP rooms were present. Before he could finish the details of his plan, Jake ran off. "I don't have time for this." He knotted his eyebrows and looked for the nearest door to the stairs that led below deck.

"Rodney, take point," Jake ordered as they neared a heavily fortified section of the deck. Rodney nodded, signaling his men to fan out and cover all angles.

Just as he disappeared on the stairs, five men came from the sides and attacked the men who had just landed on the deck. Rodney and his team, along with Vincent's men, had to hold them off so that Jake could try to save Isabella. The gunfire boomed in the air, and the constant tapering of their empty shells dissipated in the air.

Gunfire erupted as they engaged more of Rossi's guards. Jake's mind was focused, his training taking over as he fought through the onslaught. Each encounter was a brutal clash of wills, but Jake's team moved with a deadly efficiency that could not be matched.

"Jake, we're almost there," Rodney said, his voice tense but steady. "VIP quarters should be just ahead." He uttered on the radio.

Chapter 13: Comoponere Omnia

Isabella slowly opened her eyes to a painfully bright room. The harsh light stung her wounded eyes. Her whole body throbbed with waves of pain as she tried to catch a glimpse of her surroundings. Right in front of her stood a tall, floor-length mirror, reflecting her battered and exhausted form. The mirror captured every bruise and tear, highlighting her struggle and her defiant spirit.

A wave of nausea rummaged through the insides of her guts as soon as her sight locked on to her reflection in the mirror. The panic-struck, battered woman was *her* indeed. Irrespective of the pain, her eyes widened in pure horror when she saw what had become of her physical existence. The men in the basement had not shown her mercy in the slightest sense. She gasped as she focused and registered every nasty bruise. The wounds looked like red crests and were present where she had received the punches. Hints of yellow peaked from the sides, making them stand out even more.

Unconsciously, she raised her hand to where she was hit on the jaw. A sudden knot of grief unfurled in her stomach –the shock of the situation developed a sudden sob in her throat. The past few days had been brutal, even for her spirit. She took a deep breath as she assessed her reflection further in the mirror.

Someone had donned a strappy midsummer dress on her while she was passed out. The color was dyed a deep blue and stood in blaring contrast to the dried-up and mottled blood stains on her arms and legs.

Her heightened senses suddenly registered that she wore nothing underneath the dress. This sudden realization further deepened her shock as her sense of vulnerability went through the roof. She struggled against the floor, but in her weakened state, the process of standing up was futile.

"What? Don't like the new look I've given you? I think you look lovely. Better than before if you ask me." Roberto calmly looked her up and down and took a sip from his glass.

She froze. Isabella's eyes flashed in the direction of the voice. The very words made her recoil into a defensive position. She took a step back and saw the man who sat in his chair in an expensive tailored suit, unfazed.

She took a step back and brought her arms in front of her torso. She wiped the shock off her expression. Isabella was angry, and the man sitting in front of her was the reason she was in the situation in the first place.

"You…sick bastard."

"People usually start with a friendly hello." He smiled, showcasing his sharp white teeth. He looked at her with a glint of playfulness in his eyes.

She straightened up her shoulders, putting on a brave face. Despite the shock of her situation, Isabella knew she couldn't afford to show weakness. She shifted into a defensive stance, her eyes locked onto his with fierce determination. Every muscle in her body tensed, ready to defend herself. She would not let him dominate her. Not today. Not ever. She was resolved to fight, no matter the odds.

"You can't keep me here for long. Jake will come for me," she sneered, her voice hoarse but still showcasing bravery. The words were of stern determination, but her limp state suggested otherwise.

He kept his focus on her, then his face twisted. Roberto tried his best not to laugh. Stifling the chuckle with all his might, he cleared his throat and then nodded sarcastically.

"Ah, yes. But you see, I can, and I will." He took a big swig from his glass and set it down on the coffee table with a gentle thud. In every action, the man was classy and calm. He was in no hurry. He leaned back in his chair and folded his legs.

Smiling, he addressed her again. "It was time I got myself another doll to play with. Trust me..." his gaze darkened further, "I have plans to *squeeze* out every ounce of pleasure from you." His mannerisms were clear and calculated. He gestured for her to sit down on the sofa beside him, but the rage that boiled in Isabella was clear as day.

"I won't let you near me, you sick bastard," Isabella glared at him. Every second that ticked by, she gained confidence. She was not letting this man fulfill his wishes. It was as if the newfound wave of audacity rubbed Roberto off in the wrong way.

The seemingly pleased and smiling man sat on the sofa no more. His mannerisms became rigid, and his expressions went stone cold. The look in his eye was serious. The man who now perched in front of her had zero tolerance for people who didn't take his word seriously. Right now, Isabella was the epitome of defiance, someone who was not to be broken so easily. Roberto Rossi had a personal vendetta against such people.

Rossi was not just a human trafficker. He was known for making people conform to *his* ways.

Staring dead into her eyes, he slowly got up from his sofa. He adjusted his jacket and brushed off his arm. His entire attire symbolized his power and money. With slow steps, he neared

Isabella. There was a deafening silence in the room. The two were unknown to the ongoing battle outside. Isabella showed resilience; her body trembled with rage, and she showed she had no fear. Though she was in pain, she had this relentless air of courage that Roberto did not appreciate.

Strolling towards her, Rossi closed the distance between them with a predatory grace, his eyes never leaving Isabella's. He came face to face with her, a sinister smile curling his lips as he leaned in slowly, his breath hot against her skin. But Isabella was not having it. Summoning every ounce of her strength, she bolted towards the door.

Her heart pounded as she reached for the handle, desperately twisting it. The door was locked. Panic surged through her, but she refused to let it show. She turned back to face Rossi, who was now watching her with a twisted amusement. His smile widened into a cruel laugh, echoing through the room.

"Going somewhere?" he taunted, his voice dripping with mockery.

Ignoring him, Isabella scanned the room for another escape route. But Rossi was already moving. He sauntered over to a dresser, his fingers trailing along the polished wood. With deliberate slowness, he opened a drawer and pulled out a small velvet box. He turned it over in his hands, savoring the moment, before finally opening it.

Inside the box lay a gleaming set of knives. Rossi picked one up, the weapon looking almost delicate in his large hand. He picked up a particularly menacing one, its long and wickedly sharp blade. He ran a finger along the edge, testing its sharpness, before turning his gaze back to Isabella.

"You see, Isabella," he began, his voice smooth and menacing, "I like a bit of a challenge." Isabella stood her ground, her eyes darting between Rossi and the knife. She clenched her fists, her body tensed in a defensive position. She could not afford to show fear. Not now.

Without warning, he threw the knife at the door. Isabella instinctively ducked but lost her balance and fell to the ground.

"Did you really think that would work?" Rossi sneered. "It is always the same with you women."

She was on the ground, breathing heavily. Rossi's demeanor shifted, his face becoming stony and devoid of any previous amusement. He picked up another knife, this one smaller but equally deadly. He held it with a terrifying familiarity, the blade resting comfortably in his hand as if it were an extension of himself.

Isabella backed up to the door, her eyes wide with fear. Rossi's cold, unyielding gaze never left her, his expression now serious and devoid of any humanity.

"I think it's time we start this little game of ours, shall we?" he said, his voice chillingly calm.

"Now, why would you scream?" Rossi mocked, his voice dripping with false sweetness. "We're just having fun here."

He moved closer, the knife in his hand glinting under the dim light. "How about we put a smile on that face?" he suggested, his tone taking on a sadistic edge.

He brought the knife to her face, the cold metal pressing against her skin. He stroked it slowly along her cheek, the sensation sending shudders through her body. Isabella tried to remain still, but the terror was palpable.

Rossi's eyes gleamed with perverse enjoyment. "See? Isn't this fun?" he taunted. Then, with a quick flick of his wrist, he nicked her skin, drawing a thin line of blood.

Isabella gasped, feeling the sharp sting as the blood trickled down her cheek. Rossi's smile widened, his satisfaction evident. "There, now you look perfect," he said, stepping back to admire his handiwork.

"Now that's the color I like on women," Rossi said, his voice low and menacing, "fresh cherry red."

Her eyes were wide with terror, reflecting a mix of fear and desperation. She was paranoid, her body trembling as she struggled to control her breathing.

The panic was written all over her face, each moment stretching into an eternity. Rossi's humongous arms pressed her firmly against the door, his strength making any attempt to escape futile. "Let's match the other side as well," he murmured, a twisted smile on his lips. He brought the knife to her other cheek and sliced through the skin. Isabella's scream was muffled by her overwhelming fear, the pain searing through her like fire.

With a contented sigh, Rossi leaned forward and licked her cheek, removing the fresh blood. The horror had paralyzed Isabella to the point that she had stopped moving. Rossi took a little backward step, pulling his hand out of hers to gauge whether she would flee. Too afraid to even consider running away, she froze.

Her blue summer sundress caught his attention as he examined her. He casually stated, "I love that color on you," as if they were engaged in a conversation. The frightening moment was intensified by the stark contrast between his words and the brutality of his deeds. Rossi's grin widened as he used the knife to flick off the straps of Isabella's dress. The fabric slipped off her shoulders and fell to the floor. In her terror, she lost control and pissed herself, tears streaming down her face as she bawled uncontrollably.

"You've ruined the dress," Rossi sneered, his voice laced with contempt. "Let me take it off you properly."

"Shhhh," he soothed, a twisted smile on his lips as he gazed at her bruised and battered body. "I think the painting is incomplete. My boys didn't do their job well."

Isabella's sobs grew louder, her body shaking with fear and desperation. She screamed and bawled, her cries echoing through the room.

Rossi leaned in closer, his voice dropping to a deep, throaty purr. "I always tell Marco there is a trick to breaking such… spirited women." His words sent Isabella a fresh wave of terror, making her tremble even more. Isabella made an attempt to flee, but Rossi caught her and brought her to the bed, his hold on her being unbreakable by any means. He pressed the blade of the knife to his mouth for a brief second while adjusting his hold on her. He was holding the knife in one hand and forcing her down. After that, he had the audacity to climb on top of her and pin her down with alarming ease.

In a sudden moment of bravery, Isabella opened her eyes and stared directly at the mafia boss. "Jake will come for me," she whispered, her voice trembling but defiant. "Jake will come for me," she repeated multiple times, clinging to the hope of rescue.

Rossi's expression darkened. With a swift motion, he grabbed her by the neck, choking her windpipe. Isabella's defiance melted into agony as she struggled to breathe, her body trembling in pain and fear. Rossi leaned in closer, his grip tightening, and she could see the cold, ruthless determination in his eyes.

"Jake won't save you," he hissed, his voice dripping with malice. "No one will."

Isabella screamed even harder as he seized the nape of her neck. She repeatedly slapped his arm in protest, urging him to release his hold, which only made his grip tighter. With his heated breath brushing against her skin, he dipped his head towards her neck.

Their grasp hurt Isabella's already bruised arms as she fought against the man who was holding her. She gathered all her courage and will and recalled her vow to Stephanie: to fight until the end. Her motions were frantic and untamed as she attempted to twist free as Roberto approached. With a surge of determination, Isabella's spirit flared. "Get off me!" she screamed, her voice cracking but fierce. Tears streamed down her face as she cried, the sound raw and heartbreaking. Her body trembled, but her spirit refused to break.

Her eyes blazed with defiance as she stared at Roberto, her heart pounding with fear and anger. "You won't win," she spat, her voice growing louder and more resolute. "I will fight you with everything I have!" Roberto's sneer faltered for a moment as he took in the intensity of her gaze. Isabella's renewed spirit gave her the strength to push back harder, her hands clawing at his arms with a newfound ferocity. She twisted and turned, refusing to submit.

Isabella's screams grew louder, her determination fueling her resistance. "I won't let you break me!" she cried, her voice echoing through the room. Her tears mingled with the sweat and blood on her face, but her resolve was unshakeable.

Roberto loomed over her, Isabella's eyes darted frantically around the room. Her fingers brushed against a knife on the side table. With a surge of adrenaline, she seized it, holding it tight in between her fingers. Even though there was fear coursing through her veins, she didn't have time to hesitate. In a swift, desperate motion, she plunged the blade into Roberto's side. He let out a grunt of pain, staggering back and clutching his wound, his balance momentarily lost. Isabella's strike was weak, but it still broke his momentum. She noticed that the blade he cut her with had fallen on her chest. She grabbed both and got enough of a chance to push him off with all her remaining strength.

With quivering hands, she propped her balance on both her knees on the bed and took another calculated jab at the man. Just as she exerted full force toward his face, Roberto's muscular arm rose just in time. Though he missed by a few moments, and the tip of the knife made its way underneath the cheekbone.

"You little bitch," he spat, his face contorted in rage as he clutched his head, trying to maintain his balance. He grabbed her hands and squeezed the knife in them, exerting maximum pressure. Isabella screeched in pain as he dominated himself once more.

Just then, the door burst open with a deafening crash. Jake stormed into the room, eyes blazing with fury. He took in the scene in an instant, his focus locking onto Roberto. "Get away from her!" Jake roared, his voice echoing through the room.

Roberto turned, his expression shifting from anger to shock as he saw Jake. For a moment, he seemed frozen, caught off guard by the sudden intrusion. Isabella, breathing heavily, watched with a mixture of relief and fear as Jake advanced on Roberto.

Jake didn't hesitate. He crossed the room in a few quick strides, his eyes never leaving Roberto. "You picked the wrong fight," he growled, his fists clenched in readiness. Roberto, still reeling from the blow Isabella had dealt him, tried to raise his hands in defense, but Jake was faster. A primal rage had consumed Jake as he saw Isabella's battered form, and her eyes, wide with terror, met his, and that was all it took. With a roar that echoed through the room, he launched himself at Rossi. His martial arts training, specifically the disciplined techniques of Uechi Ryu, transformed him into a whirlwind of fury.

"Get away from her!" Jake bellowed, his voice filled with anguish and wrath.

Rossi barely had time to react before Jake's fist connected with his jaw, sending him staggering back. Jake followed through with a series of rapid punches, his movements precise and lethal. He grounded himself with every blow, utilizing the power of the Sanchin stance. Rossi, though taken aback, quickly regained his footing. He wasn't just any crime boss; years of training in American boxing had prepared him for moments like this.

"You think you can touch her and get away with it?" Jake snarled, his voice a growl. He advanced with renewed fury, grabbing Rossi by the collar and delivering a brutal knee strike to his stomach. Rossi doubled over, gasping for breath, but he quickly recovered, his training kicking in. Rossi threw a powerful uppercut that connected with Jake's jaw, snapping his head back. Jake stumbled but didn't fall. The two men circled each other, the tension thick in the air. Rossi's eyes were cold and calculating, while Jake's blazed with a fierce, protective instinct.

With a barrage of punches and kicks, Jake flung himself at Rossi. Even though Rossi parried most of the blows, Jake's constant barrage eventually wore him down. Jake pounded Rossi in the ribs before quickly elbowing him in the side of the head. Rossi felt himself on the brink of unconsciousness as his eyesight became fuzzy.

In retaliation, Rossi unleashed a ferocious fist swing, striking Jake in the shoulder. After taking the blow, Jake landed a vicious punch on Rossi's jaw, knocking him to the floor. With a relentless barrage of punches, Jake trailed behind him as he descended.

With his arms raised to parry the strikes, Rossi attempted self-defense, but Jake was unyielding. Thinking about Isabella and the hurt Rossi had caused drove Jake to punch harder and harder. With each increasingly forceful blow, Jake's fists made contact with Rossi's body and face.

As Rossi's efforts to fight back waned, his strength also diminished. Once again, Jake yanked him up off the floor by the collar. "This is for Isabella," Jake said as he landed a last, devastating blow on Rossi's forehead. The mob boss fell to the ground, defeated and unconscious.

"You're nothing but a coward!" Jake shouted, each word punctuated by a blow. "You prey on the weak and helpless. Not anymore!"

Rossi's attempts to shield himself were futile against Jake's fury. Blood splattered from his nose and mouth, his face a mask of pain and fear. Just as Jake was about to deliver a final, potentially lethal blow, a commanding voice cut through the haze of his rage.

"Jake, stop!"

Vincent appeared in the doorway, having witnessed the entire scene unfold from his vantage point. His presence was like a cold splash of water, momentarily breaking through Jake's red haze. Jake hesitated, his fist still poised to strike, his breathing heavy and ragged.

"Step back, Jake," Vincent ordered, his voice firm but calm. "We need him alive."

Jake's eyes flickered with conflict. Every fiber of his being screamed to finish Rossi, to end the tormentor's life. But Vincent's words slowly penetrated his rage. With a final, shuddering breath, he let Rossi go, stepping back and letting his fists fall to his sides.

Vincent moved forward, his eyes never leaving Rossi, who lay on the ground, gasping and bleeding. Vincent's presence was commanding and authoritative, his steps deliberate and filled with purpose. This was the moment he had been waiting for, the chance to end the man who had caused so much pain and chaos.

Vincent's jaw tightened as he approached Rossi, the anger in his eyes hard to hold back. Rossi, blood trickling from the corner of his mouth, tried to get up but couldn't. He snarled, "You think you can just walk in here and take me down?" His voice was weak but defiant.

A chilling, analytical stare crossed Vincent's face as he met Rossi's. "Death would be too easy for you," Vincent said, almost to himself. His boot's heel slammed down on Rossi's forehead in a vicious kick. The impact was so tremendous that it sent Rossi into a deep slumber and turned his face a deep scarlet. His eyes rolled back into his head.

Vincent made sure Rossi felt the agony but refrained from killing him as he stood over his motionless body. With bone-chilling clarity, he dipped his head close to Rossi's ear and said, "I would rather have you alive so that I can inflict more pain on you. I will become the content creator of your short life, motherfucker. Everything that happens to you from this moment on will be by my design. I command it, and I will it."

After Vincent straightened himself, he looked back to Jake, who had been watching Isabella the whole time. He could feel the emotional and physical strain that the battle had put on Jake. Vincent knew all too well the world of brutality and evil that this young man had been thrust into.

Vincent placed a hand on Jake's shoulder. "Take Isabella and get out of here. The FBI is on their way, and we can't afford to get tangled up with them."

Jake nodded, the fire in his eyes dimming but not extinguished. He rushed to Isabella's side, gently helping her to her feet. "It's over," he whispered, his voice hoarse. "You're safe now. Let's get you out of here."

As they made their way out, Vincent's eyes lingered on Rossi's unconscious form, a mixture of satisfaction and unresolved anger in his gaze. He knew Rossi would suffer, but he also knew that the battle was far from over.

Meanwhile, Marco, Rossi's son, entered the scene. He had been largely absent but now rushed to his father's side. Seeing the devastation and his father's comatose state, Marco's face twisted with a mix of horror and rage. He quickly assessed the situation, knowing he had to get his father to safety.

Marco bent down, lifting Rossi's unconscious body with surprising strength. He glanced up, seeing Jake, Isabella, and Vincent leaving the room. His eyes burned with a vengeance, a promise of retribution clear in his gaze.

While Jake and Isabella stepped off the boat, Marco fought to help his father navigate the mayhem. He was encouraged to continue by the distant sound of sirens. He needed to get away, gather his thoughts, and figure out what to do next. It would be difficult for Roberto's empire to collapse, and Marco was hell-bent on succeeding his father.

They were all on a different road now because of Vincent's choice. The cycle of violence and animosity that had engulfed Jake and Isabella would finally end, and they would get a second opportunity in life. Marco, though, saw this as merely the start. Battle lines had been formed, and the struggle for dominance and vengeance would continue for some time.

"Jake," Vincent said, his voice softer now but no less commanding. "You need to take Isabella and get out of here. The FBI is on their way, and we can't afford to get tangled up with them."

Having comprehended the sense of urgency conveyed by Vincent's comments, Jake nodded. It was Isabella who was leaning against the wall when he turned his attention to her. Although her body was battered and scarred, her spirit remained intact. "Come on," Jake replied in a soothing tone as he assisted her in standing up.

"The others are retreating; some already have, and we have to move."

As they moved toward the door, Vincent placed a hand on Jake's shoulder, stopping him for a moment. "Jake," he began, his voice serious. "I know you want to end this. But killing Rossi... it's not your burden to bear. Leave him to me. You need to focus on Isabella and yourself."

Jake looked into Vincent's eyes and saw the depth of his understanding. He nodded, the fire in his eyes dimming slightly but still burning with determination. "Thank you," Jake said quietly. "For everything."

Vincent gave a curt nod. "Just take care of her," he replied, glancing at Isabella. "And yourself. This world... it's not an easy one to navigate."

He tightened his grip on Isabella. Her body was in pain, her face bloated and bruised, and her beautiful features stained purple and blue. Her cuts and abrasions showed her suffering. Torn garments barely hung on her damaged body, showing more bruises and cuts. Isabella's tears streamed down her face, mingling with the dried blood on her cheeks. Every movement seemed to cause her immense pain, a whimper escaping her lips as she tried to steady herself. The sight of her suffering cut Jake deeply, igniting a fierce protective instinct within him.

Without a moment's hesitation, Jake shrugged off his jacket and gently draped it over her shoulders, wrapping it tightly around her fragile body. "It's okay," he whispered soothingly, his voice trembling with emotion. "I've got you."

Isabella sobbed quietly, the sound heart-wrenching. "It hurts so much, Jake," she managed to say, her voice barely above a whisper.

"I know," Jake replied softly, his heart breaking at her words. "But we're getting out of here. I won't let anyone hurt you again." He carefully slid his arms under her, lifting her as if she weighed nothing. Isabella winced, a pained gasp escaping her lips, but Jake held her snugly against his chest, ensuring she was as comfortable as possible. He could feel the tremors of her body, the physical and emotional toll of her ordeal. "Hold on to me," he instructed gently, and Isabella wrapped her arms weakly around his neck, her head resting against his shoulder. Her breaths came in shallow, uneven gasps, but she clung to Jake as if he were her lifeline.

Jake walked fast yet cautiously, taking slow, calculated steps in order to reduce the amount of anguish she felt. He muttered words of confidence to her as he carried her through the commotion of the yacht, his voice acting as a firm anchor amid the storm. "We're almost there, Bella. Just a little longer. Stay with me."

The air around the yacht was thick with tension, the hum of approaching helicopters a harbinger of the chaos to come. The FBI arrived in force, armed with a search warrant and ready to take down the criminal stronghold. As the agents disembarked, their presence was immediately noticed by both Capoli's men and Rossi's remaining forces, setting the stage for a volatile three-way battle.

"Move in! Secure the perimeter!" Agent Jackson barked, his voice amplified by the megaphone. The FBI agents spread out, their weapons at the ready, eyes scanning for any sign of resistance.

As soon as they made contact on the deck, gunfire erupted. It echoed across the water as law enforcement clashed with the two criminal factions with full force. Capoli's men, caught between retreat and retaliation, fired back at the FBI while trying to fend off Rossi's desperate guards. They had limited time. They had to keep their distance and disappear before they got surrounded.

Being the apt man he was, Vincent was monitoring the unfolding chaos from a secure vantage point. "This is getting out of hand; they should have gotten off the deck before the FBI arrived. I need my men not to make direct contact," he muttered, frustration evident in his tone. He grabbed his radio. "All units, fall back! Execute strategic retreat. Now! I do not want you to make contact."

His lieutenants were scattered throughout the yacht. They acknowledged the order with quick nods. "Create diversions and get out clean." All unit heads called out to their team. A set of flashbangs was set out, and around 5 men used the blanket of smoke grenades to disorient both the FBI and Rossi's forces. The yacht's luxurious interior got riddled with thick smoke and the acrid smell of gunpowder. FBI, who weren't well versed with the interiors, were easily thrown off and couldn't do much in this regard.

On the upper deck, the second team was under heavy fire.

"McGee! I don't like repeating myself. Get the hell out of there. Right now!" Vincent shouted at the radio, "I said no direct contact."

"Just getting my man out of trouble, sir. I don't want to get him caught." Knuckles answered. He used a diversion tactic and grabbed one of his men, who lay on his knees, covering his head. "Get the hell out of here!" he shouted, his voice filled with urgency. He grabbed him by the collar, pulling him forcefully. As the FBI agents approached the corner where Knuckles McGee used to hide, he fired empty rounds into the air. The shots echoed through the narrow alley, creating a chaotic noise that momentarily disoriented the agents and bought them precious seconds to escape. Keeping his word, Knuckles dragged the last of his men to the side deck and plunged into the deep blue sea.

The second team was out of the yacht. The water splashing over the deck was proof of the second team making it out of the clutches of the FBI.

"What is the third team taking so goddam long!" Vincent grumbled.

"Should we leave them behind?" One of the men keeping track of the monitors turned around and asked.

"Wait." Vincent was still sure his men would make it. "We leave no one behind."

As the Capoli forces pulled back, they left a trail of destruction and confusion in their wake. The FBI, caught off guard by the sudden retreat, pushed forward, securing one section of the yacht after another. One by one, every man in the Capoli detail exited the scene. Knuckles McGee, with his expertise, had arranged for smaller boats to take all of his men out. The tide was high, and escape was further assisted by the ample fog nature had gloriously arranged in the aftermath of what felt like a prolonged fight at the yacht.

"Move in! Secure the hostages!" Agent Collins shouted, her voice barely audible over the cacophony of battle. She and her team moved through the smoke-filled corridors, finding several of Rossi's men attempting to regroup.

"Drop your weapons! Now!" she commanded, her gun trained on the nearest guard. The man hesitated but complied, the fight draining from his eyes as he was cuffed and led away.

Meanwhile, Jake and Isabella had found a temporary safe haven in a secluded area of the yacht amid the chaos. Jake held Isabella close, his face set with unwavering resolve. Her tears mixed with the dirt and blood on her face, and her body shook with lingering anguish and fear.

"Jake, what's happening?" she whispered, her voice trembling.

"The FBI is here. We're going to be okay," Jake replied, trying to inject confidence into his voice. He scanned the chaotic scene, looking for a safe path. "We just need to get out of here."

As the fighting intensified, more casualties began to pile up. Rossi's men, fiercely loyal to the end, fought back with everything they had. The yacht's luxurious lounges and staterooms were now littered with the wounded and the dying, a stark contrast to their former splendor.

Realizing the situation was becoming untenable, Vincent regrouped with his top lieutenants. "We need to go. Now," he said, urgency in his voice. "The FBI will swarm this place any minute."

One of his men nodded. "The diversions are set. We'll slip out unnoticed."

Vincent gave a final look around, his eyes hardening with resolve. "Let's move. We need to get the hell out of here before the FBI storms this section of the yacht."

The Capoli forces retreated, their exit covered by the chaos they had orchestrated. Smoke and debris filled the air, obscuring their escape as they slipped away, leaving the FBI to mop up the remnants of Rossi's defenses.

In the aftermath, the scene was one of utter destruction. The once-grand yacht was a wreck, its opulent interiors marred by bullet holes and scorch marks. The FBI, now firmly in control, began the grim task of securing the area and tending to the wounded.

"Get those men to medical," Agent Jackson ordered, pointing to a group of injured guards. "And search every inch of this place. We need to find Rossi."

In the midst of the chaos, Marco Rossi had found his father unconscious and in a coma. With determination, Marco carried Roberto's limp body through the smoke and chaos, making his way to a hidden speedboat docked at the side of the yacht. The speedboat roared to life, and they sped away from the besieged vessel, the sound of gunfire and shouting fading into the distance.

As they reached a safe distance, Marco realized the severity of his father's condition. "Hang in there, Dad," he muttered, his voice filled with urgency. He decided to take Roberto to their private physician, knowing that standard medical facilities would attract too much attention.

Meanwhile, back on the yacht, Jake and Isabella were guided by the protective presence of Rodney and his team just as the turmoil began to decrease. Jake's heart hurt when he saw Isabella's face, which was covered in bruises and cuts, but the look in her eyes, filled with resolve, gave him strength.

"We're safe now," Jake murmured, holding her close. "It's over."

Isabella clung to him, her body trembling with exhaustion and relief. "I never thought... I never thought we'd make it," she whispered, tears streaming down her cheeks.

Jake tightened his hold on her, his voice soft but resolute. "We did. And we're going to be okay."

As the FBI secured the yacht, Jake and Isabella were led to safety. Vincent, who was observing the event from a distance, experienced a rare feeling of contentment. They were successful despite the disarray and the losses they had suffered, but Rossi wasn't dead yet.

"We'll see this through," Vincent muttered to himself, his gaze hardening with resolve. "No matter what it takes."

Epilogue

As Jake made his way back from the chaotic scene on the yacht, his mind was a maelstrom of emotions. The wind from the helicopter blades tousled his hair as he sat silently. Isabella nestled against his chest, her breathing shallow but steady. The adrenaline rush of the confrontation was fading, leaving behind a hollow space filled with conflicting thoughts and emotions. He had never imagined he would find himself entrenched in the world of organized crime, let alone fighting side by side with one of the most notorious families. His role in assisting the Capoli family weighed heavily on him. He couldn't shake the image of Vincent Capoli, a man who was as much a protector as he was a criminal. The Capolis were undeniably involved in illicit activities, but after witnessing the depravity and ruthlessness of Rossi's operations, Jake found himself rationalizing his alliance with them.

In the dim light of the helicopter, Jake looked down at Isabella's battered face. Her injuries were a stark reminder of the violence and cruelty they had just escaped. Despite everything, he was profoundly relieved to have her back. She stirred slightly, wincing as she adjusted her position. Jake tightened his grip around her, whispering reassurances.

"It's okay, Bella. We're safe now. Just rest."

She nodded weakly, her eyes closing as exhaustion overtook her. As Jake held her, he couldn't help but reflect on the events that had transpired. The brutality of the fight with Rossi, the sheer willpower it had taken to keep going, and the dark satisfaction he had felt when delivering those final blows. He had crossed a line he never thought he would, and it terrified him.

In the quiet moments between the rush of the mission and the calm of safety, Jake confronted the darkness within himself. He had always considered himself a man of principles, someone who stood on the right side of the law. But his involvement with the Capoli family had blurred those lines. He had willingly allied himself with criminals, justified by the need to save Isabella and take down a greater evil.

Yet, the gnawing guilt persisted. *Had he become just like them? Is a man willing to use violence to achieve his ends?* The thought made him shudder. He glanced at Isabella again, her vulnerability and strength intertwined, and felt a surge of protective rage. He had done what was necessary to save her, but at what cost to his soul?

The encounter with Rossi had forced him to confront aspects of himself he had never acknowledged. There was a part of him that reveled in the fight, that found a grim satisfaction in delivering justice with his own hands. This revelation was unsettling. It made him question his morality and the choices he had made. Jake's mind was a storm of conflicting emotions. The Capoli family, for all their criminal endeavors, had provided the resources and manpower necessary to rescue Isabella. In comparison, Rossi's operations were a nightmare of human trafficking and brutal violence.

In a world of shades of gray, the Capolis seemed to be the lesser evil. His relationship with the Capolis had been solidified by the night's events, but it was fraught with moral complexities. *How could he continue to associate with them without losing himself completely to their world?* His sense of duty and justice clashed with the reality of his actions. He knew this struggle would define him, shaping his character and guiding his future choices. The darkness within him, the capacity for violence, had been awakened. It was a part of him now, a part he would have to learn to control and understand. This internal conflict would drive him, pushing him to seek redemption while navigating the murky waters of morality.

The helicopter began its descent, the ground coming into sharper focus. Jake took a deep breath, steeling himself for the challenges ahead. He gently shook Isabella awake, her eyes fluttering open, filled with a mix of pain and relief.

"We're almost there," he said softly. "Hang on just a little longer."

As the chaos of the night began to fade, Vincent found a moment of quiet reflection. Sitting alone in his Escalade, the city lights flickering in the distance, he replayed the events in his mind. Sparing Rossi's life had been a calculated decision, one born from strategic necessity and something deeper, more personal. Vincent knew that killing Rossi would have been the easiest solution, a swift end to a persistent threat. He also understood that doing so would have pushed Jake further into the darkness that surrounded their world.

Vincent saw something in Jake that he rarely saw in those who entered his orbit: potential for goodness. Jake's fierce determination to save Isabella and his willingness to risk everything spoke of a man who had not yet been consumed by the murky ethics of their lives. Vincent's choice to spare Rossi was not just a tactical move but a safeguard for Jake's soul.

"He's not like us," Vincent murmured to himself, staring out at the city. "He still has a chance to be better."

He thought back to the look in Jake's eyes as he had fought to protect Isabella. There was a fire there, but there was also a deep-seated morality, a line that Jake was hesitant to cross. Vincent had seen too many young men lose themselves to the allure of power and vengeance. He didn't want that for Jake. There was still hope for him to emerge from this with his humanity intact.

Meanwhile, Jake and Isabella found themselves in the sterile, quiet environment of a hospital. The white walls and the soft hum of medical equipment were a stark contrast to the violence they had just escaped. Nurses and doctors moved efficiently around them, providing care and a semblance of normalcy.

Isabella lay on the examination table, her injuries being carefully tended to by a sympathetic nurse. Her face was still swollen, and her body bore the marks of her ordeal, but her eyes were clear and determined. Jake sat beside her, holding her hand and offering silent support.

"It's going to be okay, Bella," he said softly, squeezing her hand gently. "You're safe now."

Isabella nodded, her eyes filling with tears. "I know, Jake. It's just… it's all so much."

"I know. But we'll get through this. Together."

After the physical examination, Isabella was taken to a counseling room. The room was small but comforting, with soft chairs and warm lighting. A therapist sat across from her, a gentle smile on her face.

"Isabella, my name is Dr. Harris. I'm here to help you process what you've been through. This is a safe space for you to talk about anything you need."

"I want to talk about it. I need to." Isabella glanced at Jake, who nodded encouragingly. She took a deep breath, summoning her inner strength.

Dr. Harris nodded, "Take your time. There's no rush."

As Isabella began to recount her experiences, her voice trembled but grew stronger with each word. She spoke of the fear, the pain, and the moments of despair. But she also spoke of her determination, her will to survive, and her hope for the future.

"I never thought I'd make it out," she admitted, tears streaming down her face. "But Jake... he never gave up on me. And that gave me the strength to keep going."

Jake's eyes filled with tears as well, but he remained silent, letting Isabella find her voice. He knew this was a crucial part of her healing, and he was there to support her every step of the way.

Dr. Harris listened attentively, offering words of comfort and guidance. "What you went through was unimaginable, Isabella. But your resilience is incredible. You have the strength to rebuild your life, and you're not alone in this."

Isabella nodded, wiping her tears. "I will move forward. I will take control of my life back in no time."

Jake smiled at her, his heart swelling with pride. "And you will. We both will." Jake saw a feeling of serenity descend upon him as they left the counseling session. Though they still had a long way to go, they were no longer traveling alone. The fact that they had each other was what changed everything.

A new chapter in their lives had begun with Vincent's choice not to kill Rossi. It had given Jake the chance to hold onto the good and hopeful parts of himself. Jake and Isabella were able to achieve healing and atonement because of Vincent's nuanced morals and capacity to look past their initial need for retribution.

In the days that followed, Jake and Isabella started to gradually put their lives back together after they had been destroyed. By being in each other's company, they were able to find comfort and draw strength from the experiences that they had in common. They were able to navigate through the darkness with the help of Isabella's tenacity, which became a beacon of hope.

Counseling sessions and physical therapy were the activities that they participated in throughout their time spent in the hospital. During each session, we encountered new obstacles, but we also achieved new successes. Both physically and mentally, Isabella gradually regained her strength over the course of time. She got over her traumatic experiences and learned to address her worries head-on.

Jake, like everyone else, struggled with his own personal issues. Because of the events that took place on the boat, he was compelled to confront the darkness that existed inside him, to doubt his morals, and to examine the decisions that he had made. On the other hand, he was resolute in his intention to emerge from this experience more powerful and fully conscious of who he was and what he stood for.

Meanwhile, the FBI intensified its investigation into the Capoli family and Rossi's criminal activities. The chaos on the yacht provided them with a treasure trove of evidence, enough to build a formidable case. Agents meticulously combed through the crime scene, gathering data, interviewing witnesses, and piecing together the intricate web of illegal dealings. The balance of power in the criminal underworld teetered as law enforcement closed in, heightening tensions across the city.

Vincent, always a step ahead, retreated to his command center, a fortified estate on the outskirts of the city. His inner circle gathered around a massive table covered in blueprints, surveillance photos, and maps. The room was dimly lit, the atmosphere thick with anticipation and urgency.

"Listen up," Vincent began, his voice commanding and steady. "The FBI is tightening the noose. We need to clean up our tracks and protect our interests."

He turned to his trusted lieutenant, Johny. "I want you to go over every piece of evidence they might have against us. Destroy anything that can tie us to the yacht incident or any other operation."

"Consider it done, boss." Johny nodded.

Vincent then addressed the room, his eyes sweeping over his men. "We also need to ensure Jake and Isabella are kept out of this mess. They've been through enough, and I won't let them get dragged down with us."

One of his lieutenants, Luca, spoke up. "What about Rossi's men? They're scattered, but some are still loyal to him. They might retaliate."

Vincent leaned forward, his gaze steely. "We deal with them before they have a chance to regroup. Send a message that any move against us will be met with swift and deadly consequences."

As the men began to disperse to carry out their orders, Vincent motioned for Johny to stay behind. "Johny, I need you to take care of something else. We need to remove any traces of our involvement from the yacht. I'm talking about cleaning up our tracks thoroughly."

"And how do you suggest we do that? The usual way?" Johny raised an eyebrow.

Vincent's face remained impassive. "Start with the electronics. Wipe out all security footage that shows our men. Replace it with doctored videos if necessary. Make it look like a different group entirely was responsible."

Johny nodded, understanding the gravity of the task. "What about the bodies?"

Vincent's eyes narrowed with a calculated gleam. "Dispose of them. Make it look like they vanished. No bodies, no case. Thankfully, to deal with this, we do have quite a few FBI agents and authority figures on our payroll. We will have to strategically use them to help clean up this mess."

"What if some Agents start sniffing around too close?" Johnny hesitated for a moment, glancing at Vincent.

"They are on my payroll. I never make bad investments." Vincent glared at Johny, suspecting him. Understanding the gravity of the situation, Johny nodded slowly and played with his lighter.

Vincent's voice dropped to a cold, determined whisper. "Send them to the crematory. Erase all traces. No evidence, no trails. Those who make the mistake of sniffing around must find dead ends only."

"Understood. We'll handle it." With an ice-cold gaze, he agreed. Johny's mind was racing with the logistics of their next steps.

"Good. And remember, if there is any evidence that points to us, we divert. Plant false leads and send them chasing ghosts. We can't afford any mistakes." Vincent's gaze remained undeterred.

This was the time to get things done without thinking of how it may appear to be gruesome on the outside. "We'll keep them busy while we regroup. The Capoli family will not fall. It will be taken care of in a week or so, sir." Johnny clenched his jaw, ready to execute the orders.

Later that night, Vincent sat in his study, the weight of their situation pressing down on him. He poured himself a glass of vintage whiskey, staring into the amber liquid as if it held the answers he sought. His assistant came in with an urgent expression. "Sir, it's Jake. It has been a long day; should we send him away?"

Vincent took a minute to compose his thoughts. "What? No, no, send the boy in."

With a silent nod, his assistant rushed out to invite Jake upstairs to Vincent's room.

"Vincent," Jake's voice came through, a mix of gratitude and confusion. I just wanted to thank you for what you did—for sparing Rossi." Vincent gestured for him to sit and smiled at the young man with satisfaction. "Jake, you have to understand something. Killing Rossi might have solved a short-term problem, but it would have created a long-term one. For you." Vincent took a deep breath, his tone reflective.

"What do you mean?" After a moment of silence, Jake finally spoke. His voice carried a tone tinged with curiosity.

The ice in the whiskey quietly clinked against the glass. Vincent's focus was on his glass as he measured what to say next. "If you had killed him, it would have changed you. You would have crossed a line you couldn't come back from. I didn't want that for you." He took a sip and looked at Jake, reading what his response was on the matter.

"I appreciate that, Vincent. Really. But what now? The FBI is all over this." It took him a moment to absorb this. He looked at the floor and had his hands in his jacket. At the end of the day, Isabella was safe and sound- back to him. His tone softened.

Vincent's eyes hardened. "We adapt. We clean up our mess and keep moving forward. And we protect those we care about- Right?" He raised his eyebrow and asked Jake once more about his position on the matter. His eyes hardened and were on Jake, reading every aspect of his body language. The aftermath of the raid on the yacht left everyone facing the consequences of their actions. The night had been a turning point, setting off a chain reaction that would shape the future of Jake, Isabella, Vincent, and everyone involved in the criminal underworld. Each character, grappling with their own demons, found strength in their alliances as they navigated the treacherous landscape before them.

Vincent sighed and put his whiskey down. He stood up. The man was dressed in an Italian-tailored suit. He adjusted his striped jacket and looked Jake straight in the face. Vincent's stance on the matter could not have been clearer. He slowly walked to where Jake was and straightened his stature up. In a serious tone, he continued. "Jake, one of the main reasons I told you not to kill Roberto Rossi is because whenever someone kills the head of a mob family, that person's life becomes a living hell. Roberto's partners, his family, and all those loyal to him would hunt you for the rest of your life. I didn't want that kind of torment for you."

Jake listened intently, the weight of Vincent's words settling in. "I didn't realize..."

"And there's another thing," Vincent continued. "You've never killed anyone before. Taking a life changes you. It's something you carry with you forever, and I didn't want that on your conscience. You're a good man, Jake. I didn't want you to lose that."

Jake's voice was barely a whisper. "Thank you, Vincent. I understand now."

"Good," Vincent replied, his tone softening slightly. "We'll get through this. We just need to stay sharp and be ready for whatever comes next."

***

Jake stood in the hospital hallway the next day, his thoughts all over the place. The sterile environment, with its muted colors and soft hum of medical equipment, was a contrast to the chaos he had just escaped. Isabella's perseverance through yet another set of challenges is evidence of her unwavering determination. Jake attempted to make sense of all that had occurred by leaning against the nearby wall.

Vincent's words echoed in his mind: "Killing Rossi might have solved a short-term problem, but it would have created a long-term one. For you."

He understood now. The act of sparing Rossi had been a deliberate move to save Jake from crossing a line he couldn't return from. It was a reminder that even in their dark world, there were boundaries that should not be crossed. This revelation deepened Jake's respect for Vincent, highlighting the complexity of the man who had become his unlikely ally.

In another part of the city, Vincent sat in his office, his gaze fixed on the sprawling cityscape. The raid on the yacht had provided the FBI with ample evidence, and he knew they would not relent in their pursuit. The balance of power in the criminal underworld was shifting, and Vincent had to stay ahead of the curve.

Johnny entered the room, closing the door behind him. "Boss, we've started the process to clean up the yacht. Some of the FBI agents on our payroll are already complying. Much of the work is done, and we have managed to get rid of some of the bodies. The security footage has also been altered. Our guys are throwing the FBI off track as we speak."

"I expected as much. We need to stay vigilant. Have our operations run smoothly, but keep them under the radar." Vincent nodded, his expression thoughtful.

Johnny leaned against the desk, concern etched on his face. "And Jake? What's our plan for him and Isabella?"

Vincent sighed, rubbing his temples. "They need to stay out of this. We'll keep them safe, but they can't be involved in any more of our dealings. They've been through enough."

Johnny nodded in agreement. "Understood, Boss. We'll make sure they're protected."

Vincent's eyes narrowed as he continued to think about their next move. "We need to ensure the FBI has nothing to find. Keep our agents active and make sure they're doing everything to erase any evidence that points back to us."

Johnny straightened, ready to execute Vincent's orders. "We'll keep them busy chasing ghosts while we regroup."

Vincent gave a curt nod, his eyes hardening with resolve. "Good. We can't afford any mistakes. We need to be one step ahead, always."

"You really care about them, don't you?" Johny hesitated a little before asking this question.

Vincent smiled. There was a glimmer of softness in his eyes. "Jake reminds me of myself before all this. He has a chance to be different, to be better. I won't let this world destroy him."

Johny left the room, leaving Vincent alone, reminiscing his thoughts. He sat back, lost in thought. He knew that sparing Rossi had been the right decision, not just strategically but morally. It reinforced his complex sense of morality, one that balanced ruthlessness with a code of honor.

Back at the hospital, Isabella emerged from her session with Dr. Harris. Her steps were slow, but there was a newfound determination in her eyes. She saw Jake waiting for her and managed to smile weakly.

"How are you feeling?" Jake asked, his concern evident.

"Better," she replied, her voice steady. "It's going to take time, but I'm ready to move forward. We can't let this break us."

Jake nodded, his admiration for her growing. "We'll get through this together. No matter what."

As they walked through the hospital garden, they spoke about their future, tentative plans forming amid the uncertainty. The trauma of their ordeal had forged a stronger bond between them, a foundation of trust and mutual support.

Meanwhile, the FBI headquarters was abuzz with activity. Agent Jackson pored over the evidence collected from the yacht, piecing together the complex puzzle of the Capoli and Rossi operations. The raid had provided crucial information, but it was just the beginning.

"Collins," Jackson called, "I need you to follow up on the financial records we found. There's a trail of money that leads to several offshore accounts. If we can trace it, we might get a clearer picture of their network."

Agent Collins nodded, determination in her eyes. "On it, sir. We'll get to the bottom of this."

The investigation intensified, with the FBI methodically closing in on both crime families. The pressure mounted, creating an atmosphere of tension and anticipation.

In a dimly lit room, Rossi lay in a hospital bed, his body battered and broken. He was in a deep coma, his fate uncertain. The once powerful crime lord was now a shadow of his former self, a symbol of the shifting power dynamics in the underworld.

For Vincent, the days that followed were filled with strategic planning and careful moves. He held meetings with his lieutenants, ensuring that their operations remained secure and undisrupted. Each decision was a calculated risk designed to protect their interests and stay one step ahead of the law.

"Johny, I need you to tighten security around our key locations," Vincent instructed. "The FBI is relentless. We can't afford any slip-ups." His gaze hardened as he spoke. "Good. And remember, Jake and Isabella are off-limits. No one bothers them."

As Vincent navigated the complexities of their situation, he found himself reflecting on his own morality. His decision to spare Rossi had not only been a strategic move but a personal one. He saw in Jake a potential for goodness, a chance to preserve humanity in a world that often demands sacrifice. He pondered his path and the choices that had led him to this point. He understood the weight of his actions, the fine line between justice and vengeance. The future was uncertain and fraught with challenges, but he was determined to protect those he cared about.

Jake and Isabella, now more than ever, relied on each other for strength. Their journey was far from over, but they faced it with a renewed sense of purpose. They had survived the worst, and with Vincent's support, they had a chance to rebuild their lives. In the dim light of Vincent's command center, plans were made, alliances were tested, and the seeds of future conflicts were sown. The path ahead was fraught with danger but also with the promise of redemption and new beginnings.